DAM Jahrbuch **2003**

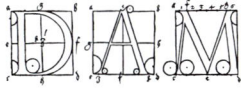

DAM Jahrbuch 2003

Architektur in Deutschland
Architecture in Germany

Thematischer Schwerpunkt: Sakrale Orte
Key Topic: Sacred Places

Herausgegeben von Edited by
Deutsches Architektur Museum, Frankfurt am Main
Ingeborg Flagge, Annina Götz

Mit Beiträgen von With contributions from
Karin Leydecker, Niklas Maak, Wolfgang Jean Stock, Inge Wolf

Mit Baukritiken von And reviews by
Markus Allmann, Julia B. Bolles-Wilson, Jochen Boskamp,
Dietmar Brandenburger, Hans-Jürgen Breuning, Manuel Cuadra,
Jörg Friedrich, Dörte Gatermann, Johannes Kister,
Wilhelm Kücker, Arno Lederer, Hilde Léon, Günter Pfeifer,
Angela Wandelt, Peter L. Wilson, Konrad Wohlhage,
Ingo Andreas Wolf, Erwin H. Zander

Prestel
München ■ Berlin ■ London ■ New York

DAM
Deutsches Architektur Museum
Frankfurt am Main

Inhalt
Contents

Vorwort
Foreword

■ Es werden wieder Kirchen gebaut. So wächst in Dresden, medienwirksam inszeniert, die Rekonstruktion von Georg Bährs Frauenkirche empor. Auch andernorts in Deutschland entstehen – jedoch in der Regel nach zeitgenössischen Entwürfen lebender Baumeister – christliche Sakralbauten, obwohl Umbauten und Renovierungen heute den Großteil kirchlicher Planungsaufträge ausmachen. Nach einer Hochkonjunktur in der jungen Bundesrepublik der Nachkriegszeit, die bis in die siebziger Jahre anhielt, kam der Kirchenbau in den achtziger Jahren beinahe zum Erliegen. Im letzten Jahrzehnt vor der Jahrtausendwende erlebte er jedoch eine Renaissance, die bis heute anhält. Die vorliegende Ausgabe des DAM Jahrbuchs widmet sich mit dem Schwerpunktthema ›Sakrale Orte‹ dieser spannenden Entwicklung.

Die Kirche hat als ehemals unumstrittene gesellschaftliche Institution an Bedeutung verloren. Die Hintergründe für das dennoch zu beobachtende Wiederaufleben der Kirchenarchitektur erläutert Wolfgang Jean Stock in einem Essay und zeigt die Bandbreite der zeitgenössischen Kirchenbauaufgaben in Europa anhand von vier exemplarischen Neubauten auf. Welchen Stellenwert hat ein heiliger Raum in unserer heutigen Gesellschaft? Dieser Frage geht Karin Leydecker in ihrem Beitrag nach und spürt zugleich den Reiz auf, welcher der Bauaufgabe ›Kirche‹ für Architekten noch immer innewohnt. Das Bedürfnis der Menschen nach Religiosität ist lebendig und spiegelt sich nicht nur in sakraler Architektur wider, sondern auch in anderen Gebäuden, die als ›Ersatzkathedralen‹ der profanierten Welt fungieren. Es gibt öffentliche und private Bauten, die Analogien zum Kirchenbau aufweisen, eine Scheinsakralität inszenieren und auf ihre Weise dem Bedürfnis nach Religiosität nachkommen – ein Phänomen, mit dem sich Niklas Maak in seinem Essay beschäftigt. Er zeigt dabei

■ Germany is experiencing a renaissance in church building. Dresden offers a good example, where reconstruction work on Georg Bähr's Church of Our Lady is progressing in a highly telegenic manner. Elsewhere in the country church buildings are rising in accordance with new designs by contemporary architects, and yet conversion and modernisation work constitutes the lion's share of building projects commissioned by the Church today. After a heyday in the early post-war years, when West Germany was still young, and a fertile period spanning the whole of the seventies, the eighties saw church building come to an almost complete halt. Not so in the nineties, when design and building activity took off again and has yet to pause for breath. This edition of the DAM Yearbook examines this exciting trend, taking 'Sacred Places' as its central focus.

Once an unquestioned social institution, lately the Church has begun to lose its significance. Church architecture has, nevertheless, gained a new lease on life, and Wolfgang Jean Stock outlines the reasons why in his essay, presenting the wealth of contemporary church building projects in Europe by means of four new, representative examples. What status does a holy space hold in society today? Karin Leydecker explores this question and puts her finger on the challenge which churches continue to pose for architects today. The human need for spirituality is alive and kicking, and finds reflection not only in religious architecture, but also in other buildings that function as 'substitute cathedrals' in the profane world. Public and private buildings that are analogous to church buildings can aid in evoking a feeling of sacredness, and in their own way serve spirituality – a phenomenon explored by Niklas Maak in his essay. He fields examples of a type of architecture that overcomes the traditional division between sacred and profane.

Beispiele einer Architektur, bei der die herkömmliche Trennung zwischen profan und sakral aufgehoben scheint.

Die Entwicklung der christlichen Sakralarchitektur nach 1945 ist neben Rudolf Schwarz eng mit dem Namen von Emil Steffann verbunden. Inge Wolf widmet sich dem Werk dieses wegweisenden Architekten, dessen Nachlass sich im Archiv des DAM befindet. Steffanns Kirchen basieren auf grundlegend neuen Überlegungen zur Liturgie und zur Positionierung des Priesters und der Gemeinde im Raum. Sie nehmen in ihrer architektonischen Gestaltung Neuerungen vorweg, die das Zweite Vatikanische Konzil 1963 formulierte.

Es gibt nach wie vor kaum Architekten, die nicht eine Kirche – neben einem Hochhaus – als Wunsch-Bauaufgabe nennen. Doch wie sehen sie die Kirchen ihrer Kollegen? In sechs Rezensionen zeitgenössischer deutscher Kirchenbauten beider Konfessionen beschreiben praktizierende Architekten ihre Eindrücke. Die Vielfalt der zum Teil gegensätzlichen Raumkonzepte aktueller Kirchenarchitektur spiegelt sich nicht zuletzt in der breiten Palette geometrischer Elementarformen wider, die den Grundrissen der ausgewählten Beispiele zugrunde liegen. Gemeinsam ist den Projekten der bewusste Einsatz von Material und Licht. Es sind zeichenhafte Gebäude, die auch ihrer traditionellen Rolle als Landmarken im Stadtbild gerecht werden – unter ihnen drei bei Erscheinen des DAM Jahrbuchs noch nicht ganz fertig gestellte, aber bemerkenswerte Projekte.

In weiteren Baukritiken resümieren ebenfalls Architekten das aktuelle Baugeschehen in Deutschland. Herausragende Beispiele anspruchsvoller Architektur etablierter sowie junger Büros stellen 2003 erneut den hohen Qualitätsanspruch der deutschen Architektenschaft unter Beweis.

Ingeborg Flagge ■ Annina Götz

The development of Christian religious architecture in the post-war era is closely associated not only with Rudolf Schwarz, but with the pioneering work of Emil Steffann as well. Inge Wolf writes about his oeuvre; the Steffann Estate is part of the DAM Collection. Steffann's churches were based on fundamentally new ideas on the liturgy and the positioning within the church building of both the priest and the congregation. This architecture pre-empts innovations that were then given official voice by the Second Vatican Council in 1963.

It is still the case that few architects fail to mention churches alongside high-rises when asked what sort of building they would most like to be commissioned to create. But how do they view the churches built by their colleagues? Practising architects describe their impressions in six reviews offered here of contemporary German church buildings. The variety of what are in part contradictory spatial concepts in current church architecture is reflected not least in the broad range of elementary geometric shapes adopted as the basis for the ground plans in examples seen here. The projects share a very carefully thought out use of materials and light. These are symbolic buildings that do justice to their traditional role as landmarks in city vistas – and they include three noteworthy projects that had not yet been completed when this issue of the DAM Yearbook went to press.

In a series of other reviews, it is once again the architects who describe the current state of the art of building in Germany. In 2003, the outstanding examples of discerning architecture created by both established offices and newcomers again attest to the high quality of German architecture as a whole.

Ingeborg Flagge ■ Annina Götz

Das Bedürfnis nach dem ›anderen Ort‹
The Need for a 'Different Place'

Wolfgang Jean Stock

Christlicher Sakralbau in Europa um die Jahrtausendwende

Christian Religious Architecture in Europe at the Turn of the Millennium

■ Kein anderer Bautypus spiegelt die wechselvolle Entwicklung der modernen Architektur seit dem Zweiten Weltkrieg besser als der Kirchenbau. Dies trifft vor allem auf Europa zu, wo sich unbeschadet regionaler Besonderheiten deutliche Parallelen bei den Neubauten für die beiden großen christlichen Konfessionen feststellen lassen. Aufgrund einer auch von katholischer Seite zunehmend gewährten Freiheit handelt es sich dabei aber nicht nur um Meisterwerke zeitgenössischer Architektur. Vielmehr stellen viele der nach 1950 errichteten Kirchen sogar Tiefpunkte im Bauschaffen dar. Bereits vor vierzig Jahren sparte der amerikanische Autor George E. Kidder Smith deshalb nicht mit Kritik am neuen Sakralbau in Europa: »Den heutigen Architekten stehen geradezu atemberaubende Möglichkeiten offen, wobei die neue Freiheit aber auch missbraucht wurde. Abschreckende Beispiele sind die modernistisch aufgetakelten Kirchen, die man besonders in neuen Vorstadtsiedlungen immer wieder antrifft.«[1]

Meisterwerke sind immer dann entstanden, wenn es auf der einen Seite Bauherren mit einem geschärften Bewusstsein für Qualität gab und auf der anderen Seite Architekten, die fähig waren, bei dieser besonderen Bauaufgabe den ›spirituellen‹ Dimensionen eine ebenso faszinierende wie angemessene Gestalt zu geben. In jenem geografischen und zugleich kulturellen Raum, den man bis zur historischen Wende von 1989 als ›Westeuropa‹ bezeichnet hat, ist dies während der letzten fünf Jahrzehnte in einer charakteristischen Abfolge von Grundströmungen geschehen. Nicht nur wegen der begrenzten Mittel herrscht in der ersten Nachkriegszeit eine bescheidene, absichtlich unmonumentale Haltung vor. Während der fünfziger Jahre werden wieder verstärkt die schon nach 1920 erprobten neuen Materialien wie Stahlbeton in den Kirchenbau eingeführt. Durch die Ausstrahlung von Le Corbusiers 1954 vollendeter Wallfahrtskapelle in Ronchamp[2] (siehe S. 19), die weithin als Wendepunkt verstanden wurde, tauchen besonders in Belgien und in der Schweiz vermehrt skulpturale Bauformen auf. Diese konkurrieren im Verlauf der sechziger Jahre mit dem häufig kubisch gestalteten Beton-Brutalismus, vor allem aber mit konstruktivistischen Konzeptionen: organoide ›weiche‹ Baukörper bilden den Gegensatz zu Montagebauten aus Stahl-Fertigteilen. Während der siebziger Jahre dominiert dann in vielen Ländern, auch als Folge der 68er-Bewegung, die Vorstellung vom kirchlichen Mehrzweckraum – die meist flachen Gebäude werden anonym bis unscheinbar. In dieser baukulturellen Krisensituation nehmen zugleich die Aufträge aus den beiden großen christlichen Kirchen rapide ab, weil eine gewisse Sättigung an sakralen Bauten erreicht ist.

Ob ein Kirchenbau gelingt oder gar neue Maßstäbe setzt, hängt nicht von der religiösen Haltung des Architekten ab. Das berühmteste Beispiel ist Le Corbusier, der auf die Frage, ob beim Bau seiner

■ No other type of building reflects the changes that have taken place in modern architecture since World War Two better than church architecture. This is particularly true of Europe where, notwithstanding particular regional characteristics, we can discern clear parallels in new edifices built for the two main Christian confessions. However, owing to the increasing liberty granted architects, especially by Catholic developers, we are left with something less than the masterworks of contemporary architecture. On the contrary, one could go so far as to say that churches constructed after 1950 represent a nadir in architectural achievement. American author George E. Kidder Smith was timely in his critique of contemporary religious architecture in Europe offered some forty years ago: "Today's architects have truly breathtaking opportunities, but this new liberty is often misused. We find terrible examples in the churches made up to look Modernist that you come across so often in new suburbs."[1]

By contrast, masterworks arose where developers had a heightened sense of quality, and there were architects at hand capable of lending this special task not only a 'spiritual' dimension, but also a fascinating and appropriate appearance. In the geographical and cultural region known before the fall of the Wall in 1989 as 'Western Europe', church architecture has evolved over the last fifty years as a characteristic sequence of basic styles. One reason for the modest, deliberately non-monumental style in the first years after the war was that funds were scarce. But it was not the only explanation. In the church architecture of the 1950s, greater use was made of new materials already tested after 1920 such as reinforced concrete. Following the favourable reception of Le Corbusier's charismatic chapel in Ronchamp (see p. 19) completed in 1954, which many people regarded as a turning point, sculptural styles increasingly make an appearance, especially in Belgium and Switzerland.[2] In the course of the 1960s these compete with the cubic forms of concrete Brutalism, but above all with Constructivist designs: organoid 'soft' structures form a contrast to the buildings assembled from prefabricated steel elements. Subsequently, in the 1970s, and partly as a consequence of the anti-authoritarian movement of the late 1960s, the idea of the multi-purpose church took hold in many nations. Typically these flat buildings are anonymous, at times nondescript. This crisis in architectural culture coincided with a sharp fall in commissions from the two big churches, since a certain saturation point had been reached in religious buildings.

Whether church architecture is successful or even sets new standards need not hinge on the architect's religious attitude alone. Take the most famous example: In response to the question of whether a belief in God was necessary for him to build the chapel in

Riepl Riepl, St. Franziskus, Innenraum, Steyr, Österreich, 2001 **Riepl Riepl, St Francis, Interior, Steyr, Austria, 2001**

Kapelle der Glaube an Gott notwendig gewesen sei, geantwortet hat: »Nein, notwendig war der Glaube an Architektur.«[3] In diesem Sinne äußerte sich auch sein Auftraggeber, der Dominikanerpater Alain Couturier: »Immer wieder erklärte er, das Ideal für eine Renaissance der christlichen Kirche wäre es, Genies zu haben, die gleichzeitig Heilige sind; da eine derartige Verbindung in der Gegenwart aber nicht vorhanden sei, sei es besser, sich an Genies ohne Glauben zu wenden als an Gläubige ohne Talent.«[4]

Ronchamp, Le Corbusier replied: "No, what was necessary was a belief in architecture."[3] His client, the Dominican friar Alain Couturier, echoed these thoughts: "He insisted that the Christian Church would achieve a renaissance by recruiting members who, ideally, combined artistic genius with a saintly spirit. Since such 'ideal candidates' could not be found at the time, it would be better, he continued, to engage individuals of genius who were no-believers rather than believers who had no genius."[4]

Riepl Riepl, St. Franziskus, Steyr, Österreich, 2001   **Riepl Riepl, St Francis, Steyr, Austria, 2001**

Katholischer Kirchenbau: Reform und Gegenreform

Selbst wenn die sakrale Architektur heutzutage als eine der wenigen gestalterisch ›freien‹ Bauaufgaben gilt, so ist sie gleichwohl nicht frei von theologisch-liturgischen Vorgaben und Ansprüchen. Dies betrifft in erster Linie den römisch-katholischen Kirchenbau, bei dem seit den zwanziger Jahren ein grundlegender Wandel hinsichtlich der innenräumlichen Disposition stattgefunden hat. Vorbereitet durch die Liturgische Bewegung und vorweggenommen in reformbetonten Neubauten wie etwa St. Laurentius von Emil Steffann in München aus dem Jahr 1955 (siehe S. 178/179), beschloss das Zweite Vatikanische Konzil 1963 ein neues Kirchen- und Liturgieverständnis. Dieser Reformschritt bedeutete eine Abkehr vom traditionellen Kirchenraum: Die Trennung in ein Presbyterium (Priesterraum, Chor) und einen Laienraum wurde aufgehoben, der Altar in die Mitte der Gemeinde gestellt. Leitidee der neuen Liturgie war die »bewusste, fromme und tätige Teilnahme der Gläubigen«[5] in einem Raum, der das Gemeinschaftserlebnis, die Communio, stimulieren soll.

Nicht zuletzt deshalb, weil historische Weg-Kirchen ›gegen den Raum‹ der neuen Liturgie angepasst wurden, mehren sich seit einigen Jahren die Stimmen jener, die eine Revision der Reform fordern. Hier ist nicht der Ort, auf die zuweilen heftige Diskussion über das

Catholic Church Architecture: Reform and Counter-Reform

For all that, contemporary religious architecture is considered one of the few areas in which the architect enjoys a certain freedom of scope, which does not mean that such projects are devoid of theological and liturgical specifications and demands. This applies especially to Roman Catholic church architecture, where the interior ground plans have undergone a substantial change since the 1920s. Anticipated by the Liturgical Movement and buildings such as the Church of St Laurence by Emil Steffann in Munich from 1955 (see p. 178–179) which expressed reformist ideas, the Second Vatican Council (1963–65) redefined the nature of the Church and the liturgy. The reforms enacted by it signified a break with the traditional church interior. The traditional division into a presbytery (room for the priests, choir), on the one hand, and space for the congregation, on the other, was abandoned; the altar was placed at the centre of the congregation. The idea at the centre of the new liturgy was the "conscious, devoute and active participation of the believers" in services designed to stimulate the joint experience, the communio.[5]

Not least of all because historical nave-based churches were adapted to the new liturgy despite the fact that their layout did not

›richtige‹ Liturgie- und Raumverständnis im Einzelnen einzugehen. Grundsätzlich lassen sich vier Parteien unterscheiden: Während die einen, unter ihnen der Kirchenarchitekt Dieter G. Baumewerd, an der zentrierten Versammlung festhalten[6] (siehe S. 23), opponieren andere geradezu fundamentalistisch gegen die gesamte Liturgiereform, so etwa der Schriftsteller Martin Mosebach, der auch den Verlust der lateinischen Sprache bei der Messfeier beklagt.[7] Als dritte Gruppe beharren Gemeinden selbst bei Neubauten auf der früheren linearen Ausrichtung – ein prägnantes Beispiel dafür ist die Herz-Jesu-Kirche in München von Allmann Sattler Wappner Architekten aus dem Jahr 2000. Die vierte Gruppe schließlich bemüht sich, eine angemessene Gestalt des katholischen Kirchenraums zu finden, indem sie die Folgen der neuen Liturgie kritisch überprüft, ohne aber den Communio-Raum als Errungenschaft des Konzils aufzugeben. Weder die Konzeption der ›Mitte‹ noch die klassische Ausrichtung des Innenraums dürften verabsolutiert werden.[8]

Protestantischer Pluralismus

Im Unterschied zur katholischen Theologie gibt es im Protestantismus keine Lehre vom ›heiligen Raum‹. Weil eine Kirche vielmehr als Haus der versammelten Gemeinde verstanden wird, steht ihre Rolle als Predigtsaal im Mittelpunkt, wobei sich der Pfarrer selbstverständlich den Gläubigen zuwendet. Deshalb zeigt sich der protestantische Kirchenbau bei der räumlichen Gliederung traditionell freier und pluralistischer. Die lutherische Liturgie stellt vor allem Forderungen an die Akustik im Raum. Wie die Schallführung von Wort und Orgel wirkungsvoll unterstützt wird, veranschaulicht beispielsweise der mehrfach gewölbte und zur Altarbühne hin ansteigende Saal in der Vuoksenniska Kirche von Alvar Aalto im finnischen Imatra (1958).

Trotz der theologisch-liturgischen Unterschiede kommt bei den Grundrissen und Raumbildern das allmähliche Annähern beider Konfessionen zum Ausdruck. Auf der einen Seite lässt sich im neueren Kirchenbau eine gewisse ›Katholisierung‹ feststellen, indem die Räume durch eine gesteigerte Lichtführung eine immateriell geprägte Sakralität erhalten. Zugleich hat sich insofern eine ›Protestantisierung‹ durchgesetzt, als bei den zunehmend schmuckloseren Kirchen der jeweilige Raum als reine Gestalt wirken soll. Diese konvergente Entwicklung bedeutet auf beiden Seiten eine Ablösung von tradierten Auffassungen.

Renaissance des Kirchenbaus

Zwar ist der Neubau einer Kirche heutzutage kein Normalfall wie noch während der fünfziger bis siebziger Jahre, als in weiten Teilen Europas mehr Kirchen als jemals zuvor errichtet wurden. Dennoch gibt es etliche Gründe, weshalb der Sakralbau seit über zehn Jahren eine Renaissance erlebt – sie reichen von neuen Siedlungsgebieten über notwendig gewordene Ersatzbauten bis hin zur Beseitigung von Provisorien. Hinzu kommen immer wieder Erweiterungen (wie die kürzlich fertig gestellte ›Kirche für eine wachsende Gemeinde‹ in

envisage the proximity of priest and congregation, calls have become vocal in recent years for a revision of this reform. This is not the place to go into detail on what is at times a vehement discussion on the 'right' definition of the liturgy or use of the interior. Basically, four groups can be distinguished: While one group, which includes church architect Dieter G. Baumewerd, is in favour of retaining the centred assembly (see p. 23), others are fundamentally opposed to the entire liturgical reform.[6] Author Martin Mosebach, for example, bemoans the loss of Latin in the celebration of the Mass.[7] A third group consists of communities which insist that even new buildings adhere to the earlier linear design – a striking example of this is the Church of the Sacred Heart in Munich by architects Allmann Sattler Wappner from the year 2000. Finally, the fourth group's interest is in finding an appropriate form for Catholic church interiors, by subjecting the new liturgy to critical examination but without abandoning the Council's idea of the communio room: In other words, there should be neither strict adherence to either the 'centre' concept nor the classic alignment of the interior.[8]

Protestant Pluralism

In contrast to Catholic theology, Protestantism does not have a concept of 'sacred space'. And, because the church is seen rather as the house of the assembled community, there is a focus on its role as a preaching room in which the priest naturally faces the congregation. This explains why Protestant church architecture typically shows greater freedom and pluralism in the interior layout. The Lutheran liturgy focuses its demands on the church's acoustics. We have an example of how the sound of both voice and organ are effectively carried in the Vuoksenniska Church in Imatra, Finland, designed by Alvar Aalto (1958), in which the room rises towards the altar and features multiple vaulting.

Despite theological and liturgical differences, it is possible to observe a gradual reconciliation between the two confessions as regards floor plan and interior design. On the one hand, a certain 'Catholisation' can be detected in more recent church architecture in that interiors are lent an immaterial religiosity through greater direction of light. Yet at the same time, a 'Protestantisation' has asserted itself in the sense that churches are becoming less ornate, and are intended to convey pure design. This convergent development points to the abandonment of traditional views on both sides.

A Renaissance in Church Architecture

Admittedly, building a new church today is no longer the everyday event it was from the 1950s through to the 1970s, an era when in large parts of Europe more churches were built than ever before. And yet there are many reasons why religious architecture has been experiencing a renaissance over the last ten years. They range from the creation of new settlement areas to the necessity of replacing

Reitermann/Sassenroth, Kapelle der Versöhnung, Berlin, Deutschland, 2000
Reitermann/Sassenroth, Chapel of Reconciliation, Berlin, Germany, 2000

Reitermann/Sassenroth, Kapelle der Versöhnung, Innenraum, Berlin, Deutschland, 2000
Reitermann/Sassenroth, Chapel of Reconciliation, Interior, Berlin, Germany, 2000

Wenzenbach bei Regensburg der Architekten Brückner & Brückner[9]) und kleinere Projekte wie ›Räume der Stille‹ in neuen Flughäfen oder auch Autobahnkapellen. Die folgenden vier europäischen Beispiele sollen das breite Spektrum der gegenwärtigen Kirchenbauaufgaben skizzieren.

Kirchenbau als Städtebau: Durch die 2001 vollendete katholische Kirche St. Franziskus hat ein Vorort der österreichischen Industriestadt Steyr erstmals eine Mitte erhalten. Von gleichförmigen Wohnbauten aus den frühen siebziger Jahren gerahmt, bildet die aus kubischen Formen komponierte Kirche auch das ideale Zentrum des Quartiers. Peter und Gabriele Riepl haben das Gebäude einladend

churches, in some cases temporary ones. Moreover, extensions are always necessary; take the recently completed Church for a Growing Community in Wenzenbach near Regensburg, Germany, by architects Brückner & Brückner, and smaller projects such as 'contemplation rooms' in new airports or motorway chapels.[9] The four examples that follow (all in Europe) should provide some insight into the broad spectrum of projects in contemporary church architecture.

Church architecture as urban architecture: The completion of the Catholic Church of St Francis in 2001 means a suburb in Steyr – an industrial town in Austria – now has a centre for the first time. Framed by monotonous residential buildings from the early 1970s, the church composed of cubic shapes creates an ideal centre. Peter and Gabriele Riepl located the building so it faces a relatively large square, inviting people to enter. A long canopy on round supports protects the fully-glazed entrance. Thanks to its clear design and also the olive green exposed concrete, the church stands out from its uninspired surroundings. Peter Riepl wanted to design a lively building: "The church is devised as a porous body in which there are spaces and niches for the full richness of life."[10] And, indeed, the baptismal chapel opens up into a glass cube which is filled at night by Keith Sonnier's work of art – his installation of coloured illuminant strips already functions as a local landmark.

Church and memorial: A small building from the year 2000 stands as a symbol of Berlin's post-war history. It is located at the exact spot where the Protestant Church of Reconciliation was built when the Wall was erected – in the city's East section but in a noman's-land between the two rings of walls. In 1985, the historicist church was dynamited by GDR border guards. When the plot of land was returned to the community after the fall of the Wall, it was decided to build a church on the same spot. Rudolf Reitermann and Peter Sassenroth won the competition. The floor plan for the new Chapel of Reconciliation is an oval intersected by two rectangles for entrance and altar niche. An egg-shaped, translucent wooden construction surrounds the oval, and also provides the outer casing. In the room of worship constructed of stamped loam, the gaze is immediately drawn to the reredos which was salvaged from the old church.

Building for the community church: Unlike the situation in Central Europe, in northerly nations Christian churches are still relatively strongly anchored in the population. The communities of the Norwegian Lutheran state church have become very involved in the building of churches as in the case of the Mortensrud Church in Oslo (completed in 2002) by architect Jan Olav Jensen from the office of Jensen & Skodvin.[11] A member of the church cultural workshop project group, Jensen was selected because he had never before built a church, and could therefore be expected to produce an unconventional design. The building rises up like a 'solid castle' on a narrow mountain ridge above the south-eastern district of the city. At the point where suburb merges with the landscape, it acts as a harmonious collage of design, material and spatial elements. A fascinating aspect is the contrast between the archaic masonry and the modern steel structure.

Reitermann/Sassenroth, Kapelle der Versöhnung, Berlin, Deutschland, 2000 **Reitermann/Sassenroth, Chapel of Reconciliation, Berlin, Germany, 2000**

zu einem relativ großen Platz orientiert, wobei ein langes, von Rund-
stützen getragenes Vordach den voll verglasten Eingang schützt.
Sowohl durch ihre klare Gestalt als auch durch den olivgrün durchge-
färbten Sichtbeton unterscheidet sich die Kirche von ihrer uninspiriert
geplanten Umgebung. Peter Riepl kam es auf ein lebendiges Gebäude an: »Die Kirche ist erdacht als poröser Körper, in dem die Fülle
des Lebens Platz und Nischen findet.«[10] So öffnet sich die Taufkapelle nach oben in einen Glaskubus, den das nachts strahlende Kunstwerk aus farbigen Leuchtstoffbändern von Keith Sonnier ausfüllt.

Kirche und Gedächtnisstätte: Ein kleines Bauwerk aus dem Jahr
2000 steht als Symbol für die Berliner Geschichte nach dem
Zweiten Weltkrieg. Es befindet sich genau dort, wo seit dem Bau der
›Mauer‹ die evangelische Versöhnungskirche stand – im Ostteil der
Stadt, aber im ›toten Streifen‹ zwischen den beiden Mauerringen.
1985 wurde die historische Kirche von den DDR-Grenztruppen
gesprengt. Als die Gemeinde nach der ›Wende‹ das Grundstück zu-

A place of communication: Built in 1998 and financed in part by
donations, the motorway chapel on the northern slip road to the
Gotthard Pass in Switzerland is dedicated to the five main world
religions. Like ritual objects left behind, larger-than-life prayer
beads and phylacteries hang above the courtyard wall of exposed
concrete. These objects turned into stone symbolise harmony between Christianity, Islam, Buddhism, Hinduism and the Jewish faith.
In designing the chapel, architects Guignard & Saner made a remote
reference to car drivers by presenting it as a religious 'milestone'.
One aspect that contributes to this effect is the strict cubic shape
and regular facades; another is the play of light in the casement
windows filled with green shards of glass. During the day these
openings reflect the sunlight, while at night the dark produces a
mysterious light in the windows illuminated from within. In the room
of worship an illuminated rock crystal is the only object indicating
the religious nature of the place.

rück erhielt, wollte sie am gleichen Platz wieder ein Gotteshaus errichten. Den Wettbewerb gewannen Rudolf Reitermann und Peter
Sassenroth. Der Grundriss der neuen Kapelle der Versöhnung ist
ein Oval, in das zwei Rechtecke für Eingang und Altarnische einge-
schnitten sind. Umgeben wird das Oval von der Eiform einer licht-
durchlässigen Holzkonstruktion, die als äußere Hülle dient. Blickfang
im Andachtsraum aus Stampflehm ist der gerettete Altaraufsatz aus
der alten Kirche.

Bauen für die Volkskirche: Anders als in Mitteleuropa sind in den
nordischen Ländern die christlichen Kirchen noch relativ stark in
der Bevölkerung verankert. Auch die Gemeinden der norwegisch-
lutherischen Staatskirche wirken bei Baumaßnahmen intensiv mit. So
gehörte der Architekt Jan Olav Jensen aus dem Büro Jensen & Skodvin bei der Planung der 2002 fertig gestellten Mortensrud-Kirche in

Church Architecture as a Coveted Task

Religious architecture was one of architecture's 'key tasks' during
the post-war period, and today it is a type of commission much cov-
eted by architects. This is attested to by numerous comments made
in recent years, for instance by Pierre de Meuron after he received
the Pritzker prize, or the Viennese office of Henke and Schreieck.
Munich architect Thomas Herzog, a great admirer of Angelo Mangia-
rotti's church in Baranzate, near Milan, concluded an interview with
the sentence: "Maybe we will even build a church some time."[12]

This wish, shared by many architects, corresponds to a growing
social need. In a blaring world that seems to have fallen prey to ma-
terialism and entertainment, churches and chapels are sometimes
the only alternative places available offering silence, meditation,

Jensen & Skodvin, Mortensrud-Kirche, Innenraum, Oslo, Norwegen, 2002 **Jensen & Skodvin, Mortensrud Church, Interior, Oslo, Norway, 2002**

Jensen & Skodvin, Mortensrud-Kirche, Oslo, Norwegen, 2002   **Jensen & Skodvin, Mortensrud Church, Oslo, Norway, 2002**

Oslo[11] zu einer von der Kirchlichen Kulturwerkstatt eingesetzten Projektgruppe. Die Wahl fiel auf Jensen, weil er noch keine Kirche gebaut hatte und deshalb einen unkonventionellen Entwurf erwarten ließ. Wie eine ›feste Burg‹ erhebt sich das Bauwerk auf einem schmalen Bergrücken oberhalb des südöstlichen Stadtteils. Im Übergang von der Vorstadt zur Landschaft gelegen, stellt es eine fein abgestimmte Collage aus konstruktiven, stofflichen und räumlichen Elementen dar. Faszinierend wirkt vor allem der Kontrast zwischen dem archaischen Mauerwerk und dem modernen Stahlbau.

liberty and not least of all sanctuary, in the case of church asylum. Only recently the working committee of the Protestant Church Architecture Congress asked that these 'other places' be kept, looked after and opened to more people. The 'Leipzig declaration' carries the appeal: "Look after your churches!"[13]

Ein Ort der Verständigung: Die 1998 mit Hilfe von Spenden errichtete Autobahnkapelle an der Nordauffahrt des Schweizer Gotthardpasses ist den fünf großen Weltreligionen gewidmet. Wie scheinbar vergessene Ritualgegenstände hängen über der Hofmauer aus Sichtbeton übergroße Gebetsketten und -riemen. Diese ›versteinerten‹ Objekte symbolisieren in Eintracht das Christentum, den Islam, den Buddhismus und den Hinduismus sowie den jüdischen Glauben. Die Kapelle selbst haben die Architekten Guignard & Saner mit Fernwirkung auf die Autofahrer als sakralen ›Meilenstein‹ konzipiert. Ein Element, das zu dieser Wirkung beiträgt, ist die strenge kubische Gestalt mit ihren regelmäßigen Fassaden, ein zweites das wechselnde Lichtspiel in den mit grünlichen Glasscherben gefüllten

Guignard & Saner, Kapelle der Weltreligionen, Hof, Gotthardpass, Schweiz, 1998
Guignard & Saner, Chapel of World Religions, courtyard, Gotthard Pass, Switzerland, 1998

Guignard & Saner, Kapelle der Weltreligionen, Gotthardpass, Schweiz, 1998
Guignard & Saner, Chapel of World Religions, Gotthard Pass, Switzerland, 1998

Kastenfenstern. Tagsüber reflektieren die Öffnungen das Sonnenlicht, bei Dunkelheit erzeugt die von innen illuminierte Verglasung
einen geheimnisvollen Leuchtkörper. Auf die Sakralität des Ortes verweist im Andachtsraum lediglich die Vitrine mit einem beleuchteten
Bergkristall.

Kirchenbau als Wunschaufgabe

War der Sakralbau in der Nachkriegszeit eine prominente ›Leitauf-
gabe‹ der Architektur, so ist er für heutige Architekten eine Wunsch-
aufgabe. Dies belegen zahlreiche Äußerungen aus den letzten
Jahren, etwa von Pierre de Meuron nach der Verleihung des
Pritzker Preises oder aus dem Wiener Büro Henke und Schreieck.
Der Münchner Thomas Herzog, ein Verehrer von Angelo Mangiarottis
Kirche in Bollate bei Mailand, hat denn auch ein Interview mit dem
Satz beschlossen: »Vielleicht bauen wir irgendwann einmal sogar
eine Kirche.«[12]

Dieser Wunsch vieler Architekten korrespondiert mit einem wachsenden gesellschaftlichen Bedürfnis. In einer lärmenden Welt, die
dem Ökonomismus wie der Unterhaltung verfallen scheint, sind Kirchen und Kapellen oftmals die einzigen alternativen Orte: Häuser der
Stille, der Meditation, der Freiheit und nicht zuletzt der Zuflucht wie
im Falle des Kirchenasyls. Diese ›anderen Orte‹ zu erhalten, zu pfle-
gen und noch weiter zu öffnen, dazu hat erst kürzlich auch der
Arbeitsausschuss des Evangelischen Kirchbautages aufgerufen.
Seine ›Leipziger Erklärung‹ ist mit dem Appell überschrieben:
»Nehmt eure Kirchen wahr!«[13]

Guignard & Saner, Kapelle der Weltreligionen, Innenraum, Gotthardpass, Schweiz, 1998
Guignard & Saner, Chapel of World Religions, Interior, Gotthard Pass, Switzerland, 1998

1 George E. Kidder Smith, *Neuer Kirchenbau in Europa,* Stuttgart 1964, S. 9.
2 Alle Kirchen und Kapellen, für die hier keine gesonderte Literatur angegeben wird,
sind dokumentiert in: Wolfgang Jean Stock (Hrsg.), *Europäischer Kirchenbau 1950–2000,*
München, Berlin, London und New York 2002.
3 Richard Weston, *The Word of God,* in: *RIBA Journal,* 2003, Heft 2, S. 16.
4 Winfried Nerdinger, *Architektur ist Bewegung. Le Corbusiers Sakralbauten,* in: Stock,
wie Anm. 2, S. 54.
5 Albert Gerhards, *Räume für eine tätige Teilnahme,* in: Ebd., S. 24.
6 Dieter G. Baumewerd, *Der liturgische Raum,* in: Benedikt Kranemann und Thomas
Sternberg (Hrsg.), *Wie das Wort Gottes feiern?,* Freiburg, Basel und Wien 2002, S. 234–
238.
7 Martin Mosebach, *Ewige Steinzeit,* in: *Kursbuch,* Heft 149, Berlin 2002, S. 9–16.
8 Siehe dazu neuerdings Albert Gerhards, Thomas Sternberg und Walter Zahner
(Hrsg.), *Communio-Räume. Auf der Suche nach der angemessenen Raumgestalt katholischer Liturgie,* Regensburg 2003.
9 Siehe Manfred Wilhelm und Wilhelm Koch (Hrsg.), *Aktuelle Architektur der Oberpfalz,*
Regensburg 2000, S. 30 f.
10 Zitiert nach Stock, wie Anm. 2, S. 207.
11 Ausführlich dazu Wolfgang Jean Stock, *Eine feste Burg,* in: *Architektur aktuell,* 2003,
Heft 1–2, S. 60–69.
12 Thomas Herzog im Gespräch mit Werner Lang, in: Ingeborg Flagge, Verena Herzog-
Loibl und Anna Meseure (Hrsg.), *Thomas Herzog. Architektur + Technologie,* München,
London und New York 2001, S. 39.
13 Leipziger Erklärung vom 6.1.2003, in: *Kunst und Kirche,* 2003, Heft 1, S. 54.

1 George E. Kidder Smith, *Neuer Kirchenbau in Europa,* Stuttgart, 1964, p. 9.
2 All churches and chapels for which no specific references are given are documented
in: Wolfgang Jean Stock (ed.), *European Church Architecture 1950–2000,* Munich, Berlin,
London and New York, 2002.
3 Richard Weston, "The Word of God", in: *RIBA Journal,* no. 2, 2003, p. 16.
4 Winfried Nerdinger, "Architecture is Movement. Le Corbusier's Sacred Buildings", in:
Stock, note 2, p. 55.
5 Albert Gerhards, "Spaces for Active Participation" in: Ibid., p. 25.
6 Dieter G. Baumewerd, "Der liturgische Raum", in: Benedikt Kranemann and Thomas
Sternberg (eds.), *Wie das Wort Gottes feiern?,* Freiburg, Basle and Vienna, 2002, pp. 234–
38.
7 Martin Mosebach, "Ewige Steinzeit", in: *Kursbuch,* no. 149, Berlin, 2002, pp. 9–16.
8 See the recent work by Albert Gerhards, Thomas Sternberg and Walter Zahner (eds.),
*Communio-Räume. Auf der Suche nach der angemessenen Raumgestalt Katholischer
Liturgie,* Regensburg, 2003.
9 See Manfred Wilhelm and Wilhelm Koch (eds.), *Aktuelle Architektur der Oberpfalz,*
Regensburg, 2000, p. 30 f.
10 Cited by Stock, note 2, p. 207.
11 For greater detail see Wolfgang Jean Stock, "Eine feste Burg", in: *Architektur aktuell,*
2003, no. 1–2, pp. 60–69.
12 Thomas Herzog interviewed by Werner Lang, in: Ingeborg Flagge, Verena Herzog-Loibl
and Anna Meseure (eds.), *Thomas Herzog. Architecture + Technology,* Munich, London
and New York, 2001, p. 39.
13 Leipzig declaration on 6 January 2003 in: *Kunst und Kirche,* 2003, no. 1, p. 54.

James Ensor, *La cathédrale,* Radierung, 1886
James Ensor, La cathédrale, etching, 1886

Nur eines erbitte ich vom Herrn,
danach verlangt mich:
Im Haus des Herrn zu wohnen
alle Tage meines Lebens,
die Freundlichkeit des Herrn zu schauen
und nachzusinnen in seinem Tempel.
Denn er birgt mich in seinem Haus
am Tage des Unheils;
er beschirmt mich im Schutz seines Zeltes,
er hebt mich auf einen Felsen empor.

Psalm 27, 4 – 5

One thing I ask of the Lord,
this is what I seek:
that I may dwell in the house of the Lord
all the days of my life,
to gaze upon the beauty of the Lord
and to seek Him in His temple.
For in the day of trouble
He will keep me safe in His dwelling;
He will hide me in the shelter of His tabernacle,
and set me high upon a rock.

Psalms 27:4 – 5

Lange, bevor man Kirchen baute, gab es die Kirche

■ Es war die Gemeinschaft der von Christus Erlösten, die Ecclesia, die sich in Privaträumen, in verborgenen Katakomben und Höhlen versammelte, um das Wort Gottes zu hören, gemeinsam zu beten und die Eucharistie zu feiern. Zwei Jahrhunderte lang wirkte die Gemeinde Gottes, ohne über eigene Kultstätten zu verfügen. Die Gemeindeglieder waren die lebendigen Bausteine des imaginären Tempels Christi.[1] Für den Zusammenhalt des Bauwerks sorgte der ›Schlussstein‹[2] Jesus Christus. Im 3. Jahrhundert entstanden erste Hauskirchen und Gemeindehäuser (domus ecclesiae = Haus der versammelten Gemeinde) nach dem Vorbild der Synagoge. Unter Kaiser Konstantin wuchsen schließlich monumentale Kirchengebäude, die man unter den Profanbegriff ›Basilika‹ (Königliche Halle)

The Church Existed Long before Churches Were Built

■ The early Church was the community of Christ the Redeemed, the ecclesia, which assembled in private rooms, in hidden catacombs and caves, to hear the word of God, to pray together and to celebrate the Eucharist. For two centuries the community of God was active without having its own places of worship. Community members were the living stones making up the imaginary temple of Christ, and Jesus Christ acted as the 'cornerstone' to ensure the building's unity.[1,2] In the third century, the first private chapels in homes and community houses (*domus ecclesiae* = house of the

Le Corbusier, Kapelle Notre-Dame-du-Haut, Ronchamp, Frankreich 1954
Le Corbusier, Notre-Dame-du-Haut Chapel, Ronchamp, France, 1954

fasste. »Die Basilika ist Wegkirche, ihr Weg aber führt in den Thronsaal Christi.«[3] Durch das christologische Moment avancierte das Bauwerk zum Symbol für das geistige Wesen der Ecclesia. Damit begann eine Entwicklung, über die wir in der Stilgeschichte der Baukunst lesen können: die Geschichte der steinernen Zeichen, die von der Anwesenheit Gottes auf Erden sprechen. Jede Zeit fand vor dem Hintergrund ihres kosmologischen Verständnisses, Theologie- und Liturgiebegriffs und nach dem jeweiligen Stand der Baukultur und -technik ihre spezifischen Zeichen. Die Romanik schuf die Gottesburg, die Gotik ihr Himmlisches Jerusalem für die metaphysische Dimension mitten im Leben und das Barockzeitalter das lichtdurchflutete Teatrum sacrum.

Heute bauen wir noch immer an diesen Zeichen. Großes ist entstanden, aber auch peinliche ›Sprungschanzen Gottes‹, die inzwischen dem Abriss preisgegeben oder umgenutzt werden. Gerade jetzt, zu Beginn des 21. Jahrhunderts, baut die Kirche wieder und gibt der Baukunst ihre Leitaufgabe zurück.

assembled community) were built, taking the synagogue as their model. It was under Emperor Constantine that monumental church buildings evolved and were referred to using the profane term 'basilica' (imperial hall). "The basilica is a wayside church, but it leads into Christ's throne room."[3] Thanks to its christological element, the basilica advanced to become the symbol for the spiritual concept that was ecclesia. This gave birth to a development about which we can read in the history of architectural styles: the history of the stone symbols that speak of God's presence on earth. Each era came up with its own specific symbols depending on its understanding of the cosmos, its concept of theology and liturgy, not to mention the respective state of its building culture and technology. The Romantic movement created the 'Citadel of God', the Gothic its 'Divine Jerusalem' for the metaphysical dimension in the midst of life, and the Baroque the light-filled 'sacred theatre'.

Today, we still base our buildings on this symbol. It has given rise to magnificence, but also to embarrassing structures that have

Helmut Striffler, Versöhnungskirche, Dachau, Deutschland, 1967   **Helmut Striffler, Church of Reconciliation, Dachau, Germany, 1967**

Kirchen für eine Gesellschaft des Mangels

Die Kirche baut für eine Gesellschaft des Mangels mitten im Überfluss. Dieser Mangel zeigt sich in einer fehlenden Verbindlichkeit der Tradition, in grassierendem Egozentrismus und einer haltlosen Säkularisierung aller Lebensbereiche. Die Orientierung an der »Würde des Menschen als in Gottes Ebenbild geschaffener Kreatur, die sich in Christus erlöst weiß und ihre Einbindung in eine prästabilisierte Gesamtordnung erkennt«[4] – diese Orientierung an der ›Mitte‹[5] ist verloren gegangen.

Die Entfremdung zwischen Gott und Mensch hat ihre Entsprechung in der wachsenden Unfähigkeit zur zwischenmenschlichen Begegnung. Ökonomismus schlägt als Herz einer Gesellschaft, die sich an flüchtigen Sensationen berauscht und permanentes Unterwegssein zur Glücksmetapher stilisiert.[6] Bleiben und Sein sind Bilder von gestern. In dieser Situation des existenziellen Mangels steht der Mensch. Die Wahrnehmung der Schutzlosigkeit in einer immer komplexer werdenden Welt ängstigt ihn, er ruft nach Sicherheit und darf diesen Ruf doch nur als Hoffnung formulieren.

Sakrale Schutzräume

Wie kann die Baukunst dieser Suche nach Schutzräumen der emotionalen Sicherheit begegnen? Die Baukunst muss sich zunächst auf eine Situation einrichten, die es zuvor so nicht gab. Selbst nach dem Trauma des Nationalsozialismus und des Zweiten Weltkrieges blieb der Kirchenbau integraler Bestandteil der Wiedererstehung von Gesellschaft und Kultur. Religiöses Wissen und religiöser Kult waren Teil dieser Kultur. Diese Verbindlichkeiten existieren in einer Welt heterogenster Interessengeflechte nicht mehr. Die Architektur kann deshalb nicht mehr nach gesellschaftlichem Konsens fragen, sie muss zurück zur anthropologischen Basis und das ureigenste Wesen des Menschen ausloten.

Aus dem Blickwinkel der Psychologie ist der Mensch unter seiner dünnen Vernunfthaut ein zutiefst steinzeitlich empfindendes Wesen geblieben, in dem archaische Verhaltensweisen und komplexe vorbewusste Strukturen wirken.[7] Es ist deshalb wichtig, zu fragen, wie der Mensch Architektur wahrnimmt und wie er auf sie reagiert. Es ist außerdem wichtig, zu begreifen, dass sich Wahrnehmung nicht auf das rein Optisch-Kognitive reduzieren lässt. »Das bloße Betrachten führt nie zu Raum.«[8] Architekturwahrnehmung ist vielmehr eine ganzheitliche Erfahrung des Menschen.[9] Architektur existiert erst durch sinnliche Wahrnehmung in der Verquickung affektiver Ebenen, die gleichsam variable Wahrnehmungsräume schaffen und die immer neu zu bilden sind. Durch sie erspürt der Mensch räumliche Dimension, Ordnung und atmosphärische Qualität der Baukunst. Die Atmosphäre eines Raumes besteht aus vielen Bausteinen: aus Geruch und Klang, aus Wärme oder Kälte, aus Licht und Schatten, aus der Struktur der Materialien und der raumbildenden Wirkung der Farbe. Der gelebte Raum entwickelt sich immer aus einem Beziehungsgeflecht »seinsenthüllender«[10] Bausteine, die im Gebrauch Empfindungswerte wecken. Kirchenbau ist deshalb

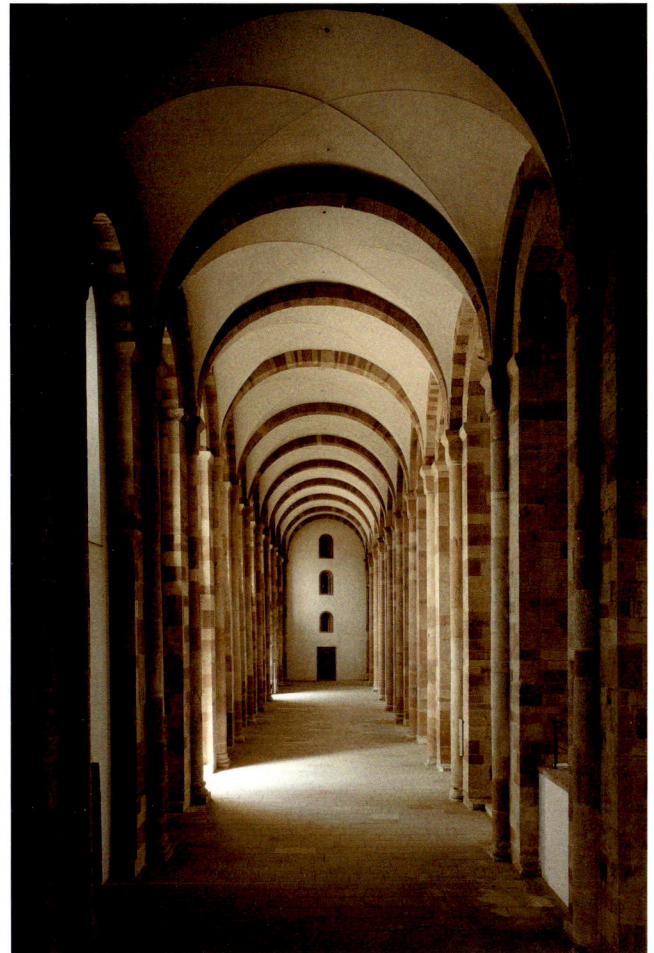

Dom, Speyer, Deutschland, 1025–1106   **Speyer Cathedral Germany, 1025–1106**

since either been pulled down or put to a different use. And now, at the start of the twenty-first century, the Church is building again, and has given architecture back its guiding task.

Churches for a Society of Privation

The Church is building for a society of privation surrounded by abundance. This privation is reflected in the absence of a link to tradition, in rampant egocentricity and the disoriented secularisation of all areas of life. Society's orientation towards the "dignity of man as a being created in God's likeness, who knows he is redeemed in Christ, and recognises his place in a pre-established overriding order" – this focus on the 'centre' – has been lost.[4,5]

Corresponding to the alienation between God and Man is our growing ineptness in the interpersonal arena. These days our society gets its highs from fleeting sensations, sees being permanently on-the-go as a metaphor for happiness, and places its faith in economics.[6] Remaining and being are outdated images. Man finds himself in a situation of existential privation. The awareness of his lack of protection in an increasingly complex world frightens him; he calls for security, but may only express this call as a hope.

Mario Botta, Kirche San Giovanni Battista, Mogno, Schweiz, 1998   **Mario Botta, Church of San Giovanni Battista, Mogno, Switzerland, 1998**

nicht allein mit dem euklidischen Raumbegriff zu fassen, sondern muss auch phänomenologische Aspekte berücksichtigen.[11]

Kirche als Wahrnehmungsraum

Vor diesem Hintergrund ist es für den Sakralbau zunächst ganz unerheblich, ob ein Kirchenraum per se ein heiliger Raum ist oder nur dann als sakral bezeichnet werden kann, wenn er der Begegnung Gottes dient. Viel wichtiger ist die Erkenntnis, dass der Mensch den heiligen Raum in seinem Alltag braucht – einen Raum, der dem allgemeinen Gebrauch ausdrücklich entrückt ist. Der Theologe Manfred

Religious Zones of Protection

How can architecture address this search for protective spaces that provide emotional security? First of all, architecture must adapt to a situation that did not previously exist in this form. Even after the trauma of National Socialism and World War Two, church building remained an integral part of the restoration of both society and culture. Religious knowledge and religious cult were part of this culture. Such connections no longer exist in a world of highly heterogeneous, meshing interests. It follows that architecture can no longer consult social consensus; it must return to its anthropological foundation and explore man's most primitive essence.

Josuttis vergleicht diese ›Wohnung‹ mit einem »symbolischen Kraft-feld, das für die Rezeption göttlicher Gegenwart wie für zwischen-menschliche Kommunikation gleichermaßen geeignet ist«.[12] Es ist eine Wohnung mit verschiedenen Zimmern: einem großen für das Fest der Gemeinde und mehreren kleinen für die Barmherzigkeit der Stille. Ronchamp ist hier das geniale Beispiel.

»In Frieden an einem geschützten Ort sein«[13] ist das Geheimnis des heiligen Raumes. Wenn der Mensch diesen Frieden mit Leib und Seele erspüren kann, dann findet Kirchenbau statt. Bei Helmut Striff-lers Versöhnungskirche in Dachau wird dieses Motiv des Bergens und Geborgenseins exemplarisch. Tief in die Erde hinein wühlt sich der graue Baukörper, um in der Dunkelheit des Raumes dem Leben eine zarte Lichtspur zu zeichnen.

Um den heiligen Raum zu gestalten, bedarf es der Demut des Architekten. Er muss sich seiner dienenden Funktion erinnern und den Satz aus Thomas Bernhards Roman *Korrektur* beherzigen: »Die Bauten, gleich welche, [...] schauten anders aus, wenn die, die sie gebaut haben, sich auch nur im geringem Maße um die, für die sie diese Bauten gebaut haben, gekümmert hätten [...].«[14] Wie also soll ein Kirchenbau sein, der sich um den Menschen ›kümmert‹? Er muss ein ›Ander-Ort‹[15] sein, eine Heterotopie, die sich von der Menge der gewöhnlichen Zeichen abhebt. Das heißt, Kirche darf kein multifunk-tionales Dienstleistungszentrum sein, kein spektakuläres Show-Biz-Gehäuse, kein marktgerechtes Event-Design, keine sterile Kontem-plationskiste, aber auch kein dekoriertes Gehäuse kindlicher Wohn-stubengemütlichkeit. ›Kümmern‹ heißt, den Menschen in seiner be-dürftigen Unzulänglichkeit ernst nehmen. Kirchenbau muss deshalb über das Funktionale hinaus Stimmungen zulassen[16] und auch her-vorrufen.

Kirchenbau muss sprechende Architektur sein, aber sie muss sprechen in den Bildern der »stummen Dinge«.[17] Diese sind die Kons-tanten der Baukunst. Das Licht als raumgestaltende Kraft ist eine solche und ihr dunkler Bruder der Schatten. Neue Kirchen, diese wohltemperierten Vitrinen des raumfüllenden Streulichts, lieben den Schatten nicht. Aber er ist wichtig, denn er ist biblische Metapher der Geborgenheit.[18] Nach C. G. Jung beschreiben Schatten die dunkle, verdrängte Seite der Seele. Auch die Umarmung des Schattens ist Gnade, nicht nur die des Lichts. Gnade, das Gesicht im Schatten zu bergen, im Zwielicht eine Kerze anzuzünden und sich für einen Augenblick wärmen zu dürfen an der Hoffnung eschatologischer Verheißung: »Ich bin das Licht der Welt. Wer mir nachfolgt, der wird nicht wandeln in der Finsternis, sondern wird das Licht des Lebens haben.«[19] In der mittelalterlichen Kirche nähert sich der Mensch nicht nur symbolisch dem ›ewigen Licht‹, sondern er wird auch ganz real auf der Via sacra des Langhauses zum Licht geführt: Vom dunklen Westtor kommend, durchschreitet er über verschiedene Helligkeits-grade das Langhaus bis zum lichtdurchfluteten Ostchor. Im romani-schen Dom zu Speyer setzt sich die Magie des Lichts bis in die Seitenschiffe fort.

Heutige Sakralarchitektur kann diese historischen Bausteine nicht einfach übernehmen, aber sie darf sie in transformierter Gestalt ›fort-schreiben‹ und aus ihnen »Orte in der Welt – aber nicht von der Welt«[20] bauen.

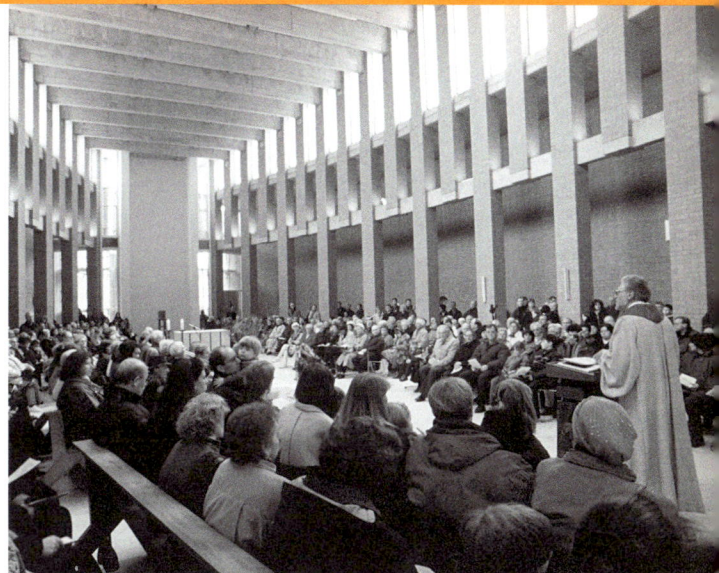

Dieter G. Baumewerd, St. Christophorus, Sylt, Deutschland, 2000
Dieter G. Baumewerd, St Christophorus, Sylt, Germany, 2000

From a psychological perspective, man has basically remained a Stone Age being in terms of emotions, employing archaic modes of behaviour and complex pre-conscious structures.[7] It is therefore vital to consider how people perceive architecture and how they respond to it. Moreover, it is important to realise that perception is not limited to the visual or cognitive levels alone. "Mere observation never produces space."[8] Rather, the perception of architecture is something experienced by the whole person.[9] Architecture only exists as a result of sensory perception in the melding of affective levels which serve to create variable perceptual spaces, and are formed anew again and again. This is the process that allows people to sense architecture's spatial dimension, order and atmospheric quality. The atmosphere of a room consists of many elements: of smell and sound, warmth or cold, light and shadow, the structure of the materials and the spatial effect of colours. How space is expe-rienced always arises from an interrelated network of "essence-revealing" elements which arouse certain emotional associations.[10] Consequently, church architecture cannot be explained using the Euclidian definition of space alone, but must also take phenomeno-logical aspects into consideration.[11]

The Church as Perceptual Space

Against this background, it is clear that for religious architecture it is totally irrelevant whether a church is holy space per se, or can only be described as religious when it serves the encounter with God. What is much more important is the realisation that people need this holy space in their everyday dealings – a space which is specifically removed from general use. Theologian Manfred Josuttis compares this 'dwelling' with a "symbolical field of force that is equally suitable for receiving the divine presence and for interper-sonal communication."[12] It is a dwelling with various rooms: a large one for the celebration of the congregation and several small ones

Ein transzendentaler Ort verlangt die Einbettung in ein klar definiertes räumliches Umfeld: die Einfriedung, den Platz. Im Idealfall gelingt die Synthese mit dem primären Ort der Landschaft. Denn »die altertümlichsten ›heiligen Orte‹, die wir kennen, bilden […] einen Mikrokosmos: eine Landschaft von Steinen, von Wassern, von Bäumen«.[21] Mario Bottas Kirche San Giovanni Battista im Tessin beschwört diesen Genius Loci. Sein Kultraum des sprechenden Lichts inmitten der gewaltigen Natur wird zum Sonnengesang der Schöpfung.

Bevor der Mensch eine Kirche betritt, hat er bereits wichtige Stationen der Prädisposition passiert: Weg, Tür und Schwelle. Sobald er Letztere überschritten hat, bleibt das Chaos des Tages draußen. In

Rudolf Schwarz, St. Fronleichnam, Aachen, Deutschland, 1930
Rudolf Schwarz, St Fronleichnam, Aachen, Germany, 1930

for the compassion of silence. Ronchamp offers an ingenious example.

"Being at peace in a protected place" is the secret of the holy space.[13] Architecture is truly religious when people can sense this peace both physically and emotionally. In Helmut Striffler's Church of the Reconciliation in Dachau, Germany, the treatment of the issues of protecting and being protected is exemplary. The grey building burrows its way into the earth in order to sketch a tender trace of light for life in the darkness of the space.

An architect needs humility to design a holy space. He must recall his serving function, and heed the observation from Thomas Bernhard's novel *Korrektur* (Correction): "Buildings, regardless of what kind they were … looked different if the people who had built them cared only slightly for those for whom these buildings were designed …"[14] What should a church that 'cares' for people be like? It must be a 'set-apart place', a heterotopia that stands out from the mass of normal symbols.[15] In other words, a church cannot be a multi-purpose service centre or a spectacular show-biz building. Nor can it be an event design in line with market requirements, a sterile contemplation box or a decorated shell containing childish living-room cosiness. 'Care' in this context means to take man's needy inadequacy seriously, which is why church architecture must go beyond the functional and also allow and evoke moods.[16]

Church architecture must be articulate architecture, but it must speak in the images of "silent things", in other words, the unchanging elements of architecture.[17] Light as a force that defines space is one such example, but also its dark brother, shadow. New churches imbued with pleasant atmosphere are showcases filled with scattered light that harbour no love of shadows. But shadow is important as the biblical metaphor for shelter and security.[18] According to Carl Gustav Jung, shadows describe the dark, suppressed aspect of the soul. There is grace in embracing not only the light, but also the shadow. Grace, to hide one's face in the shadow, to light a candle in the crepuscule and take heart for a moment in the hope of the eschatological promise, "I am the light of the world. Whoever follows me will never walk in darkness, but will have the light of life."[19] In the medieval church, man approaches the 'eternal light' not only symbolically, but also literally on the via sacra of the main building: Coming from the dark west entrance he walks along the main building, passing through various degrees of brightness until he reaches the choir at the eastern end, bathed in light. In the Romanesque cathedral at Speyer the magic of light is continued into the side aisles.

Contemporary religious architecture cannot simply adopt these historical elements, but it can continue them in a transformed guise and use them to build "places in the world – but not of the world".[20]

A transcendental place must be embedded in a clearly-defined spatial environment: an enclosure and place. Ideally, this synthesis

Peter Kulka mit Konstantin Pichler, Haus der Stille,
Benediktinerabtei Königsmünster, Meschede, Deutschland, 2001
Peter Kulka with Konstantin Pichler, Haus der Stille, Benedictine Abbey at Königsmünster, Meschede, Germany, 2001

Wohnungen der Stille
Dwellings of Silence

der Übergangszone von hell zu dunkel formen die Sinne das Bild des Raumes. Und im Erkennen entsteht eine Welt, in der die atmende Stille körperlich wird. Von fern das Licht – und plötzlich ist der Mensch mitten im Mundus sensibilis aus Tremendum und Faszinosum. Ein so ›gestimmter‹ Raum schenkt die Möglichkeit, die grelle Dimension der Realität zu verlassen und den Menschen zu sich selbst, zum anderen und vielleicht auch zu Gott zu führen.

Der Kirchenraum von heute ist primär auf das liturgisch angestrebte Erlebnis der Communio angelegt: Die Gemeinde sitzt wie eine Familie um einen gemeinsamen Tisch. Diese Vergewisserung in der Gemeinschaft der Heiligen schafft temporäre Sicherheit, aber auch diffuses Unbehagen fremder Nähe. Der Mensch braucht neben dem Band der Gemeinde vor allem intime Nischen des persönlichen Rückzugs, in denen er mit seinen ›Drinnen-Erfahrungen‹ für sich sein darf.

Äußere Einfachheit ist keine Frage konfektionären Zeitgeschmacks. Sie orientiert sich vielmehr an einer weiteren Konstante der Baukunst, an Maß und Zahl[22], mit dem Ziel eines energiegeladenen Raumes des Suchens und Fragens, den Rudolf Schwarz einst durch die »stille Ruhe großer unzerstörter Flächen« und »leergeräumte Weite«[23] charakterisierte: »Das ist keine Leere; das ist Stille! Und in der Stille ist Gott. Aus der Stille dieser weiten Wände kann eine Ahnung der Gegenwart Gottes hervorblühen.«[24]

Aber wie viel Leere erträgt der Mensch heute? Er darf immer noch auf die Schöpferkraft des leeren Raumes vertrauen. Denn die Stille des Raumes hat die Kraft, als evokatives Äquivalent zu sprechen. Das geschieht immer dann, wenn Farben, Materialien und Formen mit dem Rhythmus des Raumes aus Licht und Schatten als synästhetisches Gesamtkunstwerk wirken. »Wer einen Raum ordnet, wiederholt das exemplarische Werk der Götter«, sagt Mircea Eliade.[25] Es genügt, wenn der Architekt den bescheidenen Gedanken des großen Kirchenbauers Otto Bartning beherzigt: »Ich habe mein lebenlang Kirchen gebaut in dem bewußten und unbewußten Drange, die Menschen sanft zu überreden oder hart zu bedrohen, daß sie stille darin werden und auf die innere Stimme lauschen möchten, um alsdann hinauszutreten und aus der inneren Stille heraus stark und klar zu handeln und zu lieben.«[26]

should occur with the primary place, namely the landscape. After all, the ancient 'holy places' we are familiar with form "…a microcosm: a landscape of stones, of water, of trees."[21] Mario Botta's San Giovanni Battista church in Tessin conjures up the spirit of the place. His cultic space of the speaking light in the midst of nature is transformed into the Canticle of the Sun.

Before entering a church visitors have already passed important stations that act as a kind of preparation: path, door and threshold. Once the threshold is crossed, the chaos of the day is left behind. In the transitional zone between dark and light, the senses form an image of the interior, and this recognition creates a world in which the breathing silence becomes palpable. The light appears in the distance – and suddenly man is in the midst of a *mundus sensibilis* of *tremendum* and *fascinosum*. Such an 'atmospherically tuned' space makes it possible to leave behind the bright dimension of reality and to lead man to himself, to others and perhaps also to God.

The interiors of today's churches are primarily arranged for the liturgical experience of the communion: the congregation sits like a family around a table. This feeling of belonging to the holy community creates a temporary sense of security, but also a vague feeling of unease owing to the close proximity of strangers. In addition to the sense of unity the community provides, man needs above all secluded niches into which he can retreat, in which he can be alone with his 'inner world'.

External simplicity is not a question of mass-produced contemporary fashion or taste. Rather, it is guided by further unchanging features of architecture: measurements and figures whose aim is to create an energised domain of searching and questioning.[22] Rudolf Schwarz once referred to this as the "silent peace of large, undisturbed places" and "emptied expanse".[23] "It is not emptiness but silence! And in the silence is God. From the silence of these wide walls a sense of the presence of God can emerge."[24]

But how much emptiness can man take today? He can still trust in the creative power of empty space. After all, the silence of space has the power to speak as an evocative equivalent. That is always the case when colours, materials and shapes interact with the rhythm of the space, with light and shadow in the manner of a synaesthetic total work of art. According to Mircea Eliade, "Anyone who arranges space repeats the exemplary work of gods."[25] It suffices when the architect embraces the comparatively modest thoughts of the great church architect Otto Bartning: "I have built churches all my life with the conscious and unconscious desire to gently persuade people or browbeat them into becoming silent and listening to their inner voice so that they can go out and from that place of inner silence act strongly and clearly, and love."[26]

1   1. Korinther 3, 16 f: »Wißt ihr nicht, daß ihr Tempel Gottes seid und der Geist Gottes in euch wohnt? […] Gottes Tempel ist heilig und der seid ihr.« 1. Petrus 2, 4–6: »Lasset euch auch als lebendige Steine aufbauen als ein geistliches Haus […].«

2   Vgl. Ephesus 2, 20–22.

3   Adolf Adam, *Wo sich Gottes Volk versammelt. Gestalt und Symbolik im Kirchenbau*, Freiburg 1984, S. 24.

4   Rolf Lessenich, *Die Geistige Mitte. Sakralbauten als Zeichen des privaten und gesellschaftlichen Denkens*, in: *Kirche im Mittelpunkt?*, Fachtagung in Schwäbisch Gmünd vom 4. bis 6. September 1991, Kongressbericht, S. 15.

5   Hans Sedlmayr, *Verlust der Mitte. Die Bildende Kunst des 19. und 20. Jahrhunderts als Symbol der Zeit*, Salzburg 1948.

6   Vgl. die Ausführungen zum transitorischen Wohnen in: Hartmut Häußermann und Walter Siebel, *Soziologie des Wohnens. Eine Einführung in Wandel und Ausdifferenzierung des Wohnens*, Weinheim und München 1996.

7   Die Geschichte des Wohnens zeigt, dass der Mensch die irrationale Sehnsucht nach der bergenden Kraft der Höhle niemals verloren hat. Vgl. Hans Günther Burkhardt und Gerhard Laage, *Zur Psychologie des Städtebaus und der Architektur*, in: Hans Joachim Harloff (Hrsg.), *Psychologie des Wohnungs- und Siedlungsbaus. Psychologie im Dienst von Architektur und Stadtplanung*, Göttingen 1993, S. 3 f.

8   Franz Xaver Baier, *Der Raum. Prolegomena zu einer Architektur des gelebten Raumes*, Köln 2000, S. 90.

1   1 Corinthians 3:16f: "Do you not know that you are the temple of God, and that the Spirit of God dwells in you? …The temple of God is holy and so are you." 1 Peter 2:4–6: "Let yourselves be built like living stones into a spiritual house …"

2   See Ephesus 2:20–22.

3   Adolf Adam, *Wo sich Gottes Volk versammelt. Gestalt and Symbolik im Kirchenbau*, Freiburg, 1984, p. 24.

4   Rolf Lessenich, "Die Geistige Mitte. Sakralbauten als Zeichen des privaten und gesellschaftlichen Denkens", in: *Kirche im Mittelpunkt*, Congress in Schwäbisch Gmünd, 4–6 September 1991, congress report, p. 15.

9 Vgl. E. Bruce Goldstein, *Wahrnehmungspsychologie,* Heidelberg 1997, S. 27.

10 Jean-Paul Sartre, *Das Sein und das Nichts,* Reinbek 1962, S. 1025.

11 Vgl. Thomas Fuchs, *Leib, Raum, Person. Entwurf einer phänomenologischen Anthropologie,* Stuttgart 2000.

12 Manfred Josuttis, *Vom Umgang mit heiligen Räumen,* in: Thomas Klie (Hrsg.), *Der Religion Raum geben. Kirchenpädagogik und religiöses Lernen,* Münster 1998, S. 37 f.

13 Martin Heidegger, *Bauen Wohnen Denken,* in: Ulrich Conrads und Peter Neitzke (Hrsg.), *Mensch und Raum: Das Darmstädter Gespräch 1951* (= Bauwelt Fundamente, Bd. 94), Braunschweig 1991, S. 91.

14 Thomas Bernhard, *Korrektur,* Frankfurt/M. 1975, S. 217.

15 Helge Adolphsen, *Heiligkeit duldet keine Neutralität,* in: *Kunst und Kirche,* 2003, Heft 3, S. 134.

16 Heidegger spricht in diesem Zusammenhang von »Gestimmtheit«, die in sich transzendentale Tendenz hat. Vgl. Martin Heidegger, *Was ist Metaphysik?* 8. Aufl., Frankfurt/M. 1960.

17 Hugo von Hofmannsthal, *Brief des Lord Chandos,* in: Ders., *Gesammelte Werke. Erzählungen. Erfundene Gespräche und Briefe, Reisen,* Frankfurt/M., 1979, S. 472.

18 Vgl. Psalm 91, 1–2: »Wer unter dem Schirm des Höchsten wohnt, wer im Schatten des Allmächtigen ruht, der darf sprechen zum Herrn: Meine Zuflucht, meine Feste, mein Gott, auf den ich vertraue.«

19 Johannes 8, 12.

20 Johannes 17, 9–19.

21 Mircea Eliade, *Die Religionen und das Heilige. Elemente der Religionsgeschichte,* Salzburg o. J., S. 305.

22 Vgl. Weisheit Salomos 11, 21: »Du aber hast alles nach Maß, Zahl und Gewicht geordnet.«

23 Rudolf Schwarz zitiert nach Adolf Adam, wie Anm. 3, S. 71.

24 Romano Guardini, *Die neuerbaute Fronleichnamskirche in Aachen,* in: *Die Schildgenossen* 11, 1931, 3, S. 267.

25 Mircea Eliade, *Das Heilige und das Profane. Vom Wesen des Religiösen,* Frankfurt/M. 1984, S. 33.

26 *Otto Bartning in kurzen Worten. Aus Schriften und Reden des Architekten,* Hamburg 1954, S. 27.

5 Hans Sedlmayr, *Verlust der Mitte. Die Bildende Kunst des 19. and 20. Jahrhunderts als Symbol der Zeit,* Salzburg, 1948.

6 See the comments on transitory living in: Hartmut Häußermann and Walter Siebel, *Soziologie des Wohnens. Eine Einführung in Wandel und Ausdifferenzierung des Wohnens,* Weinheim and Munich, 1996.

7 The history of housing shows that man has never lost his irrational longing for the protective force of the cave. See Hans Günther Burkhardt and Gerhard Laage, "Zur Psychologie des Städtebaus und der Architektur", in: Hans Joachim Harloff (ed.), *Psychologie des Wohnungs- und Siedlungsbaus. Psychologie im Dienst von Architektur und Stadtplanung,* Göttingen, 1993, p. 3f.

8 Franz Xaver Baier, *Der Raum. Prolegomena zu einer Architektur des gelebten Raumes,* Cologne, 2000, p. 90.

9 See E. Bruce Goldstein, *Wahrnehmungspsychologie,* Heidelberg, 1997, p. 27.

10 Jean-Paul Sartre, *Das Sein und das Nichts,* Reinbek, 1962, p. 1025.

11 See Thomas Fuchs, *Leib, Raum, Person. Entwurf einer phänomenologischen Anthropologie,* Stuttgart, 2000.

12 Manfred Josuttis, "Vom Umgang mit heiligen Räumen", in: Thomas Klie (ed.), *Der Religion Raum geben. Kirchenpädagogik und religiöses Lernen,* Münster, 1998, p. 37 f.

13 Martin Heidegger, "Mensch and Raum. Das Darmstädter Gespräch 1951", in: *Bauwelt Fundamente 94,* Braunschweig, 1991, p. 91.

14 Thomas Bernhard, *Korrektur,* Frankfurt/Main, 1975, p. 217.

15 Helge Adolphsen, "Heiligkeit duldet keine Neutralität", in: *Kunst und Kirche,* 3/2002, p. 134.

16 Heidegger talks in this connection about "tunedness" with an inherent transcendental aspect. See Martin Heidegger, *Was ist Metaphysik?,* 8th edition, Frankfurt/Main, 1960.

17 Hugo von Hofmannsthal, "Brief des Lord Chandos", in: Ibid., *Gesammelte Werke. Erzählungen. Erfundene Gespräche and Briefe, Reisen,* Frankfurt/Main, 1979, p. 472.

18 See Psalms 91:1–2: "He that dwelleth in the secret place of the most high shall abide under the shadow of the Almighty. I will say of the Lord, He is my refuge and my fortress: my God; in Him will I trust."

19 John 8:12.

20 John 17:9–19.

21 Mircea Eliade, *Die Religionen and das Heilige. Elemente der Religionsgeschichte,* Salzburg, p. 305.

22 See the Wisdom of Solomon 11:20: "But you have arranged all things by measure and number and weight."

23 Rudolf Schwarz cited by Adolf Adam, as note 3, p. 71.

24 Romano Guardini, "Die neuerbaute Fronleichnamskirche in Aachen", in: *Die Schildgenossen 11,* (1931) 3, p. 267.

25 Mircea Eliade, *Das Heilige und das Profane. Vom Wesen des Religiösen,* Frankfurt/Main, 1984, p. 33.

26 Otto *Bartning in kurzen Worten. Aus Schriften und Reden des Architekten,* Hamburg, 1954, p. 27.

»Einige Dinge sind heilig, und andere sind es nicht.« Le Corbusier
"Some things are sacred, and others are not." Le Corbusier

Niklas Maak

Kathedralen einer neuen Öffentlichkeit:
Museum, Gericht, Konzerthalle, Autohaus

■ Der Bau steht stumm auf der anderen Seite des Ufers, fernab der hellen Stadt: eine unerbittliche, schwarze Kathedrale des Rechts. Mit der hohen, schwarz glänzenden ›Salle des pas perdus‹ betritt man eine andere Welt, die strenger ist als der laute, bunt durcheinander gewürfelte Alltag draußen. Jean Nouvels Justizpalast in Nantes ist von einer mathematischen Rigorosität, die an die Sakralbauten der Gotik erinnert. 8,10 x 8,10 Meter ist das Grundmaß dieses Gebäudes, und alle Dimensionen ergeben sich aus diesem Raster: Die Vorhalle ist 16,2 Meter hoch, 113,4 Meter lang ist der gesamte Bau – kein Millimeter, der hier nicht dem Gesetz gehorcht. Der Justizpalast ist ein Gegenbau. Er fügt sich nicht in die Stadt ein, er setzt ihr etwas entgegen, das wie vom Himmel gefallen wirkt und ein anderes, besseres Leben verspricht – und es ist genau dieser Anspruch, der den Verwaltungsbau zum Nachfolger sakraler Architektur macht.

›Sakrale Raumstimmung‹ ist kein objektivierbares Kriterium. Die feierlich erleuchtete Kathedrale, die den einen zu Tränen rührt, ist in den Augen des anderen ein dunkler Kasten, in dem es zieht. Doch es fällt auf, wie intensiv Motive der Sakralarchitektur in profanen Bauten der Gegenwart zitiert werden – und mit ihnen jene Heilsversprechen, die eigentlich längst auf der Schutthalde metaphysischer Spekulationen gelandet waren. Die gebaute Rhetorik von Konzerthallen, Museen und Gerichten ist eine im Grunde sakrale. Ein wesentliches Merkmal der Kathedralen war der Dimensionensprung, die Überrumpelung des Besuchers durch eine außerirdisch wirkende Form und Größe.

Doch nicht jeder Großbau wirkt automatisch sakral. Kaum eine Flughafenhalle, kaum ein Einkaufszentrum ruft das Gefühl hervor, man betrete eine Gegenwelt; zwischen Grillfleisch, Konservendosen und Samsonitekoffern gerät eine mögliche Atmosphäre des Sakralen unter schweren Beschuss. Schon eher rufen Museen sakrale Raumstimmungen hervor. Tadao Andos neues Kunstmuseum in Fort Worth, Texas, wirkt wie ein Bunker gegen das Banale, ein Kloster der modernen Kunst. Die Leere wirkt ungewohnt und feierlich, der Platz wird bewusst verschwendet; hier geht es um mehr als um Raumökonomie. Es ist die Erhabenheit des Verschwenderischen, die hier den Kathedraleffekt erzeugt – ebenso wie die himmelstrebende, barocke Aufwärtsbewegung in Frank O. Gehrys Guggenheim Museum in Bilbao. Eine wichtige Rolle kommt dabei der Inszenierung des Lichts zu. Schon in frühen religiösen Hymnen wurde das plötzlich aufschimmernde Scheinen, das die Architektur überflutet, als Vorstellung des Göttlichen gefeiert. Venantius Fortunatus, der als Dichter am Hofe der Merowinger tätig war, schreibt in *De ecclesia Parisiaca:* »Ein diffuses Licht überflutet von früh an die Täfelung / und leuchtet aus eigener Kraft ohne die Hilfe der Sonne.«[1] Die mystifizierende Eigenschaft des Lichts findet sich auch in profanen Bauten der Gegenwart. Gerichtsbauten wie Nouvels Justizpalast und Museen wie

Cathedrals of a New Public Realm:
Museum, Court, Concert Hall, Car Showroom

■ The building stands silently on the opposite shore, far from the bright city lights, a dark and inexorable cathedral of justice. To enter the shining, black, high-ceilinged *Salle des pas perdus* is to enter a world more ordered than the quotidian kaleidoscope of colours and cacophony outside. Jean Nouvel's Palais de Justice in Nantes possesses the mathematical rigour of a Gothic cathedral. A unit of 8.10 metres by 8.10 metres is the basis for all its dimensions, down to the very last millimetre. The portico is 16.2 metres high and the overall length of the building is 113.4 metres. It is a structure that does not fit in to the urban fabric, but contrasts with it instead, like something that has come to earth with the promise of a different and better life. Indeed, this is precisely what places this administrative building in the tradition of religious architecture.

A 'sacred atmosphere' is not an objective criterion. The solemnly lit cathedral that moves one visitor to tears will seem like a cold and gloomy box to another. Yet it is striking that the motifs of religious architecture should be so frequently quoted in the secular buildings of the present day, and that these references should be so intensely imbued with a promise of salvation since abandoned on the scrapheap of metaphysical speculation. The architectural rhetoric of concert halls, museums and law courts is a fundamentally religious one. Cathedrals have always been characterised by their sheer size, which overwhelms the visitor with an other-worldly sense of form and scale.

Not every large building, however, automatically has a religious air. An airport terminal or a shopping mall is unlikely to give us a sense of entering a different world. Between the meat counter, the canned foods and the Samsonite suitcases, any potential feeling of religious awe is quickly thwarted. Tadao Ando's new art museum of Fort Worth, Texas, seems like a bulwark against banality, a monastery of modern art. Its emptiness is unaccustomed and ceremonious, its lavish expansiveness of space no mere design feature. It is the sublimity of extravagance that creates the 'cathedral effect' – as in the baroquely soaring movement of Frank O. Gehry's Guggenheim Museum in Bilbao. The handling of light plays a crucial role in this. Early religious hymns celebrate the sudden shimmer of brightness that floods architecture with a sense of divinity. Venantius Fortunatus, bard of the Merovingian court, wrote in his *De ecclesia Parisiaca*: "A diffuse light floods the panelling from the early hours / and shines by its own strength without the aid of the sun."[1] The mystic quality of light can also be found in contemporary secular buildings. Law courts such as Nouvel's Palais de

Jean Nouvel, Justizpalast, Nantes, Frankreich, 2000
Jean Nouvel, Palais de Justice, Nantes, France, 2000

Tadao Ando, Modern Art Museum, Fort Worth, Texas, USA, 2002 **Tadao Ando, Modern Art Museum, Fort Worth, Texas, USA, 2002**

Stephan Braunfels' Pinakothek der Moderne in München spielen gleichermaßen mit dem Überwältigungseffekt eines plötzlich einfallenden Lichts.

Der sakrale Raum des Automobils

Doch sakrale Architektur ist heute auch jenseits traditioneller Bauten zu finden; die kryptoreligiösen Räume der Gegenwart können sogar auf vier Rädern daherkommen. Bereits 1955 schrieb Roland Barthes in seinem Essay *Der neue Citroën,* das Auto sei heute das genaue Äquivalent der gotischen Kathedralen: von unbekannten Künstlern erbaut, von einem ganzen Volk bewundert und als magisches Objekt verehrt.[2] Heute, gut ein halbes Jahrhundert später, durchdringt die Rhetorik des Sakralen sowohl das Auto selbst als auch die Architektur, die seinem Image und somit seinem Verkauf dient. Zum Beispiel die Autostadt Wolfsburg: Angelegt als veloziferisches Disneyland, ist sie jedoch kein Rummelplatz, sondern ein modernes Mysterienspiel. In der Sepultur reihen sich die mythischen Vorfahren der neuen

Justice and museums such as Stephan Braunfels' Pinakothek der Moderne in Munich also use the overwhelming effect of a sudden deluge of light.

The Sacred Space of the Automobile

Today, religious architecture can also be found beyond the bounds of traditional buildings; the crypto-religious spaces of the present can even have four wheels. As early as the 1950s, in his essay "The New Citroen", Roland Barthes described the car as "almost the exact equivalent of the great Gothic cathedrals: …the supreme creation of an era, conceived with passion by unknown artists, and consumed in image if not in usage by a whole population which appropriates them as a purely magical object."[2] Today, half a century later, the rhetoric of religion permeates not only the car itself, but also the architecture that serves its image and marketing. Take, for example, the car manufacturing city of Wolfsburg, Germany. Designed as a velociferous Disneyland, it is not so much a fairground as a modern

Frank O. Gehry, Guggenheim Museum, Bilbao, Spanien, 1997 **Frank O. Gehry, Guggenheim Museum, Bilbao, Spain, 1997**

Autos, im Mittelpunkt steht, als Prophet, der VW-Käfer. In einem eigenen Tempel findet die Epiphanie der Technik statt: Wie aus dem Nichts erscheint, auf einer Drehscheibe in der Wand, der neue Lamborghini. Der Stier von Sant'Agatha ist das Goldene Kalb: ein bewunderter, vergötterter Fetisch der technischen Moderne. Dazu trägt auch sein plötzlicher Auftritt bei – seit jeher ein wichtiger Bestandteil des Sakralen. Das Heilige bricht immer mit hohem Tempo herein und überrumpelt die Ungläubigen. Ob Verkündigungsengel oder der heilige Ranieri Rasini in Sassettas berühmtem Gemälde von 1437–1444, auf dem der Heilige wie eine zentaurische Rakete ins Bild donnert: Immer offenbart sich das Jenseitige plötzlich. Wie eine leuchtende Gottheit taucht auch der Lamborghini in seinem Techno-Tabernakel auf, eine Erscheinung aus einer anderen Welt, unerreichbar für die unten zusammengekommenen Massen: Noli me tangere. Die Epiphanie der Technik prägt auch die architektonische Inszenierung der Endabfertigung im Porsche-Werk Zuffenhausen: Wie technoide Verkündigungsengel schweben die Sportwagen dort auf einem verglasten Förderband über den Autobahnzubringer. Auch das fabrikneue Auto ist ein quasi sakraler Raum, ein Gesamtkunstwerk, das seine

mystery play, with the mythical forebears of the new automobile arrayed at the sepulchre, and the Volkswagen Beetle at the centre as prophet. The epiphany of technology takes place in a temple of its own. The new Lamborghini appears on a wall disc as though out of nothingness. The raging bull of Sant'Agatha is the golden calf, revered and worshipped as a fetish of technical modernism. Its sudden appearance – an important element in religion – adds to its cachet. The sacred invariably arrives at high speed and overwhelms those of little faith. Be it the Angel of the Annunciation or St Ranicci in Sassetta's famous painting of 1440, thundering into the picture like a centaurian rocket, the revelation of the celestial is always sudden. The Lamborghini, too, emerges in its technoid tabernacle like a shining deity, a vision from another world, inaccessible to the masses gathering below: *noli me tangere.* The epiphany of technology also informs the architectural setting for the Porsche production works in Zuffenhausen, Germany, where sports cars hover on a glass-covered conveyor belt across the motorway access road like technoid Angels of the Annunciation. Even the brand new car is an almost sacred space, a *gesamtkunstwerk* that allows the senses no

Henn Architekten Ingenieure, Lamborghini Pavillon, Autostadt Wolfsburg, Deutschland, 2002
Henn Architekten Ingenieure, Lamborghini Pavilion, Autostadt Wolfsburg, Germany, 2002

Wurzeln in religiösen Bauten hat. Kirchen waren als Vorboten kommender Herrlichkeit Gesamtkunstwerke, die den Sinnen keinen Ausweg mehr ließen. Der Weihrauch und die Musik, die plötzliche frische Kühle, das schimmernde, in farbigen Scheiben sich bunt brechende Licht, die glänzend geschmückten Statuen, die reichen Schnitzereien – all das erzeugte eine alle Sinne angreifende Atmosphäre; benommen tritt man nach der Zeremonie wieder ans Tageslicht. Der pansensuale Theaterdonner der Kirche findet außerhalb nur noch, als infernalische Steigerung, in den Licht- und Klangbombardements der Massen bei Popkonzerten und, subtiler, in der Architektur des Automobils einen Widerhall. Ein ganzes Heer von Emotions-Ingenieuren arbeitet im Automobilbau an der haptischen Qualität der Materialien, am Klang der Motoren, und wofür in Kapellen der Weihrauch sorgte, das erfinden im Automobilbau Duft-Ingenieure, die monatelang einen Innenraumgeruch kreieren, der das Gefühl von Frische und Geborgenheit vermitteln soll. Das Innere des Autos ist ein heiliger Altar der Reinheit und des Privaten; der Gestank und Staub der Stadt wird hier ausgefiltert, und kein größeres Sakrileg ist auf der Straße denkbar, als zu einem Unbekannten ins Auto zu steigen.

escape. The incense and the music, the sudden cool breeze, the shimmering light that breaks in pools of coloured light, the shining, ornamented statues, the rich carving – all of this generates an atmosphere that touches all the senses. We emerge from the ceremony into the daylight, feeling dazed. The pansensual theatricality of the church is heightened in the bombardment of the masses with light and sound at pop concerts, and is echoed more subtly in the architecture of the automobile. An entire army of 'emotion engineers' work in the car industry, honing the tactile qualities of the materials and perfecting the sound of the engines. The incense in the chapel is tuned by aroma engineers who spend months creating the scent that makes the inside of a car seem fresh and welcoming. The interior of the car is a holy altar of purity and privacy; the stench and dust of the city are filtered out, and there is no greater sacrilege than to get into a stranger's car.

Private Chapels: the Country Retreat as Monastic Cell

As the sense of unease in public places grows, so too does the yearning to retreat into a private space. Museums and pop concert halls are places of collective experience that may bear quasi-religious traits and are, in this respect, secular cathedrals. Yet at the same time, there are intimate religious spaces that offer shelter

Stephan Braunfels, Pinakothek der Moderne, München, Deutschland, 2002
Stephan Braunfels, Pinakothek der Moderne, Munich, Germany, 2002

Graham Phillips, Skywood House, Denham, Middlesex, England, 1998 **Graham Phillips, Skywood House, Denham, Middlesex, England, 1998**

Kapellen des Privaten: Das Landhaus als Mönchsklause

Mit dem Unbehagen am öffentlichen Raum wächst die Sehnsucht nach privaten Rückzugszellen. Museen und Hallen für Popkonzerte sind Orte kollektiver Erfahrungen, die quasi-religiöse Züge tragen können, und sind in diesem Sinne profane Kathedralen. Doch ebenso gibt es die intimen religiösen Räume, die Zuflucht vor dem Kollektiv bieten, die profanen Kapellen der Gegenwart. Immer mehr Landhäuser erinnern an moderne Einsiedeleien, in denen zivilisationsmüde Städter sich von den Zumutungen der kollektiven Existenz erholen. Die Erholung auf dem Land wird immer unverhohlener religiös überhöht: Die Welle des Feng-Shui, die seit einigen Jahren wie ein vom Wahnsinn befallener chinesischer Drache durch deutsche Wohnzimmer rast, ist nur einer von vielen Versuchen, den privaten Raum mit kosmischen Gesetzen in Einklang zu bringen. Eine pantheistische Wohnkapelle ist Graham Phillips' Skywood House in Denham, Middlesex. Als habe sich der Barcelona-Pavillon in eine weiße Mönchskutte gehüllt, steht das Haus in einem zwei Hektar großen Park am Wasser; die Stadt ist ausgeblendet, die Natur als Drama der Schöpfung inszeniert: Regnet es, prasseln die Tropfen laut in den Teich vor der Terrasse, kommt Sturm auf, fängt sich das Rauschen des selbst kathedralenhaften Waldes als Hall unter dem Betondach. Im Rahmen der Architektur wird hier jedes Gewitter zum Schauspiel des Erhabenen.

Zurück zu den Ursprüngen

Die mönchische Beschränkung auf das Wesentliche, die ein reicheres Leben mit intensiverer Naturwahrnehmung mit sich bringen kann, trägt auch Stephen Atkinsons Landhaus in Zachary, Louisiana, in sich. Das kleine Haus ist als posturbanes Heilsversprechen ein archi-

from the collective, the secular chapels of the present day. More and more country houses are becoming modern hermitages where city dwellers can escape the pressure of the rat race of collective existence. Recuperating in the country is increasingly described in terms of religious fervour. The feng shui craze that stormed the living rooms of Germany like a demented Chinese dragon in recent years is just one of many attempts to bring private space into harmony with the laws of the cosmos. One example of a pantheistic chapel for living is Graham Philips' Skywood House in Denham, Middlesex. The house stands by the waterside in two acres of grounds like the Barcelona Pavilion in a white monk's habit. Here, the city is concealed from view and nature is staged like a drama of creation. When it rains, the falling drops resound loudly in the pond in front of the patio, and when there is a storm, the rustling of the cathedral-like forest echoes under the concrete roof. In this architectural scheme, every thunderstorm becomes a show of the sublime.

Back to the Roots

The ascetic reduction to essentials that can provide a richer life and a more intense perception of nature is also found in Steven Atkinson's country house at Zachary, Louisiana. The little house is something of an exception as a post-urban promise of salvation in which religious and national fantasies of redemption take the same form. Zachary is a modern-day 'Walden'.[3] Here, behind a dense oak forest on a vast expanse of meadow, city life is soon forgotten. There is a sense of how the first trappers must have felt as they set foot in unknown territory on their way westwards. A bed, a table, a fireplace, straightforward materials and nothing but nature all around: The simple metal cabin is a promise of salvation, the sanctuary of

Stephen Atkinson, Zachary House, Zachary, Louisiana, USA, 1999   **Stephen Atkinson, Zachary House, Zachary, Louisiana, USA, 1999**

tekturideologischer Sonderfall: Religiöse und nationale Erlösungs-
phantasien fallen hier in eine Form. Zachary ist ein modernes Walden.[3] Hier, hinter einem dichten Eichenwald, auf endlosen Wiesen,
ist die Stadt schnell vergessen; ein Gefühl kommt auf, wie es die
Trapper der ersten Stunde auf ihrem Zug nach Westen beim Betreten
des jungfräulichen Bodens gehabt haben müssen. Ein Bett, ein
Tisch, eine Feuerstelle, einfache Materialien und darum herum nur
Natur: Die einfache Blechhütte ist ein Heilsversprechen, das Sanktuarium des amerikanischen Traums. Die nationale amerikanische
Mythologie war, als Raumvorstellung, zunächst immer eine horizontal
expansive: Siedler zogen gen Westen und entdeckten neues Land.
Doch mit der Urbanisierung von San Francisco und Los Angeles löste sich das Versprechen der Horizontale. Das Land war erschlossen,

the American Dream. In spatial terms, the national American mythol-
ogy has always been horizontally expansive. Settlers moved westwards and discovered new land. Yet with the urbanisation of San
Francisco and Los Angeles, the promise of horizontal expansion
began to break apart. The land was opened up, and the cowboys
were ousted by high-rise architects and pilots – heroes of the
vertical. The twentieth century thrived on the myth of an upwardly
striving America with its skyscrapers, aircraft and space rockets.
The heroes of the horizontal lived on as Hollywood characters, and
those who played the roles of trappers and cowboys were revered
as saints. It is therefore hardly surprising that Hollywood actors of
the 1930s led their people, like Moses, from the West Coast back into the wilderness, back to their own mythological roots. In Palm

36

»Einige Dinge sind heilig, und andere sind es nicht.«
"Some things are sacred, and others are not."

die Nachfolger der Cowboys waren Hochhausarchitekten und Piloten, also Helden der Vertikale. Das 20. Jahrhundert lebte vom Mythos des himmelsstrebenden Amerika, von Hochhäusern, Flugzeugen und Mondraketen. Die Helden der Horizontale lebten als Hollywood-Figuren weiter, Darsteller von Trappern und Cowboys wurden verehrt wie Heiligenfiguren – und so ist es wiederum kein Wunder, dass Hollywood-Schauspieler, wie einst Moses, in den dreißiger Jahren ein auserwähltes Volk von der Westküste zurück in die Wüste und zu ihren eigenen mythischen Wurzeln führten. In Palm Springs, Kalifornien, ein paar Autostunden von der Westküste entfernt, entstanden Wochenend-Domizile, die wie die abstrahierte Wiederauflage des eben vergangenen Trapperlebens wirkten. Wo der Trapper sein Pferd stehen hatte, parkte ein offener Cadillac, wo die Quelle war, stand ein Swimmingpool, das Lagerfeuer war ein Kamin und das Zelt ein schwebendes Betondach. Palm Springs war die im modernen Gewand daherkommende Glorifizierung der amerikanischen Vergangenheit, die Feier des einsamen, gesellschaftsfernen Lebens am Busen der Schöpfung, das Mönchsidyll des amerikanischen Traums. Hollywood produzierte diese eben erst vergangene Geschichte als Film; die Luxus-Einsiedeleien von Palm Springs inszenierten sie als Architektur. Atkinson geht mit Zachary noch einen Schritt zurück. Die Bungalows von Palm Springs waren abstrakte Feuerstellen – Atkinsons Haus ist eine fast wörtliche Neuauflage. Alles ist auf das Wesentliche reduziert, kein Fernseher flimmert, nur ein archaisches Feuer brennt vor der rauen Steinwand. Wie eine jahrhundertealte Kapelle ignoriert das Haus die Zeit und wirft den Bewohner auf sich selbst zurück. Und als solle er das Heilsversprechen für die urbanitätsmüden Zivilisationsflüchtlinge unterstreichen, hat der Grundriss die Form eines Kreuzes.

Die Magie der Zukunftshöhle: Biomorphismus

Die Architekturhistorikerin Danièle Pauly erklärte einmal die hohe Akzeptanz der 1954 von Le Corbusier erbauten Kapelle in Ronchamp (siehe S. 19) bei den Gläubigen damit, dass sie das Raumgefühl der christlichen Katakomben und der alten romanischen Kirchen mit anderen Mitteln reinszeniere. Ronchamp war so fremd und futuristisch wie ein UFO und so archaisch wie eine Grotte – und vielleicht ist es die Mischung aus Futurismus und Archaik, die Ronchamp heute wie die Inkunabel aller biomorphen Wohnkapellen wirken lässt. Biomorphismus ist ein bewusst regressiver Stil. Nicht zufällig nennt der Kalifornier Greg Lynn seine Wohnblasen Embryological Houses. Architekten wie er wollen keinen städtischen Raum, sondern Schutzzellen vor den Zumutungen des Kollektivs schaffen. Nichts Hartes existiert in diesen aufgeweichten Bunkern, und wo Licht in die uteralen Techno-Höhlen eindringt, ist es stets warm gefiltert. Die biomorphe Wohnblase ist eine architektonische Feier des Jenseits in jedem Sinn: Fremd wie ein Raumschiff, abgekapselt von jeder Realität und aus einem Material, das noch erfunden werden muss – denn mit Stahl, Glas und Metall realisiert, sehen die blubbernden Wohnträume schnell aus wie Bauhauswürfel, die man zu lange über den Bunsenbrenner gehalten hat. Wie die biomorphen Bauten sich anfühlen,

Springs, California, a few hours' drive from the West Coast, one finds weekend homes built to look like abstracted reproductions of the trappers' lifestyle. Where the trapper once tied his horse, a Cadillac convertible is now parked; where there was a spring there is now a swimming pool; the campfire has become a hearth and the tent a concrete roof. Palm Springs was the glorification of America's past in modern garb, a celebration of the lone life far from civilisation – the monastic idyll of the American Dream. Hollywood has made films about this recent history with the luxury hermitages of Palm Springs as the architectural setting. Atkinson goes one step further with Zachary. The bungalows of Palms Springs were abstract reproductions, while Atkinson's house is an almost literal re-edition. Everything is reduced to the bare essentials. No television flickers here – only the flames of the archaic fire against a rough stone wall. Like a centuries-old chapel, the house ignores the passing of time and leaves its inhabitants to their own devices. And, as though to underline the promise of salvation for these refugees from the urban rat race, its floor plan takes the form of a cross.

The Magic of the Future Cave

In 1954, architectural historian Danièle Pauly explained the popularity of Le Corbusier's chapel at Ronchamp (see p. 19) among the faithful by pointing out that it reproduced, by other means, the atmosphere of the Christian catacombs and old Romanesque churches. Ronchamp was as strange and futuristic as a UFO and as archaic as a grotto – and it may be precisely this mix of the futuristic and the archaic that makes Ronchamp seem like an incunable of all biomorphic chapels for living. It is no coincidence that Californian Greg Lynn calls his bubble dwellings Embryological Houses. Architects like Lynn do not want to create urban spaces, but rather protective cells that offer shelter from the rigours of the collective. There is nothing hard in these softened bunkers, and wherever light penetrates these uterine techno-caves it is warmly filtered. The biomorphic bubble dwelling is an architectural celebration of the beyond in every sense. Strange as a spaceship, cut off from reality, and made of a material that had first to be invented – steel, glass and metal would have made these dream homes look like Bauhaus cubes that had been held under a Bunsen burner for too long. Just how these biomorphic structures feel when they leave the virtual world of computer animation was shown recently at Kunsthaus Bregenz. *Wave UFO* by artist Mariko Mori is a droplet-shaped metallic bubble some eleven metres in length. A stairway and a plexiglass eye lead into a shimmering green world in which one can lie down and be presented with a childlike fairytale voyage to visit the cute little people from Mars. Mori's *UFO* is the chapel of pop, the sanctuary of a permanently childlike culture that believes in the beatitude of plastic, curves and dreams of space. As a space-dream promise of happiness, Mori's chapel of pop is the counterpart to Atkinson's temple of nature, which seeks salvation in the hermitages of the past. Both are chapels of a hoped-for new beginning and promises of a better world.

»Einige Dinge sind heilig, und andere sind es nicht.«
"Some things are sacred, and others are not."

37

Mariko Mori, Wave UFO, Kunsthaus Bregenz, Österreich, 2003 **Mariko Mori, *Wave UFO,* Kunsthaus Bregenz, Austria, 2003**

wenn sie den materielosen Raum der Computeranimation verlassen, bekam man vor kurzem im Kunsthaus Bregenz zu sehen. Das Wave UFO der Künstlerin Mariko Mori ist eine tropfenförmige metallische Blase von etwa elf Metern Länge. Über eine Treppe und durch ein Plexiglasauge betritt man eine grünlich schimmernde Welt, in der einem im Liegen eine kindliche Märchenreise zu possierlichen Marsmenschen vorgeführt wird. Moris UFO ist die Kapelle des Pop, das Sanktuarium einer ewig kindlichen Kultur, die an die selig machende Wirkung von Plastik, Kurven und Weltraumträumen glaubt. Als weltraumseliges Glücksversprechen ist Moris Pop-Kapelle der Gegenpart zu Atkinsons Naturtempel, der sein Heil in den Einsiedeleien der Vergangenheit sucht; Kapellen eines erhofften Neuanfangs, Versprechen einer besseren Welt sind beide.

1   *Cursibus Aurorae vaga lux laquearia conplet / atque suis radiis et sine sole micat.* Fortunatus, Venantius Honorius Clementianus (530– 609 AD), poet and bishop of Poitiers. An edition of the works of Fortunatus was published by C. Brower at Fulda in 1603 (2nd ed., Mainz, 1617). The edition of M. A. Luschi (Rome, 1785) was reprinted afterwards in Migne's *Patrologiae cursus corn pletus*, vol. lxxxviii. See the edition by Leo and Krusch (Berlin, 1881– 85).
2   Roland Barthes, "The New Citroen", in *Mythologies*, translated by Annette Lavers, London 1972, p. 88.
3   Henry David Thoreau, *Walden*; or *Life in the Woods*, 1854.

1   Venantius Fortunatus zit. nach: Rosario Assunto, *Die Theorie des Schönen im Mittelalter,* Köln 1996, S. 169.
2   Roland Barthes, *Mythen des Alltags,* Frankfurt/M. 1991.
3   Henry David Thoreau, *Walden oder Leben in den Wäldern*, Zürich 1971.

Kirchen in Deutschland
Churches in Germany

Gemeindezentrum, Köln
Community Centre, Cologne

Nikolaus Bienefeld

■ Köln-Blumenberg, ein nicht gewachsener Vorort, ein Ort noch auf der Suche nach seiner Definition. 1992 gewann Heinz Bienefeld einen beschränkten Wettbewerb für ein Zentrum mit Kirche, Pfarr- und Gemeindehaus, Kindertagesstätte und Sozialstation. Es war der größte Auftrag, den er jemals per Wettbewerb erhalten hat; es wäre die umfangreichste Arbeit seines Lebens geworden. Doch nach seinem Tod 1995 musste sein Sohn Nikolaus diese Aufgabe meistern: das Erbe des Vaters verteidigen und zugleich seinen eigenen Weg suchen und finden.

Auf dem Lageplan ist eine grazile Figur auszumachen, die sich um einen nach Westen geöffneten Hof rankt. Die Gebäudeproportionen wirken schlank, gemessen an den behäbigen Baukörpern des Umfelds. In den Lageplan ist eine weiche Bogenform eingeschrieben, die den östlichen Gebäuderiegel durchsticht; nicht nur grafisch, sondern schmerzhaft körperlich. Die Gebäudeformation enthält alle Elemente urbaner Lebendigkeit: die Arkade zur Straße im Osten, die Agora zum Platz im Süden, den stillen Innenhof zwischen Kirche und Pfarrsaal, den großzügigen Spielhof des Kindergartens und die geöffnete Westseite zum kleinen Kirchvorplatz, der nur noch von Mauer und Eingangsportal bestimmt wird. Der gemauerte Turm in der Nähe des Eingangs wird dem Ensemble nach Fertigstellung darüber hinaus Prägnanz verleihen.

Auch nach den nun fast zehn Jahre dauernden mehrfachen Überarbeitungen, aufgrund der programmatischen Änderungswünsche des Bauherrn, lässt sich feststellen, dass die Grundelemente des Entwurfs den Veränderungen standgehalten haben. Die Westseite hat sicherlich wegen der Verkleinerung des Raumprogramms gelitten. Dem Spielhof des Kindergartens wird die Geborgenheit des von Gebäuden Umschlossenen fehlen. Bedauerlich ist auch die aufdringliche Nähe der Tiefgarageneinfahrt zum westlichen Kirchenportal.

Trotzdem stehen alle Baumassen mit ihren sorgfältig geplanten gelenkigen Übergängen in einer außergewöhnlichen Balance, die zwischen sakraler und profaner Zonierung erreicht wird. Raumgeometrien werden immer wieder durchbrochen. Kleine Brücken und Stege, gläserne und stählerne Gelenke verbinden Einzelteile und formen Labyrinthisches. Der östliche Durchbruch der Kirche ist in Grund- und Aufriss spürbar; im Obergeschoss überbrückt ein Steg im Laubengang der Wohnungen die Durchdringung der Kirche – eine fast metaphorische Geste.

Das streng von West nach Ost ausgerichtete Kirchenschiff, das sich um zwei Meter absenkt, bildet dabei das eigentliche Herz. Unweigerlich stößt man auf Assoziationen, warum die Grundrissform der Kirche vertraut und beunruhigend zugleich ist. Vertraut, weil sie an eine Muschel erinnert, eine jener länglichen Schalenmuscheln, die man unzählig am Strand findet. Beunruhigend aber auch in der Anmutung eines Bogens in konzentrierter Anspannung.

Die sich nach der Liturgie richtende Form der leicht gekrümmten Sitzordnung nähert sich einem Ring, der sich zum Altar öffnet. Die leicht auseinander gezogene, elliptische Form betont nicht nur die

■ Cologne-Blumenberg is a suburb still searching for a cohesive identity. In 1992, Heinz Bielefeld won a restricted competition to design a complex here comprising a church, pastoral community centre, day-care centre and social welfare unit. It was the most important contract he had ever won through a competition and would have been the biggest project of his life. However, on his death in 1995, his son Nikolaus took up the challenge of upholding his father's legacy while at the same time finding his own way.

The site plan shows a graceful figure built around a courtyard that opens to the west. The proportions of the building appear slender by comparison with the stolid structures of the surrounding area. A gentle arc is inscribed into the plan, penetrating the eastern wing of the building with a graphic clarity that is almost physical. The building formation echoes all aspects of urban life: the arcades on the street side to the east, the agora facing the open area to the south, the quiet inner courtyard between the church and the parish hall, the spacious kindergarten playground and the open west side facing the little church forecourt, defined only by the wall and the entrance portal. The masonry tower near the entrance will add further distinctiveness to the ensemble once it is completed.

Despite several revisions over a period of almost ten years – alterations carried out in response to programmatic changes requested by the client – it is nonetheless clear that the basic elements of the design hold their own. The west side has certainly suffered from the reduction of space. The playground of the kindergarten will now lack the sheltered atmosphere it would have had if it had been enclosed by other buildings. It is also regrettable that the entrance to the underground car park is so close to the west portal of the church.

Nevertheless, all the building elements with their painstakingly planned flexible transitions possess a remarkable balance of religious and secular zoning. Spatial geometries are broken time and again with small bridges and footpaths, glass and steel links that join the individual parts to form a labyrinthine whole. The eastern breakthrough of the church is evident in the floor plan and the elevation: On the upper floor, a footpath bridges the point of permeation on the access balcony to the apartments in what is almost a metaphorical gesture.

The stringently west-east oriented nave of the church, declining by two metres, forms the heart of the ensemble. It invariably triggers associations that make the layout of the church both familiar and unsettling at one and the same time: familiar because it recalls the form of a shell one might find on any beach, and unsettling in the way it suggests a permanently taut bow.

The slight curve of the seating arrangement, accommodating liturgical requirements, is like a ring opened to the altar. The slightly elongated elliptical form emphasises the spatial geometry and focuses the action on a zone between the tabernacle and the window aperture, with its scarabaeoid reveals and the altar at the centre.

Architekten Architects Nikolaus Bienefeld Architekt BDA, Swisttal-Odendorf, www.architekturbuero-bienefeld.de; Team: Eva Nawracala, Willi Nawracala, Daniel Volske, Albrecht Croy, Beatrice Rockenbach, Anke Kahlen, Markus Schultheis, Markus Kirschnick, Panja Friedrich, Hartmut Marzusch | **Bauherr Client** Katholische Kirchengemeinde St. Marien, Köln-Blumenberg | **Tragwerk Structural** Osenberg + Mertens, Köln | **HL-Technik Technical** Planungsbüro TGA, Herzogenrath-Kohlscheid | **Wettbewerb Competition** 1991 | **Ausführung Construction** 2001–2003 | **Standort Location** Schneebergstraße 2, Köln-Blumenberg

Raumgeometrie, sondern fokussiert das Geschehen auf eine Zone, die sich zwischen Tabernakel und einer Fensteröffnung mit scarpaesk abgetreppten Laibungen spannt und in deren Mitte der Altar steht.

Der Kirchenraum, vollständig in massivem Beton gegossen, mit Wandstärken bis zu einem Meter, wirkt dieser Welt entrückt. Die aus dem Sedimentgestein entlehnten monolithischen Schichtungen der Betonwände, die ihre Farbunterschiede nur durch die wechselnden natürlichen Zuschlagsmaterialien erhalten, lassen jede Art von Natursteinverkleidung vergleichsweise banal erscheinen. Durch das grobe Behauen der Wände nach dem Ausschalen erhält die Oberfläche eine durchdringende Tiefe, die den Ort auf eigentümliche Weise archaisch erscheinen lässt. Die Bogenform oder die Muschel, versteinert, in die Erde eingelassen, versunken, auch geborgen, wird bestrahlt von der konzentrierten Belichtung der leicht schwebenden Laterne über dem Mittelteil des Raums.

In der kleinen Kapelle an der Ostseite sieht man sich fast erdrückt zwischen den sich auftürmenden Massen. In dem als Krypta angelegten Raum ist das Unterirdische spürbar – aber auch der Widerspruch vertrauter Raumbilder zu dem fehlenden Inhalt der ›Grabstätte‹ und seiner Bedeutung für das liturgische Geschehen.

Nikolaus Bienefeld trug eine schwere Bürde, nicht nur wegen des eigenwilligen Vaters, sondern besonders auch aufgrund des geringen Verständnisses heutzutage für das Bewahren eines Erbes und die Neuschöpfung eines Gesamtkunstwerks. So wurde sein Wirken vor allem dadurch erschwert, dass seine handwerklichen Vorstellungen mit denen des Generalunternehmers nur schwer zu vereinbaren waren. Heinz Bienefelds Fragilität in der dialektischen Behandlung von Detail und Material ergänzt sich besonders gut mit den Fähigkeiten seines Sohnes im Umgang mit Farben, natürlichen Werkstoffen und ausgeprägt handwerklichen Techniken. Die stille innere Vereinbarung dieser beiden Architekten ist in diesem Bau ebenso spürbar wie der Konflikt mit den erzwungenen Kompromissen.

Mit Behutsamkeit und Sorgfalt gedeihen solche Arbeiten nur auf dem Nährboden eines verständigen Bauherrn, der die erforderliche Zeit gibt, Dinge entwickeln zu lassen – und das ist hier leider und gottlob keine Frage von Ökonomie gewesen.

Günter Pfeifer

The church interior, cast entirely in solid concrete, with walls up to one metre thick, seems utterly otherworldly. The monolithic layering of the concrete walls, their changing colours created by the different natural additives, is redolent of sedimentary rock and makes all other kinds of natural stone cladding seem banal by comparison. The rough-hewn finish after removal of the shuttering lends the surface a profound depth that makes the place appear strangely archaic. The shell-like curve, set into the ground, sunken and secure, is illuminated by the concentrated light of the slightly hovering lamp above the central part of the room.

In the little chapel on the east side, one feels almost overwhelmed by the towering mass. The crypt-style room has an underground atmosphere, though this seemingly familiar handling of space contrasts with the lack of an actual burial place in all its liturgical significance.

Nikolaus Bienefeld took on a heavy burden, not only because of his father's idiosyncrasy, but especially because contemporary society has little understanding of such concepts as nurturing tradition and creating a new *gesamtkunstwerk*. His work was made all the more difficult by the fact that his notions of craftsmanship did not correspond to the ideas of the general contractor. Heinz Bienefeld's delicate treatment of detail and material superbly complements his son's skilful handling of colours, natural materials and artisanal techniques. The tacit inner agreement between these two architects is as tangible in this building as the conflict with forced compromise.

Along with care and sensitivity, such works can thrive only with the client's understanding and willingness to grant the time required to let things develop – and in this case, both fortunately and unfortunately, it has not been a question of economy.

Günter Pfeifer

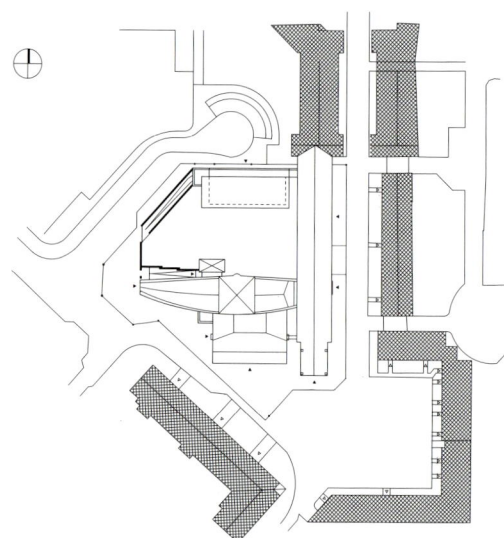

Lageplan **Site plan**

Ansicht von Südosten mit Osteingang der Kirche **View from the south-east with the east entrance to the church**

1 Kirche **Church**
2 Kapelle **Chapel**
3 Beichte **Confessional**
4 Sakristei **Sacristy**
5 Krypta **Crypt**
6 Pfarrsaal und Pfarrraum **Parish hall and parish meeting room**
7 Pfarrbüro **Priest's office**
8 Pfarrwohnung **Parsonage**
9 Kindergarten **Kindergarten**
10 Sozialstation **Welfare centre**
11 Kinderarztpraxis **Paediatrician's practice**
12 Rampe Tiefgarage **Underground car park ramp**

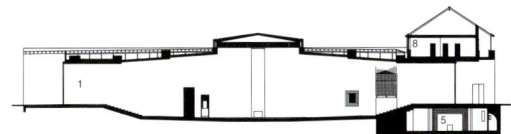

Schnitt **Section**

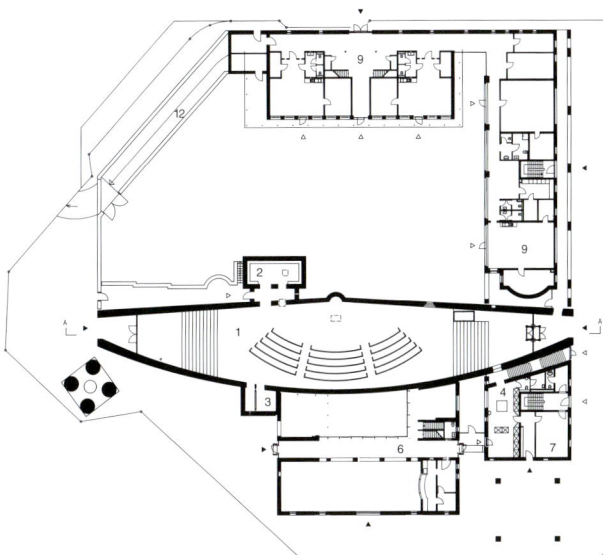

Grundriss Erdgeschoss **Ground-floor plan**

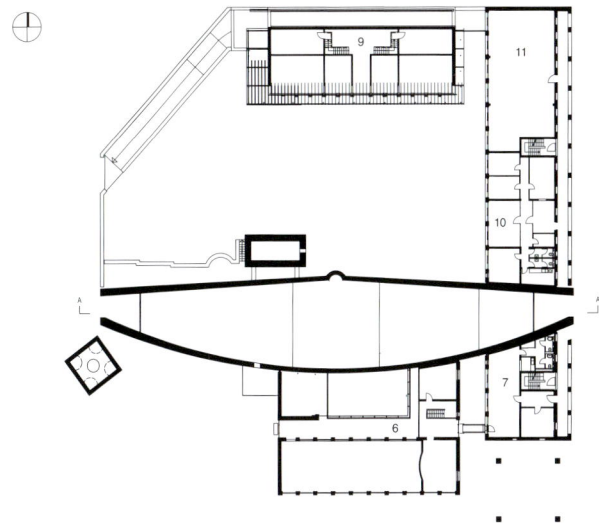

Grundriss 1. Obergeschoss **First-floor plan**

Innenhof, Blick von Südwesten
Courtyard, view from the south-west

Ansicht der Kirche von Norden
View of the Church from the north

Deckenuntersicht   **View of the ceiling from below**

Blick von der Kapelle in den Kirchenraum
View from the chapel into the church

Seiten 48/49   **Pages 48–49**
Innenraum   **Interior**

Gemeindezentrum, Köln
Community Centre, Cologne

Pfarrkirche St. Theodor, Köln
Parish Church of St Theodore, Cologne

Paul Böhm

■ Köln ist stolz auf seine Kirchenbauten, nicht nur auf den gotischen Dom, sondern auch auf die zahlreichen romanischen Kirchen. Aber auch auf der rechten Rheinseite in Kalk, Mülheim, Buchheim und Vingst finden sich gleich vier bedeutende Wiederaufbauten und Neubauten der letzten 50 Jahre, wie St. Marien mit der berühmten Kalker Kapelle von 1948 bis 1950 aus Trümmersteinen aufgebaut von Rudolf Schwarz, St. Joseph, 1951/52 von Dominikus Böhm wiedererrichtet, St. Theresia in Buchheim, 1955/56 von Gottfried Böhm als Rundkirche neu erbaut. In der dritten Generation der Kirchenbauerfamilie hat nun Paul Böhm, der jüngste Sohn von Gottfried Böhm, mit der Pfarrkirche St. Theodor in Vingst seine erste Kirche gebaut.

Vingst ist einer der jüngeren Vororte im rechtsrheinischen Köln. 1905 erhielt das damals noch kleine Dorf eine erste Notkirche an nahezu gleicher Stelle. Nachdem sich der Ort zu einer Arbeitervorstadt entwickelt hatte, wurde 1937/38 die erste große Kirche erbaut, im Krieg stark beschädigt, bis 1949 notdürftig repariert und in den fünfziger Jahren um einen Turm mit quadratischem Grundriss ergänzt. Durch ein Erdbeben 1992 wurde das Gewölbe der Kirche so stark beschädigt, dass sie wegen Baufälligkeit geschlossen und 1996 abgerissen werden musste.

Der Stadtteil Vingst gehört zu den ärmsten Vierteln in Nordrhein-Westfalen. Fast 40 Prozent aller Familien leben von staatlicher Unterstützung wie Sozialhilfe und Arbeitslosengeld. Nicht zuletzt aufgrund dieser sozialen Situation haben die karitativen Einrichtungen wie die Altkleiderkammer, die jede Woche von mehr als 70 Familien aufgesucht wird, das Möbellager, die Werkstätten für Arbeitslose sowie die Lebensmittelausgabe eine besondere Bedeutung in der Gemeinde St. Theodor. Hinzu kommen die auf demselben Grundstück vorhandene Kindertagesstätte, das Pfarrheim und ein benachbartes Seniorenwohnhaus.[1]

Noch im Jahr 1996 wurde für Architekten der Erzdiözese Köln ein Realisierungswettbewerb ausgeschrieben, an dem 162 Architekten teilgenommen haben. Paul Böhm ging mit dem Entwurf einer Rundkirche als eindeutiger Sieger aus diesem Wettbewerb hervor. Nicht nur entsprach er in allen Teilen den Anforderungen des Programms, sondern darüber hinaus ist das überlieferte Alte – der Turm und die übrigen Gebäude – in die neue Konzeption mustergültig einbezogen. In der Beurteilung schreibt die Jury: »In den Grünzug zwischen den beiden Straßenbebauungen stellt der Verfasser einen Solitärraum, ohne den städtebaulichen Zusammenhang zu verschließen. Er rückt das Gebäude nur soweit in das Grundstück, daß gegenüber fast allen anderen Entwürfen eine besonders große und nutzbare Fläche zur Straße hin und auch rückwärts zu den übrigen Gebäuden der Pfarre verbleibt.«[2]

Der Baukörper aus konzentrischen, zylindrischen Wandscheiben aus 50 cm dickem gesandstrahlten Leichtbeton, der gelblich eingefärbt ist, umfasst den Zentralraum der Kirche und schließt den alten Turm mit ein. Zwischen der äußeren und der inneren Schale schraubt sich eine Treppenrampe, begleitet von 14 Kreuzwegstationen, bis auf

■ Cologne is proud of its churches – not only its Gothic cathedral, but also its many Romanesque churches. But Kalk, Mühlheim, Buchheim and Vingst on the right bank of the Rhine can also boast four important reconstructed and newly designed churches from the past fifty years: St Marien with its famous Kalk Chapel of 1948–50, built by Rudolf Schwarz using the rubble of wartime ruins, St Joseph, reconstructed by Dominikus Böhm in 1951–52, the round church of St Theresia in Buchheim, designed by Gottfried Böhm in 1955–56 and, following in the tradition of this family of church builders in the third generation, Paul Böhm, the youngest son of Gottfried Böhm, has now built his first church, the parish church of St Theodor in Vingst.

Vingst is one of the newer suburbs of Cologne's right bank. In 1905, when it was still a small village, its first modest church was built on almost exactly the same site. Once it had grown and developed into a working-class suburb, the first full-size church was erected in 1937–38, but was badly damaged in the War. Only the most urgent repairs were carried out up to 1949, and in the 1950s a square tower was added. In 1992, an earthquake caused such severe damage to the vaulting that it was closed, and had to be demolished in 1996.

The district of Vingst is one of the most deprived urban areas in North Rhine-Westphalia, with almost forty per cent of all families dependent on state benefits and income support. Because of this, such charitable institutions as the second hand clothes depot (visited by more than seventy families a week), the furniture depot, the workshops for the unemployed and the food distribution centre play an important role in the parish of St Theodor. On the same site as the church there is also a day-care centre, parish community centre and retirement home.[1]

In 1996 a competition for architects in the archdiocese of Cologne attracted 162 entries. Paul Böhm's design for a round church was the virtually unchallenged winner. Not only did his design meet all the requirements of the programme, but it also integrated the past – in the form of the tower and remaining buildings – in an exemplary way. The jury wrote: "In the green strip between the two streets, the architect has placed a free-standing building that nevertheless forms an integral part of the urban fabric. He has situated the building on the site in such a way that it forms a large and functional area on the street side and towards the other pastoral buildings at the rear."[2]

The building, with its concentric, cylindrical wall panels of 50 cm thick sandblasted and yellow stained concrete, comprises the central church room and incorporates the old tower. Between the outer and inner shell is a ramp of steps with fourteen Stations of the Cross leading up to the church roof, culminating in the Chapel of the Resurrection in the old tower. Above that is the bell chamber. On the ground floor of the tower is the ambry with the organ built in above it. The underside of the ramp, which is visible inside the

Architekten Architects Architekturbüro Paul Böhm, Köln, www.boehmarchitektur.de; Team: Martin Amme, Henning Bertram, Mathias Wolff & Sándor Forgó, Freya Fuhrmann, Ulrike Weber, Johannes Beeh, Johannes Jaeger, Richard Frische, Mandy Sommerfeld, Florian Stuckenberg, Sabine Ziegler, Tim Klosterkamp, Wolfgang Kurz | **Bauherr Client** Katholische Kirchengemeinde St. Theodor, Köln | **Tragwerk Structural** Osenberg + Mertens, Köln | **HL-Technik Technical** Planungsgemeinschaft Haustechnik (PGH), Dormagen | **Akustik Acoustics** Graner + Partner, Bergisch Gladbach | **Wettbewerb Competition** 1997 | **Ausführung Construction** 1999–2002 | **Standort Location** Burgstraße 42, Köln-Vingst

das Kirchendach und endet in der Auferstehungskapelle im alten Turm. Darüber befindet sich noch die Glockenstube. Im Erdgeschoss des Turms liegt das Sakramentshaus, darüber ist die Orgel eingebaut. Die im Inneren der Kirche sichtbare Unterseite der Rampe wird von radialen Wandscheiben getragen, die im unteren Teil durchbrochen sind und so einen Umgang durch die entstandenen Nischen bilden. In der größten und höchsten Nische steht der Altar. Die flache Decke des Zentralraums ist von den Wänden mit einem gläsernen Ring abgesetzt und lässt Tageslicht von oben an den Wänden entlang in den Raum fließen. In den Altarraum strömt zusätzlich Licht durch raumhohe Fenster neben dem Turm.

Von Norden dringt in den Rundbau tangential ein lang gestreckter flacher Riegel ein, der sich zum Kirchenraum völlig öffnet. Darin befinden sich Bücherei, Café und Kunstgalerie sowie die Sakristei mit Nebenräumen. Mit einem Glasoberlicht ist seine Nordwand abgesetzt, wodurch sie als Ausstellungswand hervorragend ausgeleuchtet wird.

Das durch die schwierige Gründung bedingte riesige Untergeschoss von Kirche und Riegel dient den Räumen für karitative Aufgaben, die durch den Höhenunterschied des Geländes vom Pfarrhof aus ebenerdig zugänglich sind. Vom ›Empfangsplatz‹ an der Straße, an dem auch das alte Pfarrbüro liegt, gelangt man über eine halbkreisförmige Rampe um Kirche und Turm herum bequem auf die untere Ebene.

»Der Kirchenraum darf in unserem armen Viertel einfach sein, aber er ist würdig und feierlich«, heißt es bereits in der Auslobung.[3] Doch wie es Paul Böhm gelungen ist, mit minimalem Aufwand dieses hervorragende Ergebnis zu erreichen, das ist schon ein Meisterstück.

Erwin H. Zander

1   Karl Josef Bollenbeck, *Pfarrkirche St. Theodor in Köln-Vingst: 162 Entwürfe; ein Wettbewerb,* hrsg. vom Architektur-Forum Rheinland e. V., Wuppertal 1999.
2   Protokoll der Preisgerichtssitzung vom 16.4.1997, hrsg. von der Katholischen Kirchengemeinde St. Theodor, Köln, S. 9.
3   Auslobungstext vom 2.10.1996, *Der Geist des Kirchenraumes. Beschränkter Wettbewerb. Neubau einer katholischen Pfarrkirche. Bebauungsvorschlag für das Grundstück Burgstraße 42,* hrsg. von der Katholischen Kirchengemeinde St. Theodor, Köln, S. 15.

church, is supported by radial wall panels perforated in the lower part to create an ambulatory through the resulting niches. The altar stands in the largest and highest of these niches. The flat ceiling of the central room is set apart from the walls by a glass ring that allows daylight to flow in from above, along the walls and into the room. Light also streams in through the ceiling-high windows next to the tower.

A flat, elongated bar-shaped structure penetrates the round building from the north, opening into the church interior, and housing the bookshop, café and art gallery as well as the sacristy and other rooms. The north wall of this bar-shaped structure has glass skylighting, making it an excellent exhibition area.

The huge lower floor of the church and bar-shaped structure accommodates rooms that are used for charity, and are accessible from the courtyard at ground level due to the slope of the site. From the 'reception square' at the street side, where the old pastoral offices are situated, a semi-circular ramp runs around the church and the tower to the lower level.

"The church may be simple in our poor district, but it is dignified and solemn," says the design brief.[3] Paul Böhm has risen to the challenge with consummate skill, creating an extraordinary and outstanding place of worship with a minimum of pomp.

Erwin H. Zander

1   Karl Josef Bollenbeck, "Pfarrkirche St Theodor in Köln-Vingst: 162 Entwürfe; ein Wettbewerb", issued by the Architektur-Forum Rheinland e. V., Wuppertal, 1999.
2   From the report of the jury meeting of 16 April 1997, "Protokoll der Preisgerichtssitzung vom 16.4.1997", issued by the Catholic parish of St Theodor, Cologne, p. 9.
3   From the competition brief of 2 October 1996, "Der Geist des Kirchenraumes. Beschränkter Wettbewerb. Neubau einer katholischen Pfarrkirche. Bebauungsvorschlag für das Grundstück Burgstraße 42", issued by the Catholic parish of St Theodor, Cologne, p. 15.

Seiten 54/55 **pages 54–55**
Treppenrampe **Stepped ramp**

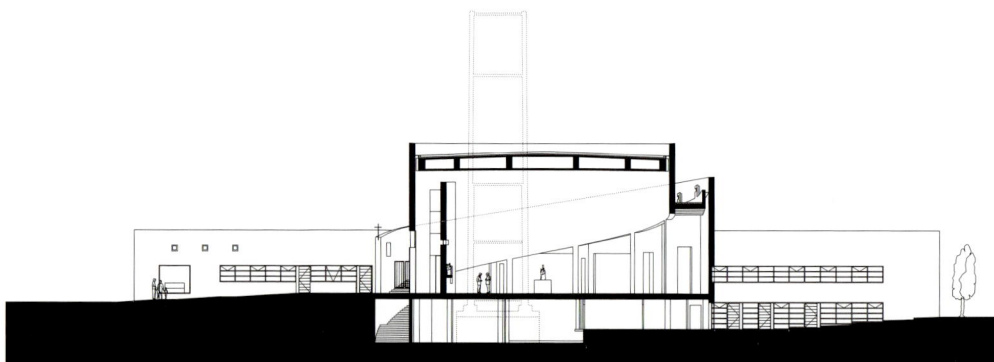

Schnitt **Section**

Ansicht von Westen **View from the west**

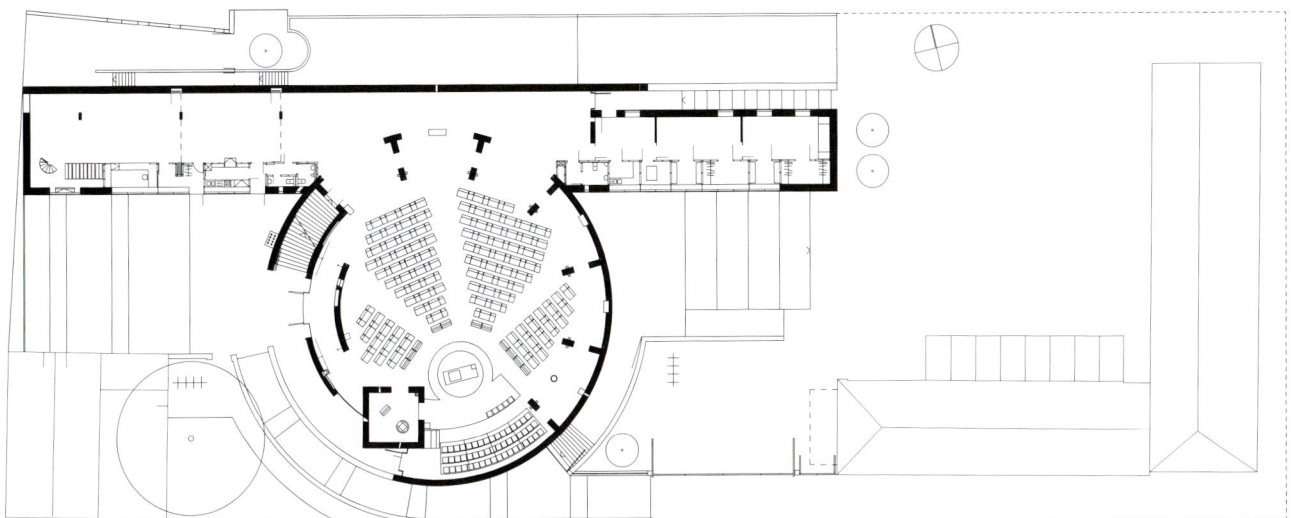

Grundriss Erdgeschoss **Ground-floor plan**

Ansicht von Süden
View from the south

Sakristei, Ansicht von Südosten
Sacristy, view from the south-east

Eingang **Entrance**

Innenraum **Interior**

Doppelkirche für zwei Konfessionen, Freiburg
Dual Denominational Church, Freiburg

Kister Scheithauer Gross

■ Protestantisch oder katholisch? In Rieselfeld, Freiburgs neuem Stadtteil, entsteht ein Gotteshaus für beide Konfessionen. Susanne Gross aus dem Büro Kister Scheithauer Gross hat einen ökumenischen Sakralbau entworfen, der Ergebnis eines Wettbewerbs ist. Doch wie sieht gebaute Ökumene aus, und kann sich Ökumene überhaupt verräumlichen?

Ökonomie und Ökumene liegen dicht beisammen. Daraus könnten Architekten Stoff für eine neue Typologie entwickeln. Nicht nur der funktionelle Aspekt wäre dafür Ausgangspunkt, auch die Frage nach der geeigneten Gestalt. Wie teilen sich außen wie innen religiöse Gemeinsamkeiten, aber auch Unterschiede mit? Wer sich auf die Suche nach geeigneten Lösungen begibt, wird wenige finden.

Die Dualität beider Einrichtungen ist architektonisch nicht ohne reizvolle Interpretationen geblieben. Das ist zum Beispiel in Städten der Fall, in denen die Gotteshäuser der beiden Konfessionen in unmittelbarer Nachbarschaft liegen oder die Kirchen über größere Distanz unterschiedliche Bezugspunkte schaffen.

Der Grundriss des Freiburger Neubaus lässt nicht unmittelbar auf einen Sakralraum schließen. Er sieht aus wie ein ärmelloses Unterhemd, an dessen Seiten zwei ›Handpaare‹ kräftig ziehen, als ob sie sich um das ›Eigentum‹ streiten. Der seitliche Saum scheint ›doppelt genäht‹ zu sein – zur Aufnahme von Neben- und Lichträumen –, ein Umstand, der die Gewissheit verleiht, dass beide Parteien zwar lange ziehen können, das Hemd jedoch nicht reißen wird.

Erhebt sich der Grundriss zum Volumen, liegen Faltungen in der Schräge. Das wird innen wie außen eine sehr schöne räumliche Wirkung haben. Um sie zu erreichen, wird vom Betonbauer eine geometrische Meisterleistung abverlangt, während den Entwerfern die Planung heute leichter von der Hand geht. Dieses mehrfach geknickte Gehäuse ist kein Einzelfall mehr, weil der Computer dem Architekten jene Unterstützung gewährt, von der Hans Scharouns Mitarbeiter nicht einmal träumen konnten. Die Faltungen bescheren diesem Sakralbau in der Realität einige Vorteile, die einerseits die Bauaufgabe selbst betreffen, andererseits die Einbindung in den städtebaulichen Kontext. Im Neubaugebiet des Freiburger Rieselfelds, in dem eine Vorherrschaft rechtwinkliger Wohnbauten existiert, steht eine bemerkenswerte Plastik auf der Ecke und sagt unmissverständlich etwas über ihren besonderen Inhalt aus.

Im Grunde genommen ist die Grundrissdisposition denkbar einfach: Rechts und links eines mittleren Foyers liegen die katholische und die evangelische Kirche, die Nebenräume sind peripher untergebracht. Gäbe es den ›verzogenen‹ Raumzuschnitt nicht, könnte man von einer klassischen Dreiteilung sprechen, wobei es entsprechend den Gemeindegrößen unterschiedlich große Bereiche gibt. Der westliche, katholische Kirchenraum ist hinsichtlich seiner Kontur und Lichtführung sehr expressiv. Das Foyer und der östliche, protestantische Kirchenraum sind dagegen zurückhaltender gestaltet. Die Architektin hat vielleicht an einen neuen Gebäudetypus gedacht, der insbesondere der Teilung sowie der Verschmelzung bei-

■ Protestant or Catholic? A church for both is currently under construction in Rieselfeld, a new district of Freiburg. Susanne Gross of Kister Scheithauer Gross Architects devised an ecumenical religious building that promptly won the architectural tender. But what does ecumenicalism look like when translated into architecture? Can it be rendered in spatial terms in the first place?

Economics and ecumenicalism connect in a way that could offer material for a new typology. Both the appropriateness of the shape and the functional aspects of such a building must be considered carefully. How can the interior and the exterior symbolise the similarities and the differences between these two branches of Christianity? Anyone seeking a suitable solution to these problems will have a hard job finding answers.

However, exciting architectural interpretations of the duality of these two Christian institutions do exist. They can be found in towns where churches of both confessions are located close to one another, and in places where the two churches are far apart but still from different points of reference.

The ground plan of the new building in Freiburg is not necessarily indicative of a religious edifice. In fact, it resembles an undershirt without sleeves. Two pairs of hands are pulling on either side, as if engaged in a tug of war. Ancillary rooms and illuminated areas are incorporated into the seam on the edge of the shirt, which appears to be sewn double. This conveys the feeling that the parties in question can pull as long and as hard as they like, but they will never be able to tear the fabric.

Once the outline is transformed into three dimensions, folds appear on the surface. This has a very pleasant effect both inside and out. To achieve this outcome, a geometric work of genius was required on the part of the engineer handling the concrete. It is much easier to draw up such plans today. Architects are now able to incorporate creases into a building's design using computerised support that Hans Scharoun's staff could only dream of. The folds offer several advantages. Some are related to construction techniques, and others are relevant to integrating the building into its urban surroundings. As rectangular buildings predominate in Freiburg's new district, this unusually sculpted building makes an unequivocal statement about its extraordinary contents.

The utilisation of space within the complex is easily understood. The Protestant and Catholic churches are located to the right and left of a central foyer, respectively, and subsidiary rooms are on the periphery. If the division of space were not 'distorted' we could refer here to a classic trinity, with each section varying in size in accordance with the different congregations. The Catholic section lies to the west, and its contours and use of light are very expressive. The foyer and eastern side of the church are dedicated to Protestantism, and display a much more reserved style. Perhaps the architect was considering a new kind of building, one that would simultaneously accommodate disparity and synthesis. The three sections of the

Architekten Architects Kister Scheithauer Gross, Köln; Prof. Johannes Kister, Reinhard Scheithauer, Susanne Gross; Entwurf **Design** Susanne Gross; Team: Sándor Forgó & Jim Cassidy, Étienne Fuchs, Bastian Giese, Jörn Knop, Eric Mertens, Maren Meyer, Barbara Schaeffer, Dagmar von Strantz, Nathan Ward, Klaus Zeller | **Bauherr Client** Evangelische Maria-Magdalena-Gemeinde, Freiburg; Katholische Kirchengemeinde St. Maria Magdalena, Freiburg | **Projektsteuerung Project Management** Klotz & Partner, Freiburg | **Tragwerk Structural** Wolfgang Naumann, Köln | **HL-Technik Technical** Planerwerkstatt Hölken Berghoff, Vörstetten | **Licht Lighting** Planungsgruppe Burgert, Schallstadt | **Wettbewerb Competition** 1999 | **Ausführung Construction** 2002–2004 | **Standort Location** Maria-von-Rudloff-Platz, Freiburg im Breisgau

der Kirchen Rechnung trägt. Den Zusammenhalt erhalten die drei Raumeinheiten durch das Stakkato der in regelmäßigen Abständen geplanten Holzbalken, die das Volumen horizontal überspannen. In Längsrichtung sind Lichtbänder integriert, die für jeden Raum eine harmonische und differenzierte Ausleuchtung ermöglichen. Schwierig sind solche Lichtführungen immer dann, wenn sich durch den Zusammenschluss der Einheiten, hier also von Foyer und beiden Kirchenräumen, ein ebenso stimmungsvolles Ganzes ergeben soll. Hinzu kommt die nicht ganz einfache Bewältigung der Fugen, die der Führung der beweglichen Schiebewände dienen.

Bei der Ausführung der Pläne stellen sich jene Schwierigkeiten ein, die man auch im Umgang mit Partituren hat. Denn entscheidend ist, wie die Bauausführung den Plan umsetzt beziehungsweise interpretiert. All das, was man jetzt festzustellen glaubt, kann erst in einem halben Jahr nachgeprüft werden. Noch befindet sich das Kirchengebäude im Bau, und außer den Umfassungswänden aus sorgfältig gegossenem Sichtbeton ist wenig zu sehen. Eine gewisse Präzision in der Realisierung ist schon deshalb wünschenswert, weil es einige Stellen gibt, die eine nachlässige Ausführung nicht zulassen. Zu ihnen gehören die Führung der Schiebewände, die Anschlüsse der Oberlichter, aber auch so banale Dinge wie die Türöffnungen. Es gibt einen Zusammenhang der Öffnungen mit dem länglichen Zuschnitt des katholischen Kirchenraums. In ihm endet die Raumsequenz nicht ganz eindeutig. Türen liegen unmittelbar an den Engstellen des Raums, im nördlichen Teil sieht man wie über einen Lettner zur Außenwand.

Die gebaute Ökumene tut sich schwer: Die Unterschiedlichkeit beider Konfessionen lässt sich in jedem noch so schön gezeichneten Plan nicht verbergen. Dieser neue Kirchenbau scheint gerade die Polarität zum Thema zu nehmen und trägt nicht einer Harmonie Rechnung, die es (noch) nicht wieder gibt. Die Botschaft der letzten Enzyklika im Ohr ist das Haus eine gute Metapher für den Stand der Unterschiedlichkeit, aber auch der Gemeinsamkeit von Protestanten und Katholiken.

Arno Lederer

church are united by a staccato of regularly recurring wood beams which span the building horizontally. Strips of lights extend its length, providing distinct yet harmonious illumination of the various sections. This kind of lighting makes it difficult to create the proper mood at the point where the three sections intersect, where the foyer and the two areas within the church come together. The grooves for the moveable walls further complicate the question of lighting.

The implementation of such plans can be compared to a conductor preparing to coax music from a score. What is decisive is how the construction managers interpret and carry out the plans. After all, nothing that is decided at this point can be tested until building starts six months later. The church is still under construction, and apart from the chuted curtain walls erected in fair-faced concrete, there is little to see. Some elements of construction will require great precision; their success depends on the work being carried out very carefully. These include the grooves for the moveable walls, the connections for the overhead lights, and even such banalities as the space for the doors. There is a connection between these door openings and the long shape of the Catholic space. In this part of the church, the space has no definitive end. Doors are located where it is narrowest, and in the north section one can look over what amounts to a choir screen at the exterior wall.

Transforming ecumenicalism into built form is not without its difficulties. Despite the architect's best efforts, there is no hiding the differences between the two confessions. The main thrust of the architecture seems to be the very polarity that the structure was intended to harmonise. Bearing the Pope's most recent encyclical in mind, this church is a good metaphor for the differences as well as for the similarities between Protestants and Catholics.

Arno Lederer

Seiten 62/63 **Pages 62–63**
Ansicht von Norden **View from the north**

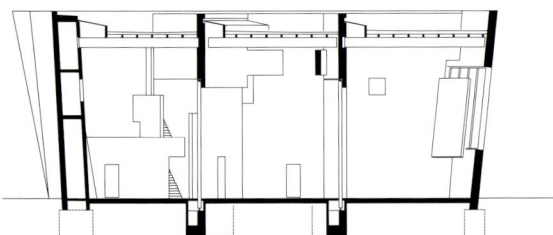

Schnitt **Section**

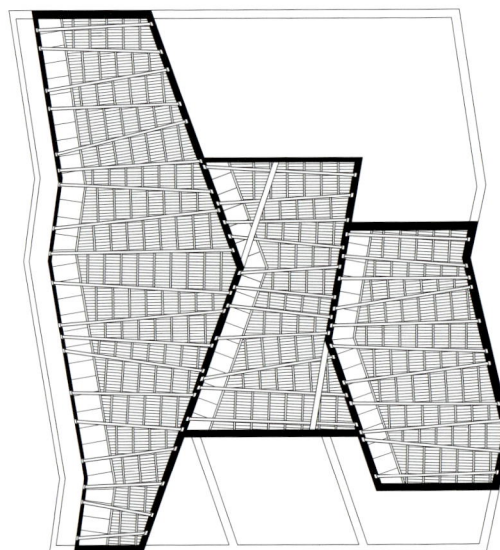

Deckenuntersicht **View of the ceiling from below**

Ansicht von Nordosten **View from the north-east**

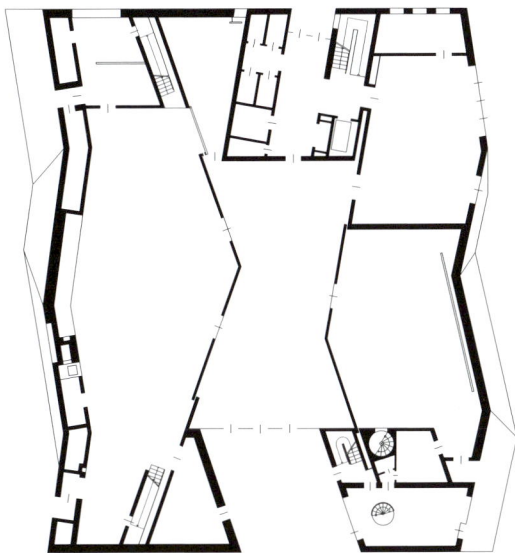

Grundriss ›Zwei Kirchen‹ **Ground plan, 'Two churches'**

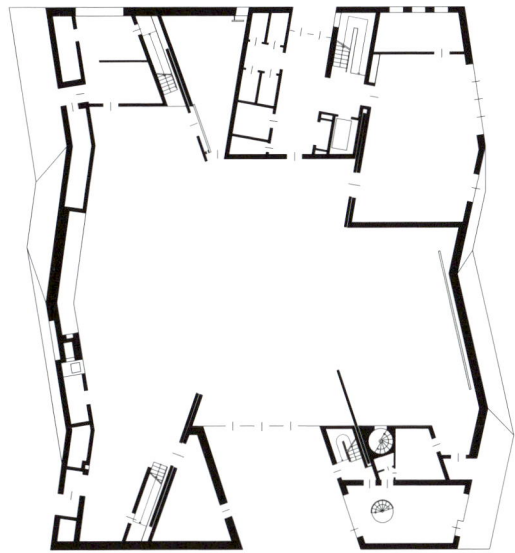

Grundriss ›Eine Kirche‹ **Ground plan, 'One church'**

Detail der Fassade **Detail of the facade**

Südliche Kapelle **Southern chapel**

Nördliche Kapelle
Northern chapel

Pfarrzentrum St. Franziskus, Regensburg
Parish Community Centre of St Francis, Regensburg

Königs Architekten

■ Von dem Altstadtwunder Regensburg sieht der aus Richtung München erwartungsfroh sich Nähernde zunächst nichts. Stattdessen empfängt ihn auf der Anhöhe, die von der Autobahn Nürnberg–Passau durchquert wird, ein Wildwuchs neuzeitlicher Stadterweiterung, wie man ihn sich wüster kaum vorzustellen vermag. Auch die breite Fernverkehrsstraße kann dem keinen Einhalt gebieten, längst schwappt er breiartig über und beginnt die Dörfer des Umlands wie Burgweinting unter sich zu begraben.

Inmitten solchen Chaos sucht hier nun ein neuer Kirchenbau mit franziskanischer Askese, seinem Patrozinium angemessen, sich davon abzusetzen und seinen eigenen Ort zu bestimmen. So ruht er da: erdenschwer, ein erratischer Block, ein gestreckter Quader aus hell geschlämmtem Ziegelmauerwerk von fast monolithischer Geschlossenheit. Nur wenige Lichtöffnungen, unregelmäßig gesetzt, mindern diesen Eindruck nicht, sie werfen eher Fragen nach dem Inhalt auf. Das Besondere dieses Bauwerks springt zwar inmitten der bedrängenden Banalität ins Auge, die gewohnten Merkmale seiner sakralen Bestimmung fehlen jedoch. Gäbe es nicht den zeichenhaften Glockenträger, der den kubischen Kirchenbau – wohl aus Respekt vor dem auch nicht höheren Turm des benachbarten alten Dorfkirchleins – nur wenig überragt. Er flankiert die unruhige Ortseinfahrt, während sich der von Pfarrhaus und Pfarrheim gesäumte Kirchenvorplatz von ihm abwendet und sich damit zur geplanten Besiedlung in westlicher Richtung öffnet. Die Ostung kam dieser Lösung entgegen.

Die dem rechten Winkel verpflichtete Kubatur der Kirche lässt eine ihr entsprechende Räumlichkeit erwarten. Umso größer die Überraschung für den unvorbereitet Eintretenden! Er findet im Inneren zwar dieselbe Materialität vor, die geschlämmten Ziegelmauern, aber sie sind nicht mehr rechtwinklig und senkrecht angeordnet, sondern schließen sich zu einem Rundraum zusammen, dessen Stereometrie jedoch nur schwer zu erfassen ist. Ursache dafür sind die Wände, die sich mit wechselnden Radien krümmen und auch noch schräg nach hinten weg in unterschiedlichen Neigungswinkeln weichen.

Ein Blick auf die Pläne verrät das Entwurfsprinzip: Die eigenwillige Stellung der Wände ergibt sich, weil Boden- und Deckenkontur nicht übereinstimmen. Die räumliche Begrenzung muss zwischen einer annähernd eiförmigen Grundfläche und einer etwas weiteren ovalen Deckenöffnung vermitteln. In ein rektanguläres Gehäuse ist mit Abstand ein Rundbau inkorporiert. Ein Zwischenraum von unregelmäßigem Zuschnitt entsteht, in dem sich das unterbringen lässt, was bei einer Kirche an Hilfseinrichtungen notwendig ist und gewöhnlich zu Anbauten der doch stets angestrebten Großform führt.

Mit der formalen Divergenz von äußerer Erscheinung zum Innenraum wird durchaus bewusst gegen eines der so genannten modernen Dogmen verstoßen. Aber haben das Innen und das Außen denn nicht unterschiedliche Bedingungen? Die Reaktion auf die vorhandene Umgebung ist das eine, die Kreation eines Andachtsraums doch etwas ganz anderes! Die Architekten berufen sich auf ein barockes Vorbild: San Carlo alle Quattro Fontane von Francesco Borromini in

■ Driving in from Munich there is little to be seen of the famous historic centre of Regensburg. Instead, what one sees from the hill traversed by the Nuremburg-Passau motorway is a sprawling modern suburb that could hardly be more desolate. Not even the broad swathe of the motorway holds it in check as it spills over and threatens to swamp the villages of the surrounding area, such as this one, Burgweinting.

In the midst of this chaos, a new church building imbued with Franciscan asceticism now stands apart and stakes out its own place, a heavy, erratic block, an elongated mass of pale brick masonry of almost monolithic closedness. A few apertures set at irregular intervals let in the light but do nothing to alleviate this impression, tending instead to pose questions as to its content. Although the distinctiveness of this building is clearly evident in the midst of so much concentrated banality, the usual characteristics of religious function are missing – except for the emblematic bell tower which rises only slightly above the cubic body of the building, probably out of respect for the tower of the adjacent old village church. The new church flanks the restless approach road, while the square out in front, bounded by the ministry and pastoral community centre, turns away from it, opening up towards the planned housing estate to the west. This solution has been accommodated by building in an eastward direction.

The cuboid angularity of the church suggests a corresponding interior: but what a surprise awaits the uninitiated visitor! Although the interior reiterates the same materials as the exterior, the forms are no longer angular and vertical, but create a rounded space whose stereometry is difficult to grasp. The reason for this are walls that curve on different radii and incline backwards at varying angles.

A glance at the plans reveals the underlying design principle: The outlines of floor and ceiling do not correspond, thereby creating unexpected wall alignments. The handling of space has meant mediating between an almost ovoid floor plan and a slightly wider oval ceiling aperture. In short, a round building has been incorporated into a rectangular shell. Between the two lies an irregularly shaped space that accommodates all the services a church requires, facilities which are normally housed in extensions to the church that increase the impression of sheer size.

The divergence between external appearance and interior space deliberately flouts so-called modern dogma. But do not the interior and the exterior have different requirements? Responding to the existing surroundings is one of them, while creating a contemplative space is something entirely different indeed. In this, the architects have looked to a Baroque precursor, San Carlo alle Quattro Fontane by Francesco Borromini in Rome, a church also reminiscent of Johann Balthasar Neumann's Vierzehnheiligen with its complex interactive spatial curvatures set within a very stringent structural volume.

Architekten Architects Königs Architekten, Köln; Ulrich Königs, Ilse Maria Königs; Team: Claudia Pannhausen, Thomas Roskothen, Volker Mencke, Ilka Aßmann, Christoph Schlaich, André Rethmeier, Bernd Jäger, Sabine Bruckmann, Christoph Michels, Max Illigner | **Bauherr Client** Katholische Kirchenstiftung, Regensburg-Burgweinting | **Tragwerk Structural** Arup GmbH, Düsseldorf | **Akustik Acoustics** Graner + Partner, Bergisch Gladbach | **Licht Lighting** Lichtplanung Dipl.-Ing. Annette Hartung, Köln | **Künstler Artist** Robert Weber, Grafling | **Wettbewerb Competition** 1998 | **Ausführung Construction** 2001–2003 | **Standort Location** Obertraublinger Straße 18, Regensburg-Burgweinting

Rom. Zudem fällt einem spontan Vierzehnheiligen von Johann Balthasar Neumann mit seinen sich kompliziert durchdringenden Raumkurvaturen innerhalb eines gestrafften Bauvolumens ein.

Der ellipsoide Kirchenraum vermittelt erfolgreich zwischen traditioneller Axialität und Zentralraumidee und schafft so die räumliche Voraussetzung für die Nähe von Gemeinde und Altar, die von der katholischen Liturgie heute gefordert wird. Der individuellen Andacht aber bietet er Geborgenheit und Konzentration.

Die Raumgeometrie stellte hohe Anforderungen an die Detailplanung und die handwerkliche Ausführung, die von einer sonst kaum noch anzutreffenden Qualität ist. Im Vergleich zum scheinbar doch so formbaren Sichtbeton sahen die Architekten im Ziegel das geeignetere fehlerfreundlichere Material, das ihnen wegen seiner Textur und Maßstäblichkeit mehr behagte.

Von außen unsichtbar überdeckt ein Shedtragwerk den Bau. Darunter spannt sich frei über den ganzen Raum eine transluzente Membran, die den Blick in die Dachkonstruktion verhindert, das Tageslicht diffus filtert und die eher ›weiche‹ Raumstimmung entscheidend beeinflusst.

Bei Redaktionsschluss war der Kirchenraum noch durch Gerüste verstellt und verdunkelt, das Mauerwerk noch unbehandelt. Nicht einmal den Rohzustand konnte man also als Ganzes wahrnehmen. Deshalb habe ich zunächst gezögert, mich auf eine Baukritik einzulassen. Doch das Projekt hat mich spontan angesprochen: Ich erkannte darin eine geglückte Synthese aus minimalistischer Architekturhaltung und raumkünstlerischer Sensibilität, die dem reduktionistischen Bauen sonst eher fehlt. Mit dem Besuch der Baustelle und im Gespräch mit den beiden motivierten Architekten gewann ich schnell das Vertrauen, dass es ihnen gelingen wird, ihre Intentionen im Bauwerk auch Wirklichkeit werden zu lassen.

Wilhelm Kücker

The ellipsoid church room successfully bridges the gulf between traditional axial alignment and the notion of the central room, thereby creating a space in which the congregation can gather close to the altar, as required by contemporary Catholic liturgy. It also offers a sheltered atmosphere of concentration for individual prayer.

The spatial geometry demanded the painstaking planning of details and high standards of craftsmanship rarely found today. In comparison to the more malleable exposed concrete, the architects found brick better suited to the task as a material with a more appropriate texture and scale.

The load-bearing shed structure that covers the building is invisible from the exterior. Beneath it, suspended freely across the entire room, is a translucent membrane that conceals the view into the roof structure, filtering the natural daylight diffusely and, most importantly, creating a 'soft' atmosphere.

At the time of going to print, the interior of the church was still obscured by scaffolding, and the masonry was untreated. In other words, it was not even possible to gain an overall view of the building in its unfinished state. For this reason, I was initially reluctant to attempt any critical review of the architecture. Yet the project appealed to me at first sight: I recognised in it a happy synthesis of minimalist architecture and creative sensitivity in the handling of space, so often lacking in reductionist buildings. A visit to the building site and a discussion with the two highly motivated architects soon persuaded me that they will succeed in turning their architectural intentions into reality.

Wilhelm Kücker

Seiten 70/71   **Pages 70–71**
Ansicht von Westen   **View from the west**

1   Vorhalle   **Entrance hall**
2   Raum der Stille   **Room of silence**
3   Marienkapelle   **Lady chapel**
4   Friedhofskapelle   **Cemetery chapel**
5   Taufkapelle   **Baptistry**
6   Andacht   **Pray room**
7   Beichte   **Confessional**
8   Sakristei   **Sacristy**
9   Orgel   **Organ**
10   Chor   **Choir**

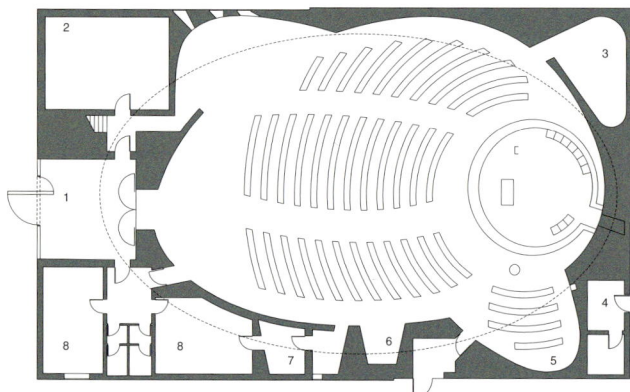

Grundriss Ebene ±0,00 m   **Ground-plan level ±0,00 m**

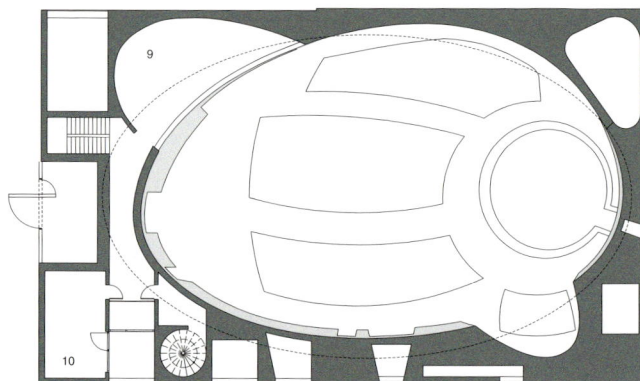

Grundriss Ebene +3,58 m   **Ground-plan level +3,58 m**

Gesamtanlage, Modell **Overall complex, model**

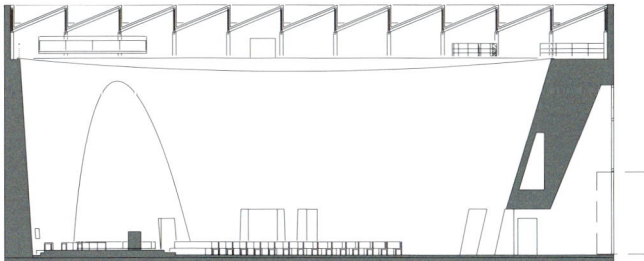

Längsschnitt **Longitudinal section**

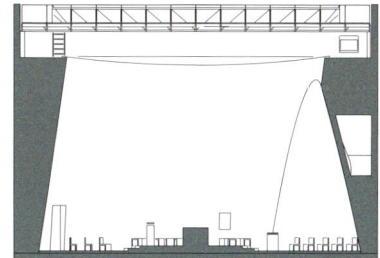

Querschnitt **Cross section**

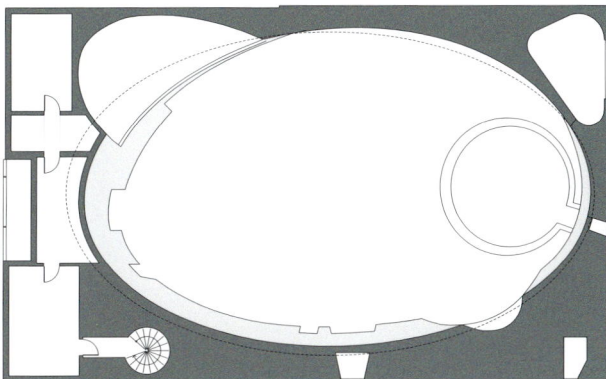

Grundriss Ebene +8,00 m **Ground-plan level +8,00 m**

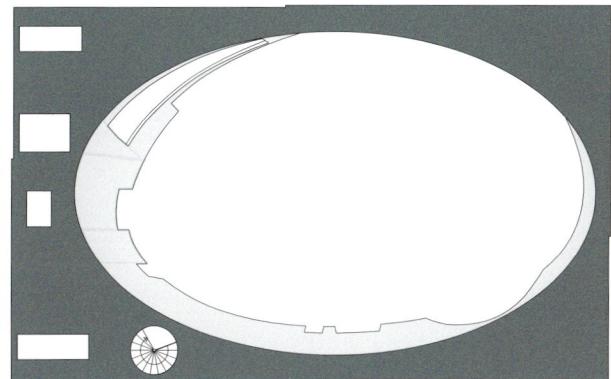

Grundriss Ebene +11,58 m **Ground-plan level +11,58 m**

Sheddach   **Shed roof**

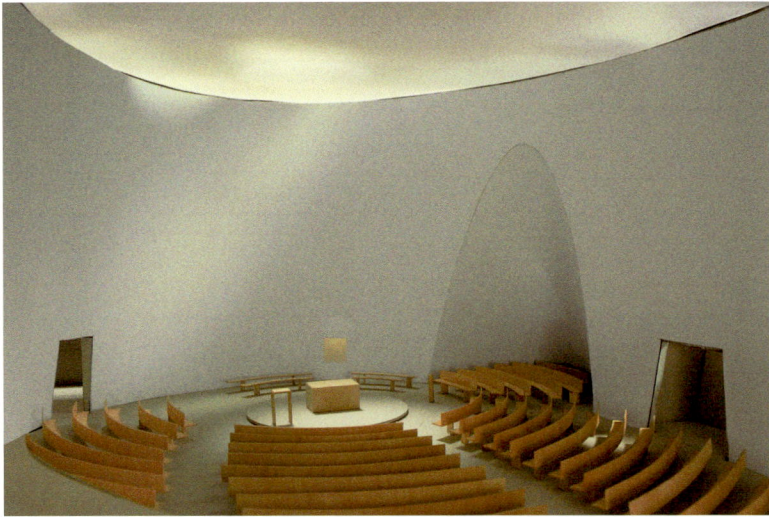

Innenraum
Interior

Innenraum, Modell   **Interior, model**

Innenraum vor Einbau der Membran   **Interior prior to installation of the membrane**

Gemeindekirche Christus König, Radebeul
Parish Church of Christ the King, Radebeul

Staib Architekten mit with Günter Behnisch

■ Fährt man in den Weinbergen Radebeuls die Borstraße zwischen natursteinernen Mauern hangabwärts, erblickt man hinter einer solchen Mauer eine silbrig schimmernde Fassade. Wüsste man es nicht genauer, könnte es sich auch um etwas anderes als eine Kirche handeln. Doch eigentlich ist die den Gemeindehof umschließende übermannshohe Mauer aus Naturstein das Überraschende, welches ganz selbstverständlich das Plakative des ›Natur-ins-Innere-Holen‹ vielschichtig macht. Ein Hortus sanctus, gebildet aus einer Gartenmauer und einem eingestellten solitären Baukörper. Schade, dass das Tor entfernt wurde.

Eigentlich sind es zwei Baukörper, denn das alte Pfarrhaus steht noch, längs zur Straßenfassade, und teilt den gepflasterten Gemeindehof in zwei Bereiche: Es bildet das Rückgrat, vor dem – ohne sichtbaren Bezug – der flache dreieckige Kirchenbau steht. Warum eigentlich ein Dreieck? Man assoziiert mit ihm das Sinnbild der Dreifaltigkeit, ein Zeichen, so geläufig wie das des Kreuzes. Der dreieckige Grundriss ist zugleich eine Variante der konzentrischen Raumform des Zentralbaus, die bereits von Leonardo da Vinci als Form der ›idealen Kirche‹ bezeichnet wurde.

Der Baukörper dominiert nicht wie ein Rundbau, er ordnet nicht, weil er keine Achsen aufnimmt. Er stellt sich nicht als Monument dar, weil die Fassaden auszuweichen scheinen. Das sieht nach einem ›Behnisch‹ aus. Vielerorts ist der Name Programm, und man kann erleben, wie das Erwartete die physische Präsenz des Bauwerks bedrängt und überlagert. Es gehört zur Kunst des Baumeisters, dem Vorhersehbaren etwas in die Quere zu stellen. Rein funktionale und technische Lösungen sind letztlich von begrenztem Interesse, nur die Form kann über Konventionelles hinaus wirken. Es liegt wohl an der äußeren Gestalt, dass die Frage nach der Bedeutung der Kirche in und für die Gesellschaft gestellt scheint: Ist dies ein unangreifbarer Ort, dessen Fassade nach bester Festungsbaukunst keine Breitseite zeigt und der infolge der Spiegelungen einen kristallinen Rückzugsbereich für die Gemeinde bietet? Oder wird hier auch von der Sehnsucht nach einem Ort erzählt, an dem die Seele leichter scheint und in sie ein Strahl der Erleuchtung fällt?

Es scheint, als ob die Dreiecksfigur als zusammengestellter Schirm transluzenter Wände zu verstehen ist, die eher einen Ort markieren, als eine zentralisierte Raumgeometrie bilden. Die von mir bewunderte Kirche San Ivo della Sapienza in Rom von Francesco Borromini ist aus gegeneinander verdrehten Dreiecken komponiert. Die Raumverteilung ist dabei entgegen aller Erwartung nicht eine stark nach außen in Richtung der Ecken gerichtete Bewegung, sondern gerade das Gegenteil. Die Negativ-Ecken erzeugen eine Kompression des Raums, die unmittelbar spürbar über dem kleinen Grundriss eine vertikale Bewegung erzeugt: ein gebauter Prototyp koordinierter Dynamik.

Derartiges ist der Kirche Christus König fremd. Die dynamische Geometrie des Barocks ist zur Ruhe gekommen, fast spröde in der äußeren Form erstarrt. Stattdessen kommt hier mit dem Besucher die

■ Walls of undressed stone line Borstrasse as it traverses the vineyards of Radebeul, and one such barrier conceals a facade that shimmers silver. If you didn't know better, you could be forgiven for thinking that this was something other than a church. Yet it is the over two-metre-high undressed stone wall circumscribing the churchyard that is the real surprise. It clearly confers several levels of signification to the otherwise superficial character of 'bringing nature indoors'. The result is a sanctuary consisting of a garden wall and a stand-alone building. It is a shame that the gate has been removed.

In fact, there are essentially two edifices here as the old vicarage is still standing, parallel to the street, dividing the paved churchyard into two sections and thus forming a backbone without there being any legible connection to the flat, triangular church in front. Now why a triangle? The shape is associated with the trinity, a symbol as common as the cross. The triangular ground plan is also a variant of the concentric layout of the central building, something which Leonardo da Vinci once described as the 'ideal form' for a church.

This shape is not as dominating as a round building would be, and, as it has no axes, it does not impose a specific order on the setting. It does not lay claim to being a monument because the facades seem strangely evasive – in fact, it looks like a 'Behnisch'. A name frequently becomes a building agenda, making it possible for the physical presence of the building to be plagued and eclipsed by any associations that may come with it. It is part of a skilful architect's job to make the predictable seem a little out of line. Purely functional and technical solutions are, in the final instance, of limited interest – only the shape itself can have an effect beyond conventionality. It is the outer shape which begs the question of the meaning of the church in and for society. Is this an unassailable bastion, a place with a facade constructed by a master fortress builder bereft of a broadside and which, thanks to the reflections, offers the congregation a crystalline retreat? Or must we speak of the desire for a place where the soul seems lighter and can be reached by a ray of enlightening illumination?

It seems as if the triangular shape should be understood as a screen of translucent walls intended to define a place rather than create a centralised spatial geometry for the location. I much admire the Church of San Ivo della Sapienza in Rome by Francesco Borromini, a building composed of juxtaposed distorted triangles. The division of space in this church is, however, the opposite of what one would expect because there is no strong movement outward towards the corners. In fact, precisely the opposite is the case. The negative corners produce a compression of space which results in the visitor sensing a pronounced vertical movement rising up from the small footprint of the church – a constructed prototype of coordinated dynamism.

The likes of this are not to be found in the Church of Christ the King. Here, the dynamic Baroque geometry has come to rest; the

Architekten Architects Staib Architekten, Stuttgart; Prof. Gerald Staib mit **with** Prof. Günter Behnisch, Stuttgart; Team: Christoph Kimmich, Ingmar Menzer, Effi Schneider unter Mitwirkung von **with the assistance of** Prof. Christian Kandzia | **Künstlerin Artist** Sabine Staib | **Bauherr Client** Katholisches Pfarramt Christus König, Radebeul | **Tragwerk Structural** Fischer & Friedrich, Stuttgart | **Landschaft Landscape** Krokenge & Ritter Landschaftsarchitekten, Dresden | **Wettbewerb Competition** 1998 | **Ausführung Construction** 2000/01 | **Standort Location** Borstraße 11, Radebeul

Bewegung in die Kirche. Der Grundriss der Empore und die Trennwand zur Sakristei, die sich um die Beichtnische einrollt, erscheinen wie die gebaute Arabeske einer Kordel: Allegorie einer Weinrebe und Nachklang des Dresdner Barocks. Die Sichtbetonwand und der zum Altar abgesenkte Estrichboden erinnern für einen kurzen Moment an Ronchamp. Le Corbusiers Lichtwand mit ihren tiefen Laibungen (siehe S. 19) ist nun einer Wand aus Doppelstegplatten gewichen, in deren Hohlräume farbige Glas- und Kunststoffstreifen eingeschoben sind. Die Paravents, transparent oder mattiert, beleben den Raum durch die Art des Lichteinfalls. Bei schnell vorbeiziehenden Wolken und gleißendem Sonnenlicht spielen die Farben und die Reflexe im Innern der Kirche. Man ist nicht allein.

Die Idee des Sakralen der Kirche Christus König erwächst nicht aus der großen Geste der äußeren Erscheinung, sondern wie bei vielen Kapellen am Wiesenrain aus dem gerichteten Innenraum. Die Distanz zwischen Altar und Taufstein legt gleichsam eine Wegführung nahe – präsent, aber nicht dominant, da man vom Eingang kommend erst auf diese einschwenken muss. Die Achse ist eingeschrieben in ein umhüllendes Ganzes, in dem verschiedene Orte liturgischer Handlungen im Raum zugeordnet sind. Auf diese Weise erlangt der Kirchenraum eine Vieldeutigkeit und etwas von der Komplexität eines mehrschiffigen Kirchenraums mit seinen Altarnischen, die der Individualität des Gläubigen Raum im Raum bieten.

Angenehm ist die Atmosphäre dieses Kirchenraums, und schön sind die natürlichen Materialien, die nur sparsam behandelt wurden. Der rohe Estrich des Bodens, die matte Lasur der Hölzer, die Schlosserarbeiten des Emporengeländers verraten den sicheren Umgang mit Material und Detail.

Die Gemeinde hat mit den Architekten gehadert und selbst einen ganz unchristlichen Streit nicht gescheut. Das lässt sich für den Außenstehenden nicht nachvollziehen, da in der Kirche doch Grundsätzliches offenbart wird: Das Licht der Welt. Womit soll ein Architekt sonst umgehen?

Johannes Kister

building is almost stiff and brittle in its outer form. Instead, movement enters the church with the visitor. The outline of the gallery and the wall separating the sacristy, which winds around the confessional niche, resemble an architectural arabesque of a length of cord – an allegory of a grapevine and an echo of Dresden's Baroque. The fair-faced concrete wall and the sunken screed floor in front of the altar are reminiscent of Ronchamp. Le Corbusier's wall of light with its deep recesses (see p. 19) has given way to a wall made of twin-webbed panels whose hollows are filled with coloured glass and plastic strips. Transparent and stained room dividers animate the space depending on the angle of light. When clouds pass by quickly, or when the sun glares, the inner church dances in colours and reflections: You are not alone.

The concept of sacredness in the Church of Christ the King does not grow out of some grand demeanour imparted by its outside appearance, but, as is the case with many roadside chapels in the country, it derives from the arrangement of the interior. The distance between the altar and baptismal font is suggestive, so to speak, of a path ahead of us – present but not dominant since one has to turn in this direction when entering the church. The axis is inscribed in a surrounding whole in which liturgical events are assigned to different parts of the room. In this way, the building generates some of the ambiguity and complexity of a church with several naves complete with side altars, granting the individuality of each believer a space within the space.

The atmosphere within this church is pleasant and the natural building materials, treated only sparingly, are attractive. The rough screed of the floor, the dull varnish of the wood, and the locksmithry of the gallery banister betray a familiarity with the materials and with detail.

The congregation had its difficulties with the architect, and did not shy away from engaging in some rather un-Christian arguments. This is hard to comprehend for someone on the outside for the simple reason that something fundamental is revealed within the church, namely the light of the world. What else is there for an architect to tackle?

Johannes Kister

Schnitt **Section**

Gemeindekirche Christus König, Radebeul
Parish Church of Christ the King, Radebeul

Ansicht von Südwesten **View from the south-west**

1   Sakristei **Sacristy**
2   Beichte **Confessional**
3   Taufkapelle **Baptistry**
4   Orgel **Organ**
5   Chor **Choir**

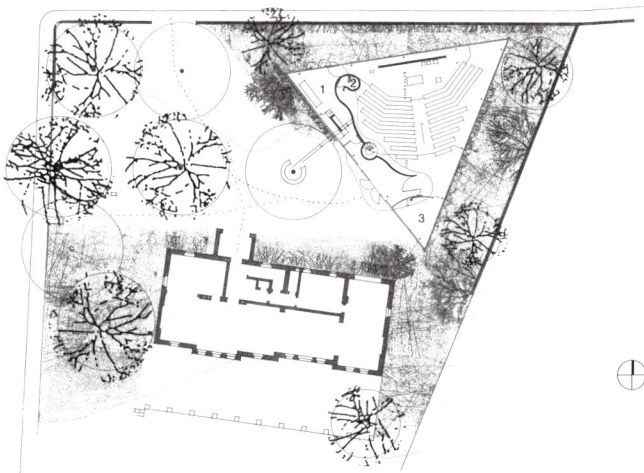

Grundriss Erdgeschoss **Ground-floor plan**

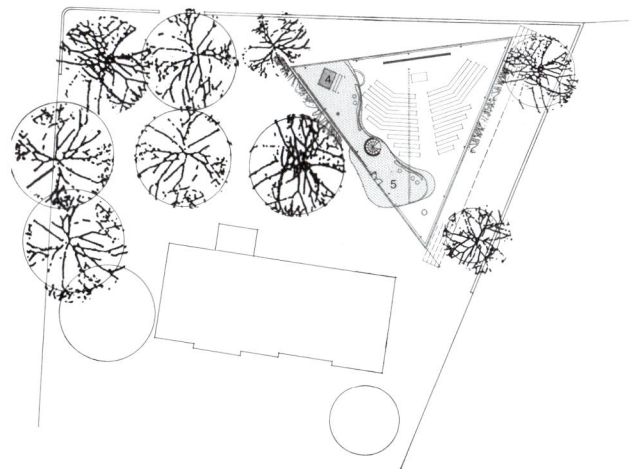

Grundriss Empore **Ground plan, gallery**

Ansicht von Nordosten **View from the north-east**

Empore **Gallery**

Innenraum **Interior**

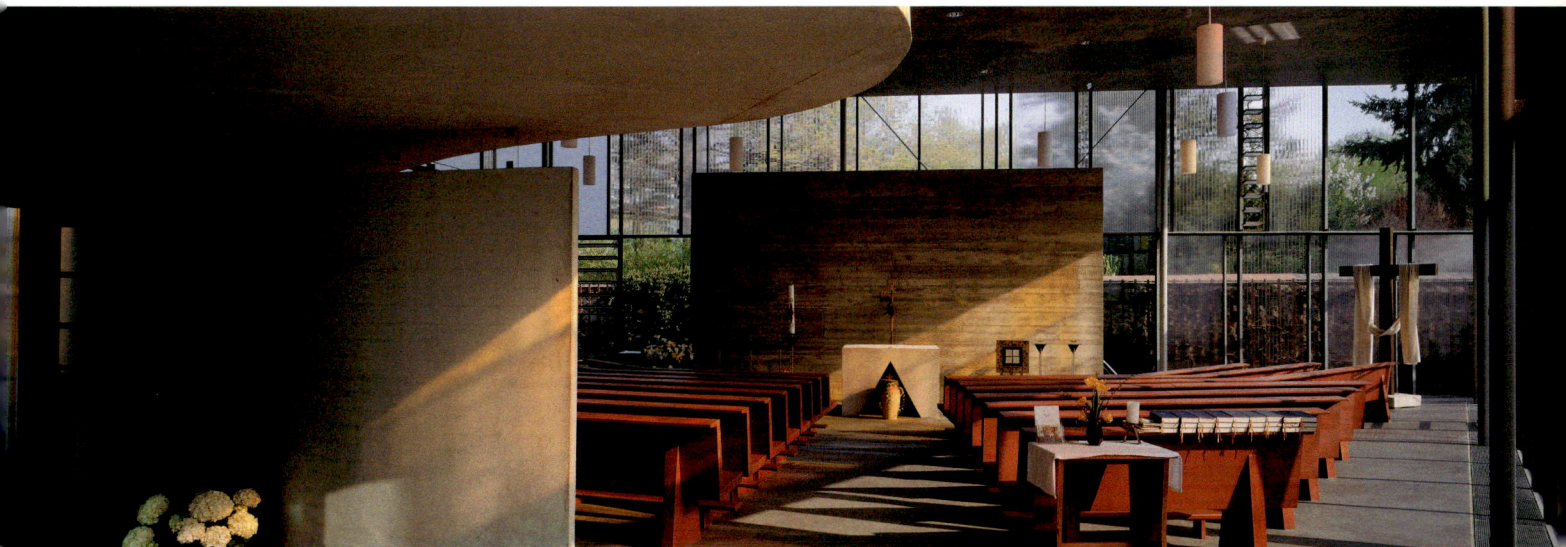

Blick auf den Altar **View of the altar**

Autobahnkirche, Medenbach
Highway Chapel, Medenbach

Hans Waechter

■ Die Autobahn zwischen Köln und Frankfurt ist wieder einmal völlig überlastet. Der Verkehr rast, hektisches Überholen, Lichthupen. Plötzlich entdecke ich auf der rechten Seite das Schild, das zur Autobahnkirche Medenbach weist. Schon mehrmals habe ich mich gefragt, welche Bedeutung eine Autobahnkirche in unserer Zeit wohl haben mag. Und wie man eine solche Aufgabe heute architektonisch wohl lösen würde. Jetzt wurde ich gebeten, über diese Kirche zu schreiben.

Mein Fahrer drängelt sich, auf mein Bitten hin, ganz nach rechts und kann gerade noch an der Tankstelle abfahren. Ich halte nach der Kirche Ausschau, ein Schild weist weiter geradeaus. Bereits zuvor hatte ich eine ungewöhnlich fremde Gebäudeform von der Autobahn aus gesehen, die nicht recht in das Repertoire einer Tankstelle und Raststätte zu passen schien. Hinter dem Tankstellengebäude bin ich völlig allein, kein Auto, kein Mensch. Schräg vor mir ragt ein Gebäudekeil in den Himmel: die schon von ferne gesehene fremde Form. Allein ein Kreuz weist auf die sakrale Funktion des Gebäudes hin. Ich überquere eine Straße, gehe erst über ein Rasenstück und dann durch Arkaden in einen kiesknirschenden Vorbereich. Die Umfassungsmauern sind sorgfältig betoniert. Arkaden, Rückwand und Bänke, dazu der Kiesboden und sieben Bäume, die im Sommer sicherlich ein Schattendach bilden. Jetzt ist Winter, kein Laub, kein Mensch, nur das laute Rasen der Autos in der Nähe. Eine große Öffnung in der Betonwand führt mich in einen inneren Hof, der von einem gedeckten Umgang umgeben ist. Eine lange Betonbank steht an einer Seite, der Ziegelkeil an gegenüberliegenden.

Über eine Glasfuge zwischen der den Hof umgebenden Betonwand und dem Ziegelbau trete ich in den Vorraum der Kirche. Schräge Schnitte in der Mauerwerksumwehrung verstärken den Eindruck des Massiven beim Eintritt in den Kirchenraum. Der umhüllende, archaisch wirkende Ziegel verstärkt diesen Eindruck, der zugleich von einem steilen, den Himmel freigebenden Glasdach wieder aufgehoben wird.

Ein introvertierter, aber beinahe heiter wirkender Innenraum erschließt sich dem Betrachter. Vermeintliche Kargheit wird durch die Reduktion der Materialien erzeugt: Glas, wenig Metall, Ziegel und Betonplatten für den Boden werden durch kubische Holzblöcke zum Sitzen und einen völlig schnörkellosen Altar ergänzt. Er besteht aus einem massiven Granitblock von Nikolaus Gerhart, in den zentrierte Öffnungen geschnitten wurden und der in diesem Raum überzeugt. Selbstverständlich sind Schwere und Konzentration spürbar. Der Altar wird in seiner räumlichen Wirkung durch kleine Betonplatten an der rückwärtigen Ziegelwand verstärkt. Sie stehen aneinander gereiht und lassen ein Kreuz frei. Der gesamte Raum ist in ein leichtes blaues Licht getaucht, das von einer zentral im Dach befindlichen Glasarbeit von Johannes Schreiter herrührt. Diese Arbeit erschließt sich mir zwar nicht, das gefärbte Glas verstärkt aber die entrückte Stimmung.

Ein schmaler Schlitz im Mauerwerk lässt als einzige Öffnung den horizontalen Blick frei. Fast magisch zieht es mich zu ihm. Der Blick

■ Once again, the motorway between Cologne and Frankfurt is inundated with traffic. Cars swerve in and out of the fast lane, frantically trying to overtake. Suddenly I notice a sign on the right pointing the way to the Medenbach Highway Chapel. How many times have I asked myself what the sense of a motorway church is in our day and age? And what architectural solution would be found if such a church were to be commissioned today? Good, too, for now I have been asked to describe this very church.

In response to my request, my driver forces his way across into the far-right lane, just in time to exit at the petrol station. I have my eyes peeled, and a sign indicates that we should continue straight on. Just a few moments earlier, I had spotted a strangely shaped building from the motorway. It didn't seem to fit into the repertoire of petrol stations and motorway service areas. Behind the petrol station, I am all alone: no car encompassing me, no one beside me. At an angle in front of me, a wedge-shaped building looms into the heavens – the strange entity I had seen from afar. Only a cross indicates that the building has a religious function. I traverse a street and a section of grass, and pass through an arcaded area before crunching through the gravel in front of the chapel. The surrounding walls have been carefully made of cement. There are arcades, a back wall and benches, not to mention the gravel and seven trees which no doubt form a shaded roof in summer. It is now winter. There are no leaves and no people; only the whine of cars travelling close by at high speed. A large opening in the cement wall leads me to an inner courtyard enclosed by a covered ambulatory. On the one side is a long concrete bench, and the brickwork wedge is on the other.

Through a glass seam between the cement wall of the courtyard and the brick edifice I enter the anteroom of the chapel. Slanted slits in the bulwark of the walls intensify the massive feel of the building when I enter the sanctuary's main space. This impression is further enhanced by the seemingly ancient brick cladding, yet also elided by the steep glass roof with its view of the heavens.

An introverted but somehow cheerful interior opens up to the visitor. Ostensibly, sparseness is produced through a reduction in materials – glass, little metal, bricks and a floor made of cement flagstone are complemented by cubic wooden blocks as seats and an altar completely bereft of ornamentation. Nikolaus Gerhart crafted the massive block of granite into which centred openings have been cut, a persuasive presence in this space. Of course, gravity and concentration are tangible. The spatial impact of the altar is enhanced by small cement plates on the brick wall behind it. They are placed in rows, and the space left in-between forms a cross. The entire room is steeped in a slightly blue light that emanates from a glass work of art positioned in the centre of the roof, the brainchild of Johannes Schreiter. I cannot really fathom what the artwork is about, but the coloured glass strengthens the sense of remoteness surrounding the interior.

Architekten Architects Prof. Hans Waechter, Dipl.-Ing. Architekt BDA, Mühltal; Team: Sibylle Waechter, Felix Waechter, Klaus Witzel, Silke Rossbach, Peter Stiebahl | **Bauherr Client** Evangelische Kirchengemeinde Medenbach, Wiesbaden | **Freianlagen Landscape** Ute Lienemeyer-Russell, Frankfurt am Main | **Künstler Artists** Prof. Johannes Schreiter, Langen; Prof. Nikolaus Gerhart, München | **Tragwerk Structural** Krebs und Kiefer GmbH, Darmstadt | **HL-Technik Technical** Planungsbüro für Ingenieurwesen Herbert, Darmstadt | **Wettbewerb Competition** 1998 | **Ausführung Construction** 2000/01 | **Standort Location** Raststätte Medenbach, A3

wird in den Hof gelenkt. Gleichzeitig erhält das Buch mit kleinen und großen Alltagssorgen, den Bitten und Danksagungen vor dieser geschlossenen Tür zwischen innen und außen eine noch größere Bedeutung. Der Blick wandert weiter in das geschlossene Atrium. Im Hintergrund grummelt viel zu laut der gleichmäßige Fluss der Autobahn. Warum hat Hans Waechter die Türen nicht besser abgedichtet?

Beim Verlassen des Kirchenraums nehme ich im Vorraum einige Infobroschüren mit. Draußen setze ich mich kurz auf eine Betonbank. Es ist kalt, und ich bin noch immer der einzige Besucher. Man kann sich gut vorstellen, dass hier im Sommer viele Menschen sind, um zu picknicken und unter dem Baumdach zu sitzen. Vielleicht werden sie ins Atrium gehen, herum um neun sprudelnde künstliche Wasserquellen im Boden. Dann werden sie durch die Glastüren den Vorraum betreten, um in den Kirchenraum zu gelangen. Sie werden zu den Wolken aufsehen, zum Anliegenbuch gehen und auf das Wasser im Atrium blicken. Statt der Autobahn wird nur das gleichmäßige Rauschen des Wassers zu hören sein.

Mein Fahrer hat getankt und mich zwischen Tankstelle und Raststätte gefunden. Wir starten wieder, der Verkehr rast erneut an uns vorbei. Wir schieben uns mit voller Beschleunigung zwischen zwei große Lastkraftwagen und dann mit viel Gas auf die linke Spur in die Hektik der Autobahn.

Dörte Gatermann

A small horizontal slit in the wall is the only opening. It exudes an almost magical attraction and directs the eye to the courtyard. At the same time, the request book containing everyday problems, both large and small, as well as wishes and notes of thanks gains special importance, placed as it is in front of this closed door, between the inside and the outside. The eye wanders on to the enclosed atrium. In the background: the never-ending and far-too-loud noise of the cars flowing along the motorway. Why did Hans Waechter not insulate the doors better?

When I leave the main room of the church, I take some informational leaflets from the anteroom with me. Outside I sit briefly on a cement bench. It is cold, and I am still the only visitor. One can well imagine that in summer there are many people here, enjoying picnics and sitting in the shade of the trees. Perhaps they will go into the atrium and see the nine bubbling fountains in the ground. Then they will go through the glass doors to enter the anteroom and the main room of the chapel. They will look up to the clouds, go to the request book and gaze at the water in the atrium. Instead of the motorway, the only sound will be the steady gurgling of water.

By now my driver has filled the tank and located me between the petrol station and the restaurant. We continue our journey as the traffic races by once again. He puts his foot to the floor and we squeeze in between two juggernauts. Back in the fast lane, we rejoin the frenzied pace of the motorway.

Dörte Gatermann

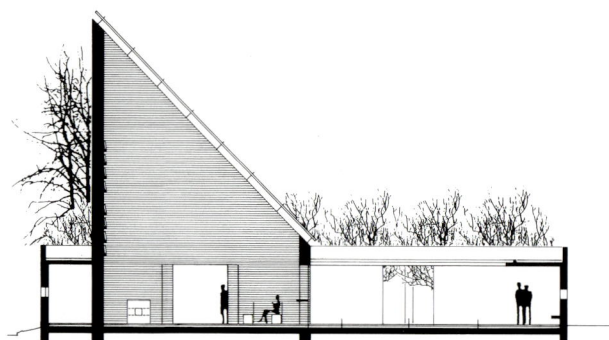

Längsschnitt **Longitudinal section**

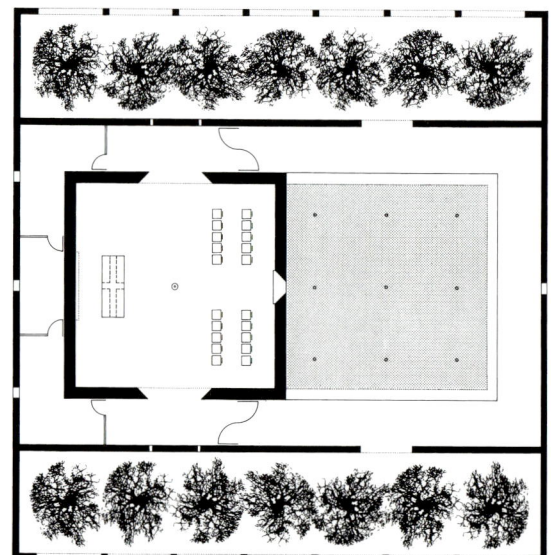

Grundriss **Ground plan**

Autobahnkirche, Medenbach
Highway Chapel, Medenbach

Ansicht von Osten **View from the east**

Innenhof **Courtyard**

Autobahnkirche, Medenbach
Highway Chapel, Medenbach

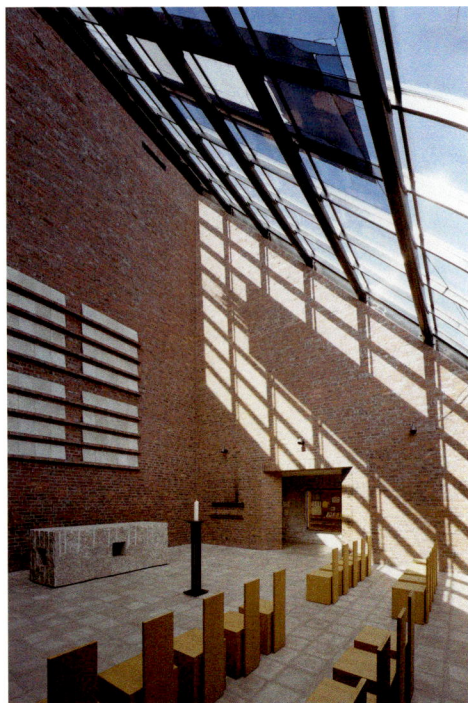

Innenraum bei Tag   **Interior by day**

Innenraum bei Nacht   **Interior by night**

Architektur in Deutschland
Architecture in Germany

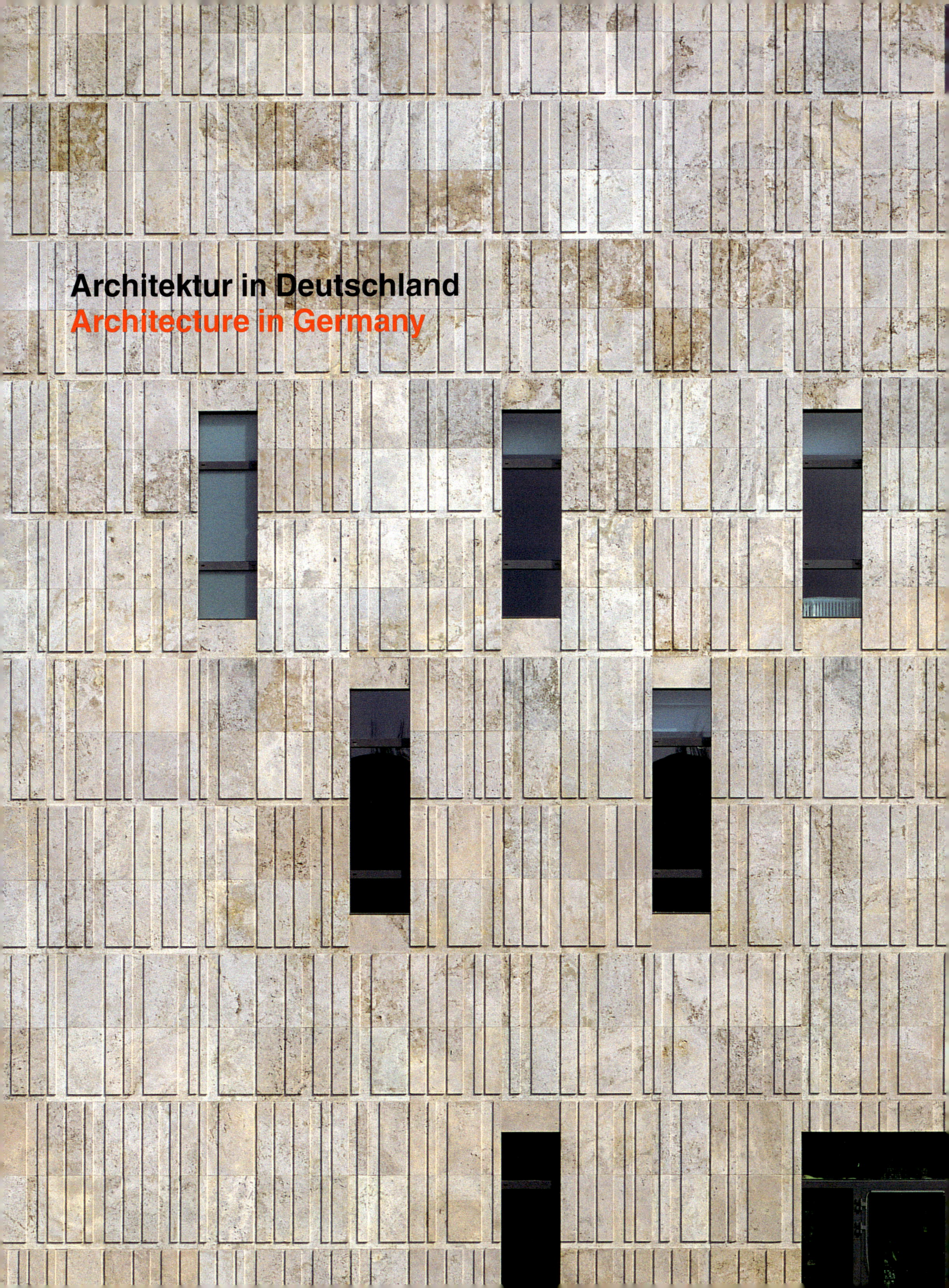

Verbandsgebäude der Südwestmetall, Reutlingen
Südwestmetall Federation Building, Reutlingen

Allmann Sattler Wappner

■ Drei silbern schimmernde Körper aus Edelstahl stellen sich als scharfkantige Blöcke in die Nachbarschaft braver Stadthäuser. Die fast vollkommen geschlossenen Metallfassaden des Verbandsgebäudes der Südwestmetall, hinter denen sich die raumhohen Verglasungen von Büro- und Schulungsräumen verbergen, verstärken diesen Eindruck des Monolithischen. Ohne Auskragungen und Rücksprünge demonstrieren die über gläserne Brücken verbundenen Neubauten perfekte Flächenbündigkeit – zwischen Dach und Wand gibt es keine Differenzierung mehr. Aus den klassischen Fensterlaibungen wurden bündig eingepasste Metallflächen, perforiert von lasergeschnittenen Schlitzen. Millimetergenau wurden diese Flächen in die Metallhaut gesetzt. Regenrinnen und Tonziegel, schmucke Vordächer oder verspielte Erker, all das hat diese Architektur wie unnötigen Ballast abgeworfen. Ihr metallisches Blattwerk umschließt nicht nur das Sockelgeschoss, sondern faltet sich auf die kleinen Freiflächen vor den Gebäuden hinaus: Die eigenwillige Fassade wird zum Bodenbelag. Das Spiel der Transformationen und Irritationen beginnt: Die vertraute Form ist nur noch eine leise Spur der Bebauungsvorschrift. Denn obwohl die neuen Gebäude die Umrisslinien und Kubaturen ihrer Nachbarbauten aufnehmen, obwohl sie also zunächst als ganz konventionelle Stadthäuser mit gewöhnlichen Satteldächern erscheinen, sind sie durch ihre monolithische Gestaltung und ihre keramikgestrahlten Metallfassaden so vollkommen anders, dass der Kontrast zu ihrer Umgebung nicht schärfer sein könnte.

Wie in einem gigantischen Vexierbild offenbaren sich immer neue Gegensätze. Während die Nachbarn mit Zäunen ihr Terrain abgrenzen, sind es bei dem Verbandsgebäude lediglich Metallplatten, die, vor die drei Bauten gelegt, das Grundstück völlig offen lassen. Und sind es dort klare Lochfassaden, die, auf einem soliden Steinsockel ruhend, das vertraute Bild eines Wohnhauses vermitteln, so stellt man bei der Annäherung an die metallischen Blöcke überraschende Veränderungen fest. Das matt schimmernde, leicht wirkende Blattwerk, das den gesamten Sockelbereich zu umranken scheint, steht nicht nur in Kontrast zu den klassisch-schweren Sockeln seiner Nachbarn, sondern das vermeintlich klare Bild löst sich auf und ist nur noch als abstraktes Muster lesbar. Dominiert aus der Ferne die kompakte Geschlossenheit der Körper, so erkennt man erst aus der Nähe die fragile (vier Millimeter starke) Membran aus Metall. Die demonstrative Flächenbündigkeit der Fassade wird durch die dahinter liegenden Glaswände gestört. Was zuvor als Fläche wirkte, erhält nun räumliche Tiefe. Konsequent und spannungsreich ist das Konzept der subversiven Verfremdung verwirklicht. Das besondere Interesse an der Gebäudehülle, die konzeptionelle Schärfe in der baulichen Umsetzung und die Entwicklung eines architektonischen Themas aus der Bauaufgabe heraus offenbaren Analogien zu den Arbeiten von Herzog & de Meuron.

Fein ausgearbeitete Details tragen dazu bei, das Exklusive dieser Architektur selbst bis in den kleinen Maßstab spürbar zu machen. Alles ist hier mit großer Sorgfalt entwickelt: Oberflächen aus glattge-

■ Three stainless-steel bodies shimmering silver act as sharp-edged blocks in a neighbourhood of stolid town houses. The monolithic impression is emphasised by the almost completely hermetic metal facades of the Südwestmetall Federation's building, behind which the floor-to-ceiling windows of the office and training rooms are concealed. Bereft of protrusions or indentations, the new buildings, linked by glass bridges, demonstrate a perfect seamless continuity – there is no longer any distinction between roof and walls. The classical window reveals have given way to flush-fitted metal surfaces, perforated by laser-incised slits. These surfaces have been precisely positioned in the metal skin down to the last millimetre. Rain gutters and clay roofing tiles, decorative canopies or playful oriels – this architecture has shed them all like so much unnecessary ballast. The metallic panelling extends not only to the basement, but also unfolds on the small free surfaces in front of the buildings: The idiosyncratic facade becomes a floor covering. And so begins the game of transformations and irritations. The familiar shape is only a vague memory of the building permission issued. The new buildings reiterate the outlines and cubing of the neighbouring edifices, and therefore initially appear to be quite conventional city houses with the usual saddle roofs. Their monolithic design and ceramic-blasted metal facades are, however, so completely different that they could not contrast more sharply with the surroundings.

The eye continuously spies new contrasts as if viewing a gigantic puzzle. While the neighbours stake out their terrain with fences, at the Federation's building metal sheets laid out in front of the three edifices leave the grounds completely open. And while the clear, perforated facades resting on a solid stone plinth convey the familiar image of a residential house, upon closer inspection, the metallic blocks reveal surprising changes: the matt, shimmering, seemingly light foliage that seems to entwine the entire base contrasts with the heavy, classical base sections of the neighbouring buildings, and what once appeared as a clear picture dissolves into an abstract pattern. Whereas from a distance the compact, hermetic character of the building stands out, only when up close do you recognise the fragile (4 mm thick) metal membrane. The demonstrative smoothness of the facade is interrupted by the glass walls behind. What initially seemed to be a surface now transpires to have depth. The concept of subversive alienation has been achieved logically and is very exciting. Analogies to the works of Herzog & de Meuron become evident if we consider the special attention paid to a shroud for the building, the conceptual acuity in the architectural design and how and architectural theme has been developed out of the task commissioned.

Finely treated detailing helps to render the exclusive qualities of this architecture tangible even at the most minute level. Everything here has been devised with great care: Surfaces made of fair-faced concrete blasted smooth, doors, floors, ceilings and walls in light

Architekten Architects Allmann Sattler Wappner Architekten, München, www.allmannsattlerwappner.de; Markus Allmann, Amandus Sattler, Ludwig Wappner; Team: Helgo von Meier & Georg Rafailidis, Angela Hertel, Bettina Mutzenbach, Susanne Rath | **Bauherr** Client Südwestmetall, Verband der Metall- und Elektroindustrie Baden-Württemberg e.V., Stuttgart | **Bauleitung** Construction Management Erich H. Fritz, Stuttgart | **Grafik** Graphics Design Roswitha Allmann Mediendesign, München | **Tragwerk** Structural Sobek Ingenieure GmbH, Stuttgart | **Fassade** Facade Fuchs R + R, Ingenieurbüro für Fassadentechnik, München | **Energie** Energy Transsolar Energietechnik GmbH, Stuttgart; Schreiber Beratende Ingenieure, Ulm | **Wettbewerb** Competition 1999 | **Ausführung** Construction 2000–2002 | **Standort** Location Schulstraße 23, Reutlingen

strahltem Sichtbeton, Türen, Fußböden, Decken und Wände in dezentem Lichtgrau oder Weiß nehmen das Prinzip der bündigen Flächen wieder auf und verdeutlichen, dass auch in den Innenräumen die Reduktion auf das Wesentliche mit Akribie verfolgt wurde. Die raumhohen Fenster in den allseits verglasten Büros erlauben den überraschend großzügigen Blick nach außen – selbst bei dicht verschlossener Fassade fällt ausreichend Tageslicht durch das enge Raster der kleinen Schlitze in der Metallhaut. Betritt man einen der beiden Konferenzsäle unter dem geneigten Dach, wird wieder erfahrbar, dass man sich eigentlich in einem ganz ›normalen Haus‹ mit Satteldach befindet – doch schnell erscheint auch dies nur als gekonnte Camouflage. Die räumliche Dramatik durch die abgerundeten Übergänge zwischen Dach- und Wandflächen und die enorme Höhe des Raums (maximal 9,60 Meter) verleihen diesem eine völlig neue Wirkung, die mit der vertrauten Vorstellung eines Dachraums bricht. Die gekonnt inszenierte Verfremdung beginnt ihr Spiel mit dem Vertrauten. Wenngleich sich die drei neuen Häuser mit ihren gleitend gelagerten Metallfassaden wie selbstverständlich in die Baulinie ihrer Vorgänger stellen, so tanzen sie doch merklich aus der Reihe. Die Neubauten brauchen ihre braven Nachbarn wie der Artist sein Publikum. Als perfekt gestaltete Körper wirken sie wie autonome Objekte, die vor allem ihrer eigenen Ästhetik gehorchen und auf spürbare Distanz zur Stadt gehen. Objekte, die sich auch gerne ein bisschen selbst feiern, die sich mit ihrem gänzlich eigenen Materialkanon ein kaum sichtbares Podium errichten und dadurch den Bezug zum Außenraum bewusst verfremden. Dort wachsen streng geometrisch gepflanzte Chinesische Wildbirnen zwischen den Metallplatten empor. Ein surreales Szenario? Nein, nur die konsequente Fortsetzung dieser kompromisslosen Sprache.

Die Verbandsgebäude der Südwestmetall überzeugen nicht nur durch die Synthese aus Aufgabe und Material, sondern auch deshalb, weil diese besonderen, mit feinem Kalkül entwickelten Häuser stets Überraschungen bereithalten. Weil sie in ihrer Wahrnehmung ständig changieren und genau damit ihre eigene gestalterische Strenge persiflieren.

Hans-Jürgen Breuning

grey or white reiterate the principle of seamless surfaces and highlight the fact that in the inside rooms, great attention has been paid to reducing everything to the essentials. The floor-to-ceiling windows in the fully glazed offices offer a surprisingly generous view of the outer world – even with the densely hermetic facade, sufficient daylight shines through the close grid of small slits in the metal skin. If you enter one of the two conference rooms beneath the angled roof you realise again that you are actually in a quite 'normal' house with a saddle roof – although that impression quickly proves to be clever camouflage. The spatial dynamism, thanks to the rounded transitions from roof surface to wall and the room's immense height (maximum 9.60 metres), lend it a completely new feel that shatters any familiar notions of a loft. The inventively staged alienation of the usual begins to undermine the familiar. Even though the three new houses with their smooth sliding metal facades occupy the same positions on the street as their predecessors, they dance noticeably out of line. The new buildings need their good neighbours like an artist needs an audience. As perfectly designed bodies they act as independent objects which have an aesthetic all their own and manifestly distance themselves from the city. They are objects that enjoy celebrating themselves, that deploy a materials canon of their very own to create an almost invisible podium and in this way deliberately eliminate any reference to the outside space. There, wild Chinese pears, planted in a strictly geometrical fashion, reach for the sky between the metal sheets. A surreal scenario? No, only the logical continuation of this uncompromising formal idiom.

The Südwestmetall buildings are convincing not only in the way they create a synthesis of task and material, but also because these specially designed houses, designed with such refinement, constantly surprise you. For the perception of them changes all the time, and in this way they poke fun at their own design stringency.

Hans-Jürgen Breuning

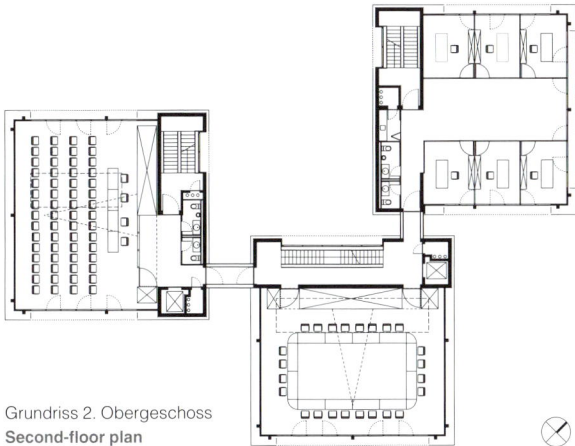

Grundriss 2. Obergeschoss
Second-floor plan

Grundriss 1. Obergeschoss
First-floor plan

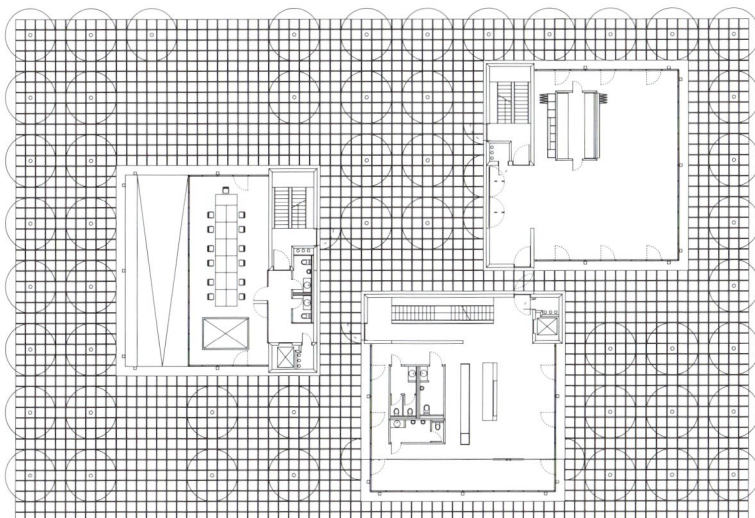

Grundriss Erdgeschoss **Ground-floor plan**

Gläserne Brücke
Glass bridge

Empfang **Reception**

Treppe **Staircase**

Büroräume **Offices**

Schattenwurf der Fassade
Shadow cast by the facade

Domviertel, Magdeburg
Cathedral District, Magdeburg

Bolles+Wilson

■ Wenn in einer bissigen Kritik dem Neubau der NORD/LB in Magdeburg der Architekten Julia B. Bolles-Wilson und Peter L. Wilson die Qualität eines »Ozeandampfers, der auf Sand gelaufen« ist, bescheinigt wird[1], vermutet der unvorbereitete Besucher eine architektonische Tragödie. Der Artikel liest sich wie eine Philippika gegen ein zeitgenössisches Architekturprojekt in unmittelbarer Nähe zum grandiosen gotischen Magdeburger Dom, in der den Architekten – neben allgemeinem Versagen – zumindest entschuldigend als ein Grund des Scheiterns der qualvolle Anpassungsprozess unter dem Druck öffentlicher Empörung und der denkmalpflegerischen Auflagen zur »Animation einer Dachlandschaft«[2] zugestanden wurde.

Eine anspruchsvolle städtebauliche Schließung des Domplatzes in Magdeburg durch den Neubau der NORD/LB lässt die Kritik verblassen. Ein gespannt-nervöses manieristisches Städtebaukonzept durchzieht urbane Blöcke mit einem komplizierten Raum- und Gassensystem; doch erweist sich der Block als klares Prinzip, welches die Gespanntheiten im Inneren der Anlage verkraftet. Im Gegenteil: Die vielfältigen Durchgänge, die Vor- und Rücksprünge, die Dachaufsätze laden das traditionelle Blockprinzip mit einer Energie auf, die den Stadtraum um den Magdeburger Domplatz souverän fasst. Kompliziert im Detail und zugleich einfach in der Struktur, möchte man dieses städtebauliche Konzept einfach nur ›schön‹ nennen.

Dass diese urbanistische Schönheit eine komplizierte ist, spürt man beim Durchwandern der Geschosse. Herkömmliche zwei- und dreibündige Bürogrundrisse müssen sich um diesen Städtebau ›herumwinden‹. Der Fluss der Geschosse und die räumliche Dynamik innerhalb der Baublöcke werden gebremst. Der verordnete Bürozellenbau nimmt viel von der räumlichen Kraft, die im Innern der Anlage steckt. Die Architekten reagieren auf die Repetition im Bürobau mit einem beliebten Mittel: Jede Situation wird individuell designed. Keine Linie, kein Prinzip existiert ohne Brechung. Situativ wird die Eigenständigkeit, das Individuelle des architektonischen Gewebes in den Vordergrund gestellt. Bewundernswert, wie die Architekten ihre Detailbesessenheit durchhalten, wie sie ihre Fantasie ausleben. Auffällig ist die große Unterschiedlichkeit in der Entwurfsmetaphorik des Neubaus: Jede Ecke, jede Seite, jedes Geschoss, jede Fassade, selbst die ›Säulenordnungen‹ sind je nach Situation und Lage unterschiedlich. Alison und Peter Smithson haben das Prinzip der Unterschiedlichkeit als Qualität in ihrer Kritik an der Moderne eingefordert: »[…] um uns an unserem Territorium wirklich erfreuen zu können, benötigen wir ein Gewebe, das eine große Anzahl von ›Unterschieden‹ zur Verfügung stellt. Das Gebäude hat Wände, Decken, Böden, die sich krümmen und verspringen, auf- und abgehen, sich schlängeln und aufeinander wirken […]. Die ›First-Rippen-Dacharchitektur‹ wurde entdeckt, wie die sichtbaren Wirbel bei einigen Knochenfischarten oder auf dem Rücken einiger Dinosaurier.«[3] Der ›Knochenfisch‹ ist nun auf dem Dach der NORD/LB gelandet. Welchen Kampf muss es um dieses Attikageschoss gegeben haben, wenn es – völlig abweichend von dem darunter liegenden Hauptgebäude – den ›ge-

■ In a biting criticism of the new building for the Norddeutsche Landesbank in Magdeburg, one commentator claimed that architects Julia B. Bolles-Wilson and Peter L. Wilson had created an edifice with the qualities of a "beached ocean liner".[1] The unprepared visitor may therefore be forgiven for expecting to encounter an architectural disaster. The article reads like an invective against a contemporary architectural project that is located very close to the grand Gothic cathedral of Magdeburg. The architects are charged with general incompetence, and a reason cited for their failure (and perhaps an excusable one at that) is a tortuous adaptation process triggered by public outcry and conditions set by the monuments office as regards the "animation of the skyline".[2]

The criticism pales when one actually sees the Norddeutsche Landesbank, a project that offers an ambitiously discerning completion of the layout of Magdeburg's cathedral square. The tense, nervous, Mannerist concept of town planning here means that the blocks of the downtown area involve a complex system of spaces and streets. Yet, the block itself establishes a principle of clarity that easily absorbs the suspense created in the interior of the complex. In fact, the multiple passageways, the projections and indentations, as well as the superimpositions on the roof give the traditional office block concept an energy which provides a masterful solution to the problem of handling the space of Magdeburg's cathedral square. Complicated in detail and simultaneously simple in structure, one could easily call this concept for solving the planning issues involved 'beauty'.

One perceives how complicated this urban beauty is while wandering through the various floors. Traditional clusters of two and three flush office spaces have to 'twist' around the urban structure. Inside the block, the flow of floors and the dynamics of space are arrested. The prescribed need for office cells takes much from the power of the space innate in the interior of the complex. The architects have resorted to a preferred means to counter repetition in the office building: Every situation is individually designed. No lines and no principles exist without interruption. Each setting is defined by its independence, and the individuality of the architectural fabric is foregrounded. The way the architects have maintained their obsession with detail is admirable. They have lived out their fantasies. The immense differences in the metaphoric qualities of this building are striking. Every corner, every side, every floor, every facade, even the 'orders' of the columns differ according to setting and location. In their critique of Modernism, Alison and Peter Smithson have called for the principle of difference as a quality to be upheld: "…in order to really enjoy our territory, we need a fabric which gives us a great number of 'differences'. The building has walls, ceilings and floors which are crooked and uneven, which go up and down, which wind and interact…. 'Ridge-rib roof architecture' was discovered, like the visible vertebrae of some skeletal fish or the back of some dinosaurs."[3] The "skeletal fish" has now landed on the roof of the

Architekten Architects Bolles+Wilson, Münster, www.bolles-wilson.com; Peter L. Wilson, Prof. Julia B. Bolles-Wilson; Team: Andreas Polzer, Axel Kempers & Susanne Asmuth, Manfred Kieler, Kersten Schagemann, Cornelia Nottelmann, Cäcilia Reppenhorst, Andrea Janietz, Ruth Thörner, Thomas Wagener, Christian Veddeler, Ellen Krampe | **Bauherr** Client NORD/LB Immobilien Holding GmbH & Co Objekt Magdeburg KG, München | **Projektsteuerung** Project Management Arge Saleg, Magdeburg; NILEG, Hannover | **Tragwerk** Structural ASSMANN Beraten + Planen GmbH, Magdeburg | **HL-Technik** Technical NEK Beraten + Planen GmbH, Groß Glienicke | **Licht** Lighting a·g Licht Gesellschaft beratender Ingenieure für Lichtplanung, Bonn | **Wettbewerb** Competition 1998 | **Ausführung** Construction 2000–2002 | **Standort** Location Domplatz 10–12, Breiter Weg 7, Magdeburg

strandeten Knochenfisch‹ auf dem Dach als Gestaltungselement be-
nutzt? Mir scheint der ›Knochenfisch‹ der reifste Teil dieser Arbeit
von Bolles+Wilson zu sein. Endlich spielt der Bau sich frei, luftiger
sind der Raumschnitt und Lichtfluss zwischen innen und außen.
Irgendwie fremd wirkt nunmehr der Blick hinunter auf die hellblau
geäderte Natursteinverkleidung in Azul Macauba der Fassade. Nicht
die Materialität, sondern die feine blau schimmernde Lichtstimmung
aus dem Innern des gotischen Doms wird in die farbige Natursteinverkleidung des Neubaus übersetzt: für den Betrachter gewöh-
nungsbedürftig. Das gilt auch für die in die sechziger Jahre zurück-
weisende Baubronzefassade des Erdgeschosses, die dem Gewicht
des historischen Gegenübers des gotischen Doms und der barocken
Domplatzbebauung beinahe trotzig ein eigenes Design entgegenset-
zen möchte. Davon zeugt die materiale Überinstrumentierung, die
mit vielfältigen Öffnungen die städtebaulich abgestimmte Blockkon-
zeption des Neubaus im abwechslungsreichen Detail weiter aufladen
möchte. Manchmal ist dieser Detailreichtum verwirrend: Der Unterschied zwischen innen und außen scheint aufgehoben. Selbst bei
der Verkleidung der Stützen der Kolonnaden zum Domplatz wechseln die Materialien der Oberflächen von vorpatinierter Baubronze im
unteren Bereich zu hinterleuchteten Glasverkleidungen im ›Kapitell-
bereich‹ der Stützen: Design für Innenräume, vielleicht im Außenraum ein wenig zu viel, meint man, wenn man oben auf der Reling
des Casinos befreit stehen und über Magdeburg blicken kann.

Eine großartige Metamorphose von einem eher konventionellen,
aber wertvollen Bank- und Bürogebäudedesign zu einem ›Fisch auf
dem Dach‹. Ich mag diesen manieristischen Bau, seine hohe gestalterische Qualität im Detail, seine Widersprüche, diese ständig wechselnden Interpretationen von Stütze, Öffnung, Wand, Dach und
Raum. Hier wird eines der bedeutendsten Stadtensembles Deutschlands souverän vollendet.

Jörg Friedrich

1 Dankwart Guratzsch in: *Die Welt,* vom 13.3.2003.
2 Ebd.
3 Alison und Peter Smithson, *Italienische Gedanken,* Braunschweig 1996, S. 150.

Norddeutsche Landesbank. What a battle there must have been over
this attic floor, which (departing totally from the building under-
neath) uses a 'stranded skeletal fish' on the roof as a defining
shape! For me, the 'skeletal fish' is the most mature part of this
design by Bolles+Wilson. The edifice swims free of the surroundings
here: There is an airy use of space and flow of light between inside
and outside. By contrast, the view down to the light blue grained
natural stone facade in azul macauba seems somehow strange. It is
not the material, but the fine blue shimmering aura of light from the
interior of the Gothic cathedral which is transposed into the
coloured stone facade of the new building. And it needs some get-
ting used to. This is equally true of the architectural bronze facade
of the ground floor, reminiscent of the 1960s. It is an individual idea
which stubbornly contrasts with the massive history of the Gothic
cathedral and the Baroque square. This is evidenced by an extreme
use of different materials which further enhance the coordinated urban conception of the new building with its diverse openings and
rich variety of detail. Sometimes this richness of detail is confusing.
The difference between inside and outside seems to be elided. Even
the cladding for the pillars in the colonnade leading to the cathedral
square changes from pre-patinated bronze on the lower parts to
back-lit glass coverings around the 'capitals'. A design for interiors
which is perhaps too much for exterior use, one might think, while
catching one's breath by the railing atop the casino and taking in
the view of Magdeburg.

A splendid metamorphosis from a somewhat conventional but
useful design for a bank and office building into a 'fish on the roof'. I
like this Mannerist building, its high-quality detailing, its contradic-
tions, its constantly changing interpretations of supports, openings, walls, roof and space. One of Germany's most important urban
ensembles has been masterfully completed.

Jörg Friedrich

1 Dankwart Guratzsch in *Die Welt,* 12 March 2003.
2 Ibid.
3 Alison and Peter Smithson, *Italienische Gedanken* (*Italian Thoughts*), Braunschweig,
1996, p. 150.

Seiten 104/105 **Pages 104 – 105**
Ansicht von Südosten
View from the south-east

Grundriss Erdgeschoss **Ground-floor plan**

Blick auf St. Sebastian **View of St Sebastian**

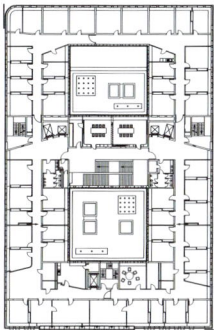

Grundriss 2. Obergeschoss **Second-floor plan**

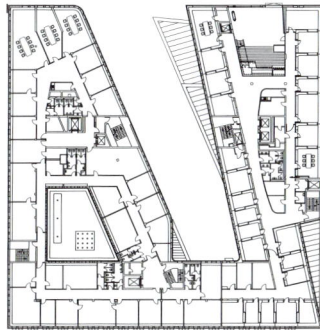

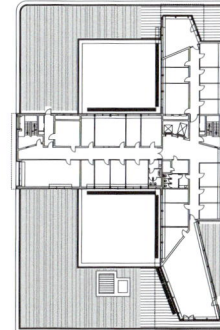

Grundriss 5. Obergeschoss **Fifth-floor plan**

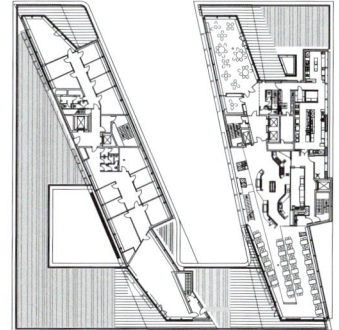

Eingang Kassenhalle   **Entrance, banking hall**

Kassenhalle   **Banking hall**

Atrium **Atrium**

Kantine **Canteen**

Haus S, Ludwigsburg
House S, Ludwigsburg

Bottega + Ehrhardt

■ »Um etwas zu zeigen, male ich viel weg«, sagt der belgische Maler Luc Tymans. Dieser Strategie haben sich auch Bottega + Ehrhardt bei der Planung des Hauses S in Ludwigsburg bedient. Auf diese Art ist ein kraftvolles Objekt entstanden, das für Aufsehen sorgt, aber auch für so manche Irritation.

Gerade unter den Nachbarn ist der ›Betonblock‹ umstritten. Zwar ist außen praktisch kein Beton zu sehen, und den ›béton brut‹ im Inneren werden die meisten Passanten kaum zu Gesicht bekommen haben, doch sprechen die Kragkonstruktion und die materielle Homogenität des Gebäudes eine eindeutige Sprache. Vor allem aber unterscheidet sich das Haus S deutlich von den Nachbarhäusern und lässt es in den Augen der Menschen vor Ort als Fremdkörper erscheinen – als ›Betonblock‹ eben.

So mancher Fremde wird jedoch weniger Befremdliches an diesem als an den kleinbürgerlichen Häuschen der Umgebung erkennen können. Aus der Distanz betrachtet, will die von diesen suggerierte, aber nicht wirklich eingelöste Idylle wenig zur Unwirtlichkeit der Lage des Hauses unmittelbar an einem Eisenbahndamm passen. Die Fassade zu den Gleisen hin geschlossen zu halten, wie bei Haus S, erscheint hier schon aufgrund des Lärms notwendig. Genauso vernünftig ist es, Autos auf dem eigenen Grundstück zu parken, wie hier – vielleicht ein wenig zu demonstrativ – auf einem von Leitplanken flankierten Vorplatz möglich, statt sie halb auf dem Bürgersteig abzustellen. Schließlich stellt der neue Baukörper auch formale Bezüge zur Umgebung her: durch seine Maße, die annähernd denen der Nachbarbauten entsprechen; durch seine geneigten Dachflächen; durch das matte Olivgrün des wasserdichten Putzes, mit dem das Haus einheitlich versiegelt wurde – ein Grün, das man vor Ort vielfach wiederfindet.

Was schon auf den ersten Blick nicht in die alles andere als feine Umgebung passen will, ist der Bauherr. Als erfolgreicher Jungunternehmer und Werbefachmann unterscheidet sich Herr S sehr von den hier lebenden kleinen Leuten. Seine Welt ist die der visuellen Kommunikation und des Designs, des auffälligen Auftritts und der permanenten Repräsentation. Davon zeugt sein Haus S, insbesondere durch seine Symbolik. Wenn der Baukörper eher an den Kontrollturm eines Flughafens denn an ein trautes Heim denken lässt, dann soll dies wohl zusammen mit dem großzügigen Parkplatz als Hinweis auf einen durch Mobilität gekennzeichneten, aufregend modernen Lebenswandel des Bewohners verstanden werden. Bewusst so inszeniert oder nicht, ist der Wille zur prägnanten Großform unübersehbar.

Allerdings steht die Einheitlichkeit der äußeren Erscheinungsform im Gegensatz zur Kleinteiligkeit im Inneren. Bei Haus S handelt es sich nämlich wider Erwarten nicht um eine Villa, sondern um ein Mehrfamilienhaus. Bedingt durch die Hanglage, befindet sich eine Mietwohnung eine Treppe tiefer auf Gartenniveau, eine weitere liegt ebenerdig, und die Wohnung des Bauherrn selbst beansprucht schließlich das erste und zweite Obergeschoss. Allein diese weicht in ihrem Anspruch von den marktüblichen Standardlösungen ab.

■ "In order to show something, I paint a lot out," explained the Belgian artist Luc Tymans. Bottega + Erhardt have developed a similar strategy in designing House S in Ludwigsburg. The result is a compelling structure that draws both attention and controversy.

For the neighbours, this 'concrete block' is a bone of contention. Although there is hardly any concrete visible on the outside, and while it is unlikely that passers-by would glimpse the *béton brut* within, the cantilever construction and material homogeneity of the building speak an unambiguous language. Above all, however, House S differs so much from the surrounding buildings that it seems like a foreign body – it sticks out like a 'concrete block'.

Others might find House S more familiar than the petty bourgeois architecture of houses nearby. Seen from a distance, these dwellings evoke a certain idyll that they ultimately fail to deliver. In this respect, they are somewhat incongruous in this rather unappealing setting adjacent to a railway cutting. Creating a closed facade towards the railway tracks, as in House S, appears to be a mandate here on the grounds of noise alone. It is also a sensible idea to create a space for the car on the site, as here – albeit a little too demonstratively, perhaps – parked on a forecourt bounded by guardrails rather than with two wheels on the pavement. Finally, the new building also responds to the surroundings – its scale and approximate sloping roof of the neighbouring buildings, and the matt olive green of the watertight plaster used to seal the house is commonly found here.

What does not seem to fit in to this less than prestigious area is, at first glance, the client. A successful young businessman in advertising, Mr S is very different from his neighbours. His is the world of visual communications and design, a world in which making the right impression counts. House S reflects this, especially in its symbolism. If the building looks more like an air traffic control tower than home sweet home, this is probably a reference – like the spacious parking area – to an excitingly modern lifestyle of mobility. Whether or not this impression is deliberate is not clear, but the will to make a mark on the large scale is evident.

Yet the unity of the outward form contrasts with the small-scale interior. Surprisingly, House S is not a villa, but an apartment block. Built on a slope, there is an apartment one floor down at garden level, yet another at ground level, and the client's own apartment is on the first and second floors. This alone sets it apart from the solutions one usually finds in the building sector.

All in all, this is a small but carefully composed design, with a narrow stair leading from the forecourt and the carport up to the first floor. On the first floor there is a single south-facing room running the entire width of the house with an open-plan living, dining and kitchen area. To the north are three small areas of flexible use which, towards the outer wall, incorporate the space under the sloped roof. A stairway leads to the upper floor with the master bedroom, bathroom and large terrace.

Architekten Architects Bottega + Ehrhardt Architekten, Stuttgart, www.be-arch.com; Giorgio Bottega, Henning Ehrhardt; Team: Matthias Siegert | **Bauherr Client** Willibald Slavicek, Ludwigsburg | **Bauleitung Construction Management** Lutz Hennig, Stuttgart | **Tragwerk Structural** Büro IMS-Bauplanung, Stuttgart | **Ausführung Construction** 2001/02 | **Standort Location** Bismarckstraße 18, Ludwigsburg

Entstanden ist hier eine kleine, aber feine räumliche Komposition mit einer betont engen Treppe, die vom Vorplatz und den Carports hinauf in das erste Geschoss führt. Dort befindet sich ein nach Süden orientierter, die gesamte Breite des Hauses einnehmender Raum zum Wohnen, Essen und Kochen. Nach Norden liegen drei kleine flexibel nutzbare Bereiche; zur Außenwand hin schließen diese nach oben den Raum unter der Dachneigung mit ein. Über eine Freitreppe erreicht man die oberste Etage mit ›master bedroom‹, Badezimmer und großer Terrasse.

Alle Räume dieser Wohnung sind von einer hohen formalen Eigenständigkeit. Interessant und schön sind sie von sich aus, und zwar auch und gerade unmöbliert. Um das Mobiliar auf das Wesentliche reduzieren zu können, verschwindet alles, was sich einbauen lässt, hinter den Klappen einer weiß lackierten Wandverkleidung. Ansonsten wurde der Beton der Wände und Decken sichtbar belassen. Sämtliche Böden bestehen aus einem leicht spiegelnden, weißen Epoxydharz.

Das raffinierte Design entspricht dem Wunsch nach einem individuellen ›Wohnen im Kunstwerk‹. Der Konflikt zwischen dem einem solchen Wunsch folgenden, elitär anmutenden Objekt und seiner biederen Umgebung ist ein kultureller Konflikt mit einem sozialen Hintergrund. Leider gehören in einer Zeit zunehmender gesellschaftlicher Segregation Konflikte dieser Art inzwischen zum Alltag. Wahrscheinlich waren sich die Architekten dieser Situation bewusst. Jedenfalls gleicht das, was ihnen gelungen ist, den Bildern Luc Tymans' und kann als architektonisches Porträt heutiger Verhältnisse, hier am Beispiel einer suburbanen Szene im schwäbischen Ludwigsburg, betrachtet werden.

Ob man das Gebäude jenseits oder wegen seines etwas theatralischen Auftritts und/oder seiner gestalterischen Qualitäten persönlich mag oder nicht mag, hängt wesentlich davon ab, wie man selbst zur heutigen Zeit steht und wo man sich in ihr positioniert.

Manuel Cuadra

All the rooms in this apartment are formally distinctive. They are interesting and beautiful in their own right – both furnished and, in particular, unfurnished. In order to reduce the furnishings to a minimum, everything that can be stored away disappears behind white wall panelling. Otherwise, the concrete of the walls and ceilings has been left visible. All the flooring consists of a slightly reflecting, white epoxy resin.

This cleverly sophisticated design accommodates the desire for individualistic 'living in an artwork'. The conflict between the elitism of a building that panders to such a wish and its petty bourgeois surroundings is a culture clash with a social background. Unfortunately, in an era of increasing social segregation, conflicts of this kind have become part of everyday life. The architects were probably aware of the situation. At any rate, what they have succeeded in doing is reminiscent of the paintings of Luc Tymans and may be regarded as an architectonic portrait of the present-day situation using the example of a suburban setting in the Swabian town of Ludwigsburg.

Whether because of its design qualities one actually likes or dislikes the building depends essentially on one's own attitudes to present-day society, as well as one's own position in it.

Manuel Cuadra

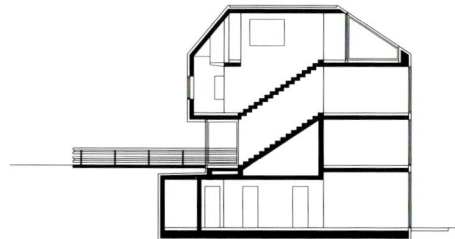

Schnitt **Section**

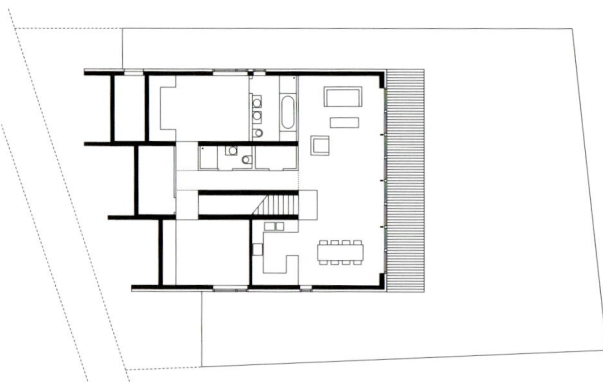

Grundriss Gartengeschoss **Ground plan, garden level**

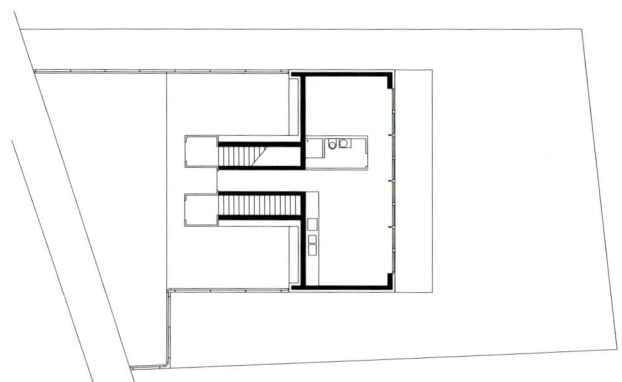

Grundriss Erdgeschoss **Ground-floor plan**

Haus S, Ludwigsburg
House S, Ludwigsburg

Ansicht von Südwesten **View from the south-west**

Eingang **Entrance**

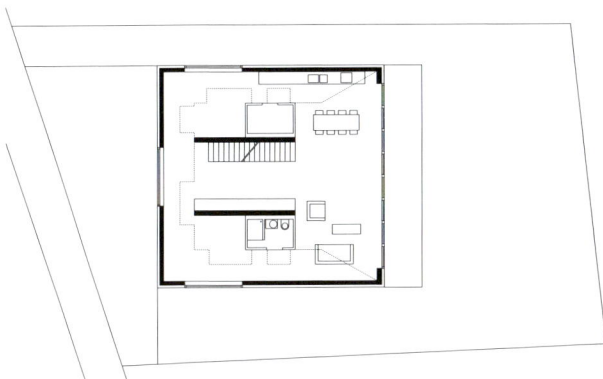

Grundriss 1. Obergeschoss **First-floor plan**

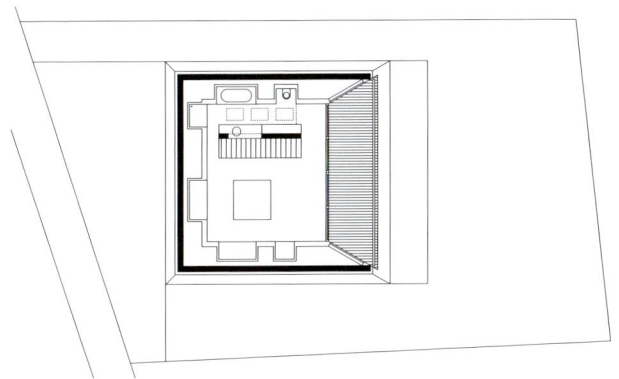

Grundriss 2. Obergeschoss **Second-floor plan**

Wohnraum 1. Obergeschoss
Living area, first floor

Treppe 1. Obergeschoss
Staircase, first floor

Ansicht von Norden   **View from the north**

Erzbischöfliches Archiv, Freiburg
Archiepiscopal Archives, Freiburg

Erzbischöfliches Bauamt Freiburg

■ Vorangestellt sei: Als Architekt über Gebäude anderer Architekten zu schreiben ist – aus Mangel an Unbefangenheit – ein Konflikt. Dass zu Tage tretende Konflikte allemal spannender sind als schweigende Glückseligkeit, mag dazu beigetragen haben, dass es zunehmend von Interesse zu sein scheint, sich innerhalb des Metiers gegenseitig zu begutachten und dies zu veröffentlichen. Die Anfrage nach einer Gebäudekritik löste daher zuerst eher Unbehagen aus, das jedoch einer durch vorab eingesehenes Bildmaterial erweckten Neugier wich.

Verlässt man das neu strukturierte Bahnhofsareal Freiburgs Richtung Osten, passiert man in der Schoferstraße den ersten Referenzpunkt – das Freiburger Münster. Der weitere Weg führt vorbei am Erzbischöflichen Ordinariat, einem bizarren Jugendstilbau, der eher an eine Kulisse für *Dr. Jekyll and Mr. Hyde* denn an den Sitz einer Kirchenverwaltung erinnert. Beiden Gebäuden gemeinsam ist roter Sandstein, der als Werkstoff für zeitgenössische Baukunst bis dato unentdeckt blieb. Durch den Neubau für das Erzbischöfliche Archiv erfährt das Material eine überzeugende Wiederbelebung. Überzeugend, obwohl Steinfassaden bei mir in der Regel eine reflexartige Ablehnung auslösen, die ihren Ursprung in der jahrelangen Betrachtung des Berliner Baugeschehens hat. Dort erinnert die willkürliche Wahl importierter Steinsorten an eine überdimensionale Baustoffmustersammlung, die ganze Stadtviertel in eine museale Leblosigkeit versetzt. Dagegen zeigt das Archiv in seiner äußeren Hülle – einer Haut und eben keiner Wand – das Potenzial des Werkstoffs Stein. Dieses liegt nicht in der motivischen Abbildung von Gediegenheit und Beständigkeit, sondern in der Darstellung einer physisch wahrnehmbaren Massivität, einer materialgerechten, geschichteten Struktur und einer, unterschiedlichen Bearbeitungsmethoden geschuldeten, differenzierten Oberfläche. In einem zweigeschossigen Sockel bleibt der Stein glattflächig, ansonsten ist er rau. In das Steingehäuse sind metallische Kästen eingesteckt, gefüllt mit Glaselementen: transparent zur Hofseite, transluzent zum Schlossbergring.

Die Qualität des Gebäudes liegt in seiner paradoxen Erscheinung. Es wirkt archaisch und zeitgenössisch, vertraut und fremd zugleich.

Der Architekt Christof Hendrich, Leiter der Neubauabteilung im Erzbischöflichen Bauamt Freiburg, empfängt mich am Eingang. Dieser ist durch einen zweigeschossigen Einschnitt an der südwestlichen Ecke des Gebäudes gekennzeichnet. Wohltuend unprätentiös ruft er durch seine Orientierung zur Innenstadt nochmals die beiden Referenzpunkte in Erinnerung. Das neue Gebäude müsse noch vollständig austrocknen, um eine Gefährdung der zum Teil wertvollen Urkunden, Taufbücher und Schriften zu vermeiden. Letztendlich werden zehn Kilometer Akten im Archiv eingelagert sein.

Mit 2,13 Millionen Katholiken ist die Erzdiözese Freiburg die zweitgrößte der 27 Diözesen Deutschlands. Der rund 3,1 Millionen Euro teure Neubau des Erzbischöflichen Archivs war notwendig geworden, weil die Magazine im Gebäude des Erzbischöflichen Ordinariats überfüllt waren und die klimatischen Bedingungen weder

■ Let me preface my remarks by saying that for an architect to write about the buildings of other architects involves a conflict of interest owing to an obvious lack of impartiality. The fact that emerging conflicts are always more exciting than silent harmony may have helped to spawn a trend that expects people of the same profession to judge one another and publish their findings. The request to review a building thus initially filled me with disquiet, but that quickly changed to curiosity as I studied the images I had been sent of the project in question.

On leaving the new Freiburg railway station complex at its eastern side, the first point of reference you pass is on Schoferstrasse, namely the Minster. The path continues past the Archiepiscopal Chancery, a bizarre building in the art nouveau style which seems more like a set for *Dr. Jekyll and Mr. Hyde* than the seat of the clerical administration. Both buildings are constructed of red sandstone which, until now, had remained undiscovered as a material employed in contemporary structures. The new Archiepiscopal Archives have granted this stone an emphatic new lease on life. I say this in the full knowledge that I usually reject stone facades, a reaction that has become automatic after years spent monitoring the building scene in Berlin. There, the arbitrary choice of imported stone is reminiscent of an outsized collection of specimen building materials which have transformed entire quarters of the city into a lifeless museum. In contrast, the Archives demonstrate the potential of this material as an exterior cover, a carapace which functions as both skin and wall. This is not achieved by some thematic illustration of pureness and consistency, but rather by the clear representation of physically perceivable massiveness, the appropriate use of material, the layered texture of the walls, and the differentiated surface, all thanks to the various methods used to work the material. The stone has been given a smooth facing at the base, which covers two floors; otherwise, it is rough. Metallic boxes have been set into the stone casing. These are filled with glass elements which appear transparent on the courtyard side, and are translucent on the side opening onto the Schlossbergring.

The building's prime quality is this paradoxical appearance. It seems to be simultaneously ancient and new, familiar and strange.

The architect is Christof Hendrich, head of the Department for New Building in the Archiepiscopal Office of Construction in Freiburg. He met me at the entrance, which is marked by a two-storey-high opening on the south-west corner of the building. Pleasantly unpretentious, its alignment towards downtown Freiburg calls the two points of reference to mind. The new building must still be allowed to dry completely, he suggests, so as not to endanger the valuable documents, baptismal records and writings which will be kept inside. At the end of the day, more than ten kilometres of files will be stored in the archives.

With 2.13 million Catholics, the Archdiocese of Freiburg is the second largest of twenty-seven dioceses in Germany. The new

Architekten Architects Erzbischöfliches Bauamt Freiburg; Team: Dr. Christof Hendrich, Anton Bauhofer & Hans-Peter Heitzler | **Bauherr** Client Erzdiözese Freiburg vertreten durch das Erzbischöfliche Ordinariat Freiburg | **HL-Technik** Technical Eckert Planungsgesellschaft mbH, Ostheim | **Tragwerk** Structural Ingenieurbüro Dr. Liermann, Freiburg | **Licht** Lighting Planungsgruppe Burgert, Schallstadt | **Ausführung** Construction 2000–2002 | **Standort** Location Schoferstraße 3, Freiburg im Breisgau

dem Archivgut noch den Mitarbeitern weiterhin zugemutet werden konnten.

Wir betreten den öffentlichen Lesesaal. Die erste Empfindung ist ein Gefühl der Geborgenheit, hervorgerufen durch die transluzenten Gläser über den Mikrofilmarbeitsplätzen, die keinen Schlagschatten ins Innere lassen. Der Raum wirkt dadurch weich, die farbliche Homogenität der raumbegrenzenden Wände aus Sichtbeton und der verputzten Decken unterstützt diese Wirkung. Die Bauteile sind mit Sorgfalt bündig zueinander gefügt, fast schon zu perfekt. Eine den Betrachter und Benutzer distanzierende museale Perfektion stellt sich jedoch nicht ein. Dazu tragen insbesondere die Einbauten aus Eiche bei. Sie formen die Arbeitsplätze, umrahmen die Schnittstellen zwischen Innen- und Außenwelt, trennen den Lesesaal von den in zwei Geschossen übereinander liegenden Einzelbüros und bergen, im Treppenkorpus integriert, das Mikrofilmarchiv. Die Büros der Mitarbeiter sind mit kastenförmigen Einbauten, ebenfalls aus Eichenholz, ausgestattet und bieten eine exquisite Aussicht auf den Garten des angrenzenden Collegium Borromaeum. Also alles bestens?

Überraschenderweise bringt gerade der Versuch, das Gebäude neben der Materialität zusätzlich über eine spezielle Ausformung der Kubatur im Kontext zu verankern, eine Problematik mit sich. Ein umlaufendes Vordach soll die Trauflinie der benachbarten Gebäude aufnehmen, Maßstäblichkeit erzeugen und ein Gegengewicht zum nördlichen Dachaufbau bilden. Sicher handelt es sich dabei auch um ein baurechtliches Zugeständnis, das aber gleichwohl bedauerlich ist. Die ansonsten selbstbewusste Haltung des Baus wird durch diese opportune Applikation geschwächt. Doch damit genug.

»Schreiben Sie freiheraus, was Sie denken«, sagt Christof Hendrich beim Abschied und gibt damit Carte blanche für eine offene Kritik. Daher in aller Offenheit: Das Archiv ist ein selbstverständliches und gelassenes Haus. Ich kann mir – und das ist selten – an diesem Ort kein anderes Gebäude vorstellen.

Markus Allmann

Archiepiscopal Archives (price tag circa € 3.1 million) had to be built because the storage area in the Archiepiscopal Chancery was full, and the climactic conditions were not suitable for its contents or its employees.

We enter the public reading room. The first feeling is one of cosiness as a result of the translucent glass above the microfilm work stations: It prevents shadows from entering the interior. As a result, the room seems soft, an effect reinforced by the homogeneous colours of the fair-faced concrete walls and the plastered ceilings. The building elements have been connected flush with great care – it is almost too perfect. However, a feeling of museum-like perfection which would distance the observer and user from the building does not arise. This is due in large part to elements of the furnishings made of oak. They form the workstations, surround the interfaces connecting the inner and outer worlds, separate the reading room from the individual offices over two floors, one above the other, and conceal the microfilm archive integrated into the body of the stairway. The staff offices are decorated with square, built-in furnishings, likewise made of oak, and enjoy an exquisite view of the garden at the neighbouring Collegium Borromaeum. So all is well?

Surprisingly, it is the attempt to embed the building in its surroundings, not only by dint of the materials used, but also by lending it a special cubistic form, that creates a problem. An overhanging roof on three sides is intended to continue the line of the eaves from neighbouring buildings, to establish a sense of a scale, and to counter-balance the staggered roof to the north. This is no doubt a concession to building codes, regrettable as it is. The otherwise self-confident demeanour of the building is weakened by this opportunistic application, but enough of that.

"Write exactly what you think," Christof Hendrich told me when we parted, giving me carte blanche for honest criticism. Therefore, in all honesty: The Archives are housed in a logical and calm building. I cannot imagine, and this is seldom the case, that another building could stand on this spot.

Markus Allmann

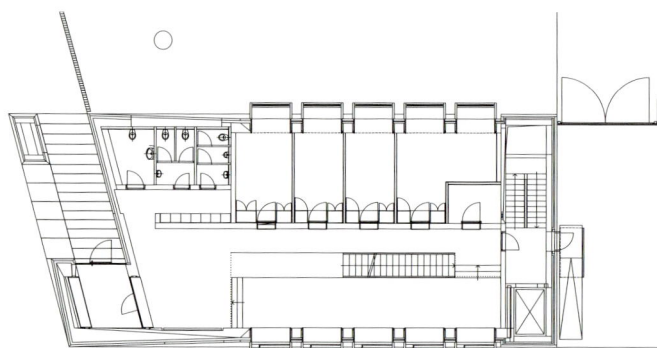

Grundriss Erdgeschoss **Ground-floor plan**

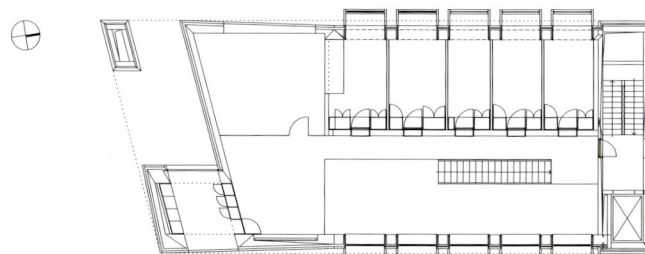

Grundriss 1. Obergeschoss **First-floor plan**

Ansicht von Osten **View from the east**

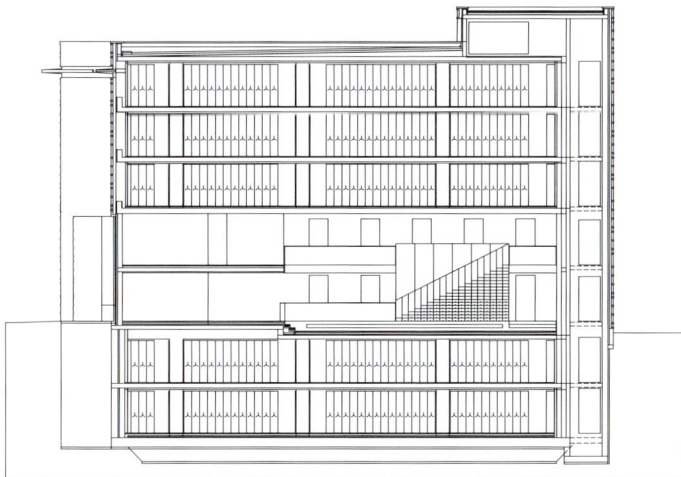

Schnitt **Section**

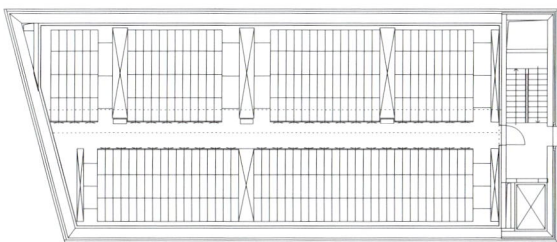

Grundriss 2., 3. und 4. Obergeschoss **Second-, third- and fourth-floor plan**

Ansicht von Süden **View from the south**

Mikrofiche-Lesehalle **Microfiche reading room**

Eingang **Entrance**

Büro **Office**

Museum und Park Kalkriese, Bramsche
Kalkriese Museum and Park, Bramsche

Annette Gigon/Mike Guyer

■ Kalkriese im Osnabrücker Land wurde als jüngst identifizierter Ort der Hermannsschlacht von 9 n. Chr. als thematisierte Landschaft inszeniert. Damals gelang es den Römern, weit nach Norden vorzudringen, heute gelingt es den Schweizern. Annette Gigon und Mike Guyer gewannen 1998 den Wettbewerb mit einer sinnträchtigen Rauminszenierung der Hermannschen Guerillataktik, die 25 000 schwer bewaffnete und auf Formation gedrillte Römer unter dem Kommando von Publius Quinctilius Varus austrickste und vernichtend schlug.

Geometrische Disziplin und schwere Panzerung bestehend aus Fassadenplatten aus wetterfestem WT-Stahl werden wie damals zu Invasoren – eine Architektur von atemberaubender konstruktiver wie intellektueller Verfeinerung, eine Architektur gelandeter außerirdischer Fremdkörper.

Es war die Landschaft, die den römischen Legionen zum Verhängnis wurde, als diese zwischen dichten Wäldern und trügerischem Moor in der Falle saßen, und es ist auch jetzt wieder die Landschaft, die den Stahlinvasoren konzeptionell entgegensteht. Drei überlagerte Wegesysteme wurden angelegt: landwirtschaftliche Wege, Mulchpfade anstelle der germanischen Angriffs- und Rückzugswege und großflächige rostige Eisenplatten für die Römerroute. Die Überlagerung gibt dem Besucher die Möglichkeit, die Seiten zu wechseln oder querschnittartig durch das (re)konstruierte Feld des Konflikts zu wandern. Unter grauem Herbsthimmel wird der Besucher entlang dieser narrativen Stahlplatten immer weiter in die nasse Landschaft geführt, die rostrote Farbe verschmilzt mit den leuchtenden Farben der gefallenen Buchenblätter. Die erhabene Schrift der gegossenen Platten erzählt aus Tacitus' Bericht, geschrieben 20 Jahre nach der Schlacht, vom Hinterhalt, vom Unwetter, von der Unmöglichkeit des geordneten Manövers auf schlüpfrigem Waldboden, von der Panik der Pferde im Moor, vom Freitod des glücklosen Feldherrn Varus. Sie begleiten den Besucher entlang des Pfades – eine aufgeladene und Bilder beschwörende Inszenierung für denjenigen, der sich die Zeit nimmt, sich mit Ort, Architektur und Inhalt auseinander zu setzen.

Die Komposition erinnert an eine von John Hejduks *Masques*, ein von autonomen Pavillons bevölkertes Territorium. Die strikte Ablehnung von Figuration oder von jeglichem didaktischen Text in den Sehen-, Hören-, Fragen-Boxen zeigt allerdings eine deutlich andere Architekturwahrnehmung als Hejduks semiologischer Spiegelgarten. Das kreative Engagement des Besuchers beruht auf Mimesis, die Pavillons werden zu Filtern, die einen ontologisch aufgeladenen Ort enthüllen. Sie sind Katalysatoren für eine phänomenologische Assimilation von Subjekt und Objekt.

Ganz automatisch bedient sich der Betrachter bei der Einordnung dieser Architektur des ›critical jargon‹ der Kunst, der Meta-Referenz für einen großen Teil der neueren Schweizer Architektur und insbesondere des Metiers von Gigon und Guyer. Der große Erfolg der minimalistischen Strategie in Kalkriese besteht in der Neutralisation der problematischen Instrumentalisierung des Mythos Hermanns-

■ Kalkriese in Osnabrücker Land, recently identified as the site of the decisive battle of 9 AD between the German tribal leader Arminius and the Romans, has been transformed into a themed landscape. Whereas, back then, it was the Romans who pushed into northern Europe, today, it is the turn of the Swiss. In 1998, Annette Gigon and Mike Guyer took the competition laurels with a metaphorical visualisation of the Teutonic guerrilla tactics that outwitted 25,000 heavily armed and highly trained Romans under the command of Publius Quintilius Varus, and inflicted a resounding defeat.

Geometric discipline and heavy armouring consisting of weatherproof WT steel facade panels take the role of the invader in an architecture of breathtaking structural and intellectual finesse – an architecture of otherworldly strangeness.

It was the landscape that caused the downfall of the Roman legions then, caught between the dense forests and the treacherous moor. And it is the landscape now that is pitted conceptually against the steel invaders. Three superimposed systems of paths have been created: agricultural paths, mulch paths in the place of the routes taken by the German tribal warriors, and huge, rusty iron panels for the route of the Romans. The interaction of the pathways allows visitors to change sides or walk a cross section of the (re-)constructed battlefield. Under a grey autumn sky, the visitor is led along these narrative steel panels into the wetlands where the rust-red of the iron melds with the brilliant hues of the fallen beech leaves. The raised lettering on the cast iron panels quotes from Tacitus' report, written twenty years after the event, telling of ambush and inclement weather, the impossibility of maintaining order on the slippy forest floor, the horses' panic in the moors, the suicide of the unfortunate Varus. The texts accompany the visitor along the pathway – a highly charged and evocative setting for anyone willing to take the time to explore the place, the architecture and the subject.

The composition recalls one of John Hejduk's Masques, a terrain populated by autonomous pavilions. However, the strict avoidance of figuration or didactic texts in the 'seeing-hearing-questioning' boxes bears witness to an architectural perception that is a far cry from Hejduk's semiological mirror gardens. The creative participation of the visitor is based on a mimetic concept in which the pavilions become filters that reveal an ontologically charged site and act as catalysts for a phenomenological assimilation of both subject and object.

In considering this architecture, the viewer automatically takes recourse to the critical jargon of art that is a meta-reference for so much of recent Swiss architecture, especially that of Gigon and Guyer. The enormous success of the minimalists' strategy in Kalkriese lies in the way it neutralises the otherwise problematic instrumentalisation of this legendary battle in German history. In Kalkriese we have moved on historically from Anselm Kiefer's traumatic figuration of the same subject in the 1970s, even if the wood-clad pavilions contain some echoes of Kiefer's work.

Architekten Architects Annette Gigon/Mike Guyer Architekten, Zürich, www.gigon-guyer.ch; Team: Volker Mencke & Massimo Wüthrich, Christian Brunner, Markus Lüscher, Christoph Loetscher, Pieter Rabijns, Sebastian Thaut, Esther Hodel, Caspar Oswald | **Bauherr Client** Varusschlacht im Osnabrücker Land GmbH, Museum und Park Kalkriese | **Kontaktarchitekt Co-Architects** pbr Planungsbüro Rohling AG, Osnabrück | **Freianlagen Landscape** Zulauf/Seippel/Schweingruber, Baden; Heimer + Herbstreit, Hildesheim | **Ausstellung Exhibition** Intégral Concept, Ruedi Bauer, Lars Müller, Paris/Baden | **Tragwerk Structural** Gantert + Wiemeler Ingenieurplanung, Münster | **Wettbewerb Competition** 1998 | **Ausführung Construction** 2000–2002 | **Standort Location** Venner Straße 69, Bramsche-Kalkriese

schlacht in der deutschen Geschichte. Wir haben uns in Kalkriese geschichtlich von Anselm Kiefers traumatischer Figuration desselben Subjekts in den siebziger Jahren weiterbewegt, selbst wenn die mit Holz ausgekleideten Pavillons an Kiefers Bilder erinnern.

Ernst von Bandels Hermannsdenkmal aus dem Jahr 1875 steht mit gehobenem Nibelungen-Schwert zwischen Detmold und Bielefeld. Die Archäologie hat nun den genauen Ort der Schlacht weiter nach Westen verlegt und, höchst zeitgemäß, direkt neben die Ausfahrt 68 der A1. Der Archäologiepark ist ein Themenpark, der mobile Besucher kann sich auch entscheiden, etwas weiter nach Süden zur Warner Brothers Movie World zu fahren. Ist also Kalkriese ein André Heller in Donald Judd-Verkleidung? Wenn ja, dann muss man Architekten und Bauherren ein Kompliment machen für ihren Widerstand gegen die kommerziellen Klischees von Themenparks und für ihre Ambition, verfeinerte Poesie für ein Massenpublikum anzubieten.

Was wir vom Sehen-Pavillon aus erkennen können, ist eine intensivierte, surreale, auf dem Kopf stehende Reproduktion der Welt draußen. Im Hören-Pavillon werden Geräusche durch ein übergroßes Hörrohr in den schalldichten Raum übertragen. Sind es vielleicht Schlachtrufe oder doch nur Kinderschreie? Der Fragen-Pavillon konfrontiert Videoclips von globalen Krisengebieten mit Sehschlitzen, die den Blick auf das überwachsene Schlachtfeld freigeben.

Sowohl die drei Pavillons wie auch das Museumsgebäude mit seinem aufgefalteten Aussichtsturm enthüllen durch fehlende Paneele in ihrer Außenhaut ein delikat geschichtetes auberginefarbiges Stahlskelett von zeichenhaftem Raffinement. Der Charakter der Innenräume wird vor allem durch monastische Zurückhaltung geprägt, ein weihevoll dunkler Raum, der seine Distanz zu den interaktiven Ausstellungswänden hält, eine Garderobe in brennendem Zinnoberrot und asketisch anmutende Toiletten. Der Aussichtsturm ist der Fokus, von dem aus das Schlachtfeld in Relation zum weiteren zeitgenössischen Raum, wie den huschenden ›just-in-time‹-Containern der nahe gelegenen Autobahn, aber auch das Potenzial von Architektur, das Gedächtnis aufzuladen und kulturellen Maßstab zu vermitteln, beobachtet werden kann.

Julia B. Bolles-Wilson
Peter L. Wilson

Ernst von Bandel's sword-wielding monument to Arminius, the *Hermannsdenkmal* of 1875, stands between Detmold and Bielefeld, both in Germany. Since then, archaeologists have located the site of the battle further to the west, appropriately enough, directly beside exit 68 of the A1. The archaeology park is a theme park, and the mobile visitor can also choose to head south to the nearby Warner Brothers Movie World. Does this make Kalkriese an André Heller in the guise of Donald Judd? If so, both architect and client must be congratulated for showing such resistance to the commercial cliché of the theme park, and for their aim of offering such poetic refinement to the masses.

What we can see from the 'Seeing' Pavilion is an intensified, surreal, topsy-turvy reproduction of the outside world. In the 'Hearing' Pavilion, noises are transmitted to the soundproofed room through a huge tube. Are they battle cries or just the shrieking of children? The 'Questioning' pavilion contrasts video clips of global crisis areas with narrow slits through which to view the overgrown battlefield.

Not only the three pavilions, but also the museum building and its unfolded outlook tower have gaps between the panels of the outer skin revealing a delicately layered, aubergine-coloured steel skeleton of great sophistication. The character of the interior is informed primarily by a sense of monastic simplicity – a dark and solemn space that remains aloof from the interactive exhibition fittings, a cloakroom of fiery crimson with ascetic toilets. The outlook tower is the focal point from which the battlefield can be seen in relation to the broader contemporary context – traffic hurtling along the nearby motorway – allowing an appreciation of the capacity of architecture to act as a vehicle of memory and cultural scale.

Julia B. Bolles-Wilson
Peter L. Wilson

Lageplan **Site plan**

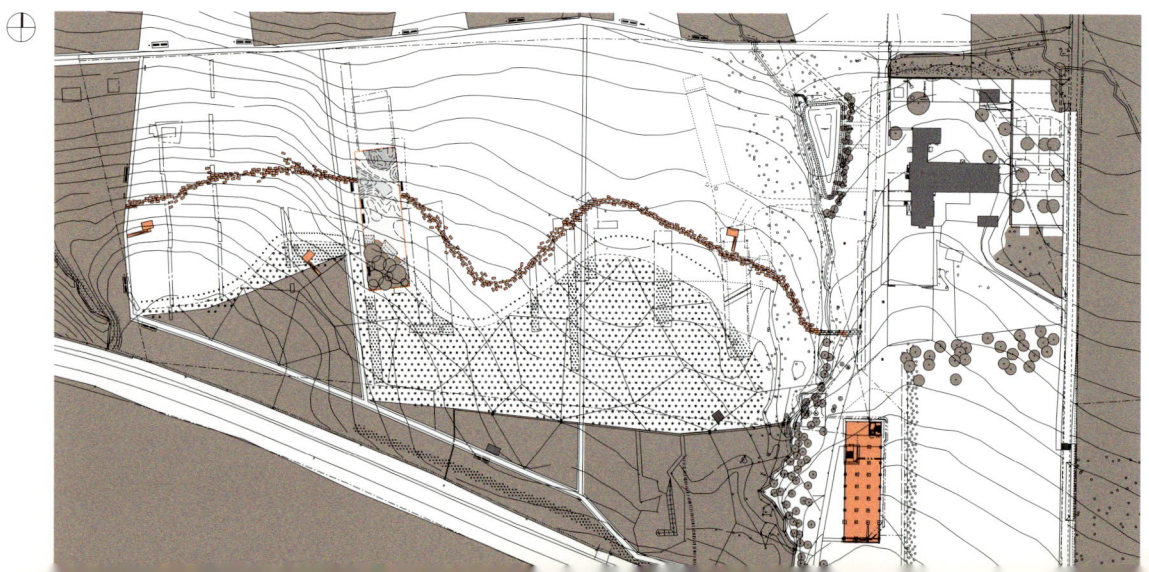

Seiten 124/125 **Pages 124–125**
Museum **Museum**

Pavillon ›Fragen‹ **'Questioning' Pavilion**

Pavillon ›Sehen‹ **'Seeing' Pavilion**

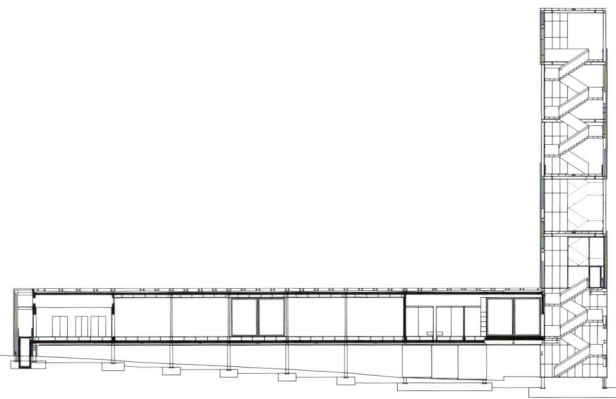
Längsschnitt Museum **Longitudinal section, museum**

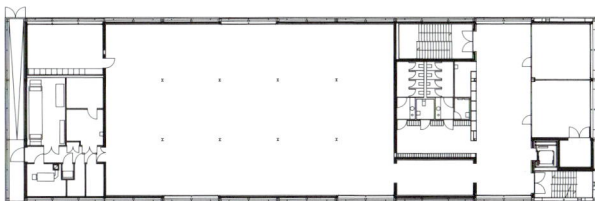
Grundriss 1. Obergeschoss, Museum **First-floor plan, museum**

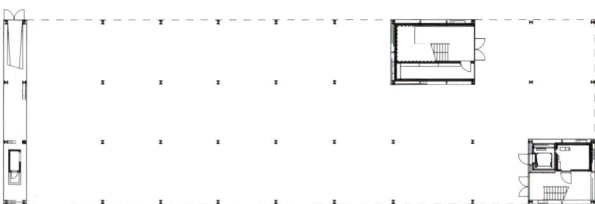
Grundriss Erdgeschoss **Ground-floor plan**

Pavillon ›Hören‹ **'Hearing' Pavilion**

Garderobe **Cloakroom**

Foyer **Foyer**

Bürogebäude Neumühlen, Hamburg
Office Building, Neumühlen, Hamburg

Grüntuch Ernst

»Lange und ausgeschlafen Gang nach Neumühlen, um den Wanderweg nun als Spülsaum zu betrachten: Stroh – Balken – Taue – angeschwemmte Dykdalben – Paletten – Tonnen – Gerümpel – eine grandideldös ausgekotzte Erntegabe des Meeres. Beim ›Lotsenhaus‹ eine der Länge nach zerspaltene Linde, die eine Hälfte in die Glasveranda gerammt. Sturm anhaltend, aber in der Dornenhecke unentmuntert Hunderte von schnäbelnden Spatzen.«[1]

Having slept well, I took a long walk to Neumühlen to see the path by the shoreline lined with debris brought in on the tide: straw – beams – rope – flotsam and jetsam – pallets – barrels – odds and ends – a grand little vomited harvest of the sea. At the 'pilot's house' I saw a linden tree split vertically in two, one half rammed through the glass veranda. Even in the storm, hundreds of sparrows were chirping in the thorny hedge.[1]

■ Neumühlen, so nennt sich ein Abschnitt des nördlichen Elbufers in Hamburg-Ottensen. Hier, am Fuße des hohen Geesthangs, befand sich früher der Westkai des Fischereihafens samt zugehörigen Equipmentbauten und einem Kaibahngleis. Der Elbwanderweg beginnt hier und verläuft flussabwärts in Richtung Blankenese; oben, auf der Geest, hat die gleichfalls hier startende ›Traumstraße‹, die Elbchaussee, dasselbe Ziel. Auf ihrer ›nassen Seite‹ wird sie anfangs von einem Teil der »großzügig geflochtenen Girlande der Elbparks«[2] begleitet.

Diese exponierte Lage innerhalb der aufgelassenen hafenwirtschaftlichen Nutzungen bewog die Stadtentwicklungsbehörde, diesen Uferstreifen ihrer Gesamtkonzeption ›Nördliches Elbufer‹ zu integrieren. Auf fünf Kilometern Länge, von Neumühlen bis zur Kehrwiederspitze, auch mit der anschließenden neuen Hafen City, wird sich mit Umsetzung der Planung eine erheblich veränderte Ansicht Hamburgs zur Elbe formuliert haben.

Dem ehemaligen Oberbaudirektor Egbert Kossak wird die jetzt nach einem internationalen Wettbewerb 1996 verwirklichte Bebauungsstruktur der Neumühlener ›Perlenkette‹ zugeschrieben. In der Tat kann man sich bei den zwar luftig gereihten und dennoch gestalterisch das Ufer festigenden vier Bürohäusern auf diese Metapher verständigen. Die U-förmigen Baukörper zeigen die gleiche Typologie, wie auch mit jeweils fünf Geschossen die gleiche Höhe. Der architektonische Glanz dieser ›Perlen‹ strahlt aber durchaus in unterschiedlicher Intensität.[3]

Im Bau ist ein die Westflanke der Uferkomposition ergänzendes längeres, winkelartiges Lofthaus von KSP Engel und Zimmermann. Der dahinter ›ausufernde‹ Kai gibt schließlich den Blick frei für das massig-hohe Wohnstift Augustinum, das – volumengleich – die Stelle des früheren und 1991 abgerissenen Kühlhauses Union einnimmt und so die gesamte bauliche Parade dominiert.

Erst nach einem nachträglichen Gutachter-Entscheid ergab sich die Forderung nach verstärktem Hochwasserschutz. Deren Folge war, dass das gesamte Ensemble auf einen auf Kainiveau zugesetzten 3,50 Meter hohen Polder gesattelt wurde. Der neue ›Garagensockel‹ aber verändert nun – nicht unerheblich – die ursprünglichen Gebäudeproportionen. Der Polderhang aus groben Schüttsteinen, der unterhalb der auskragenden Seitenflügel des Gebäudes verläuft, eröffnet nun neben der Kaimauer auf der anderen Seite der Prome-

Neumühlen is a section of the north bank of the river Elbe in Hamburg-Ottensen. Here, at the foot of the Geesthang, the west quay of the fishing port once stood, with all the usual equipment buildings and a pier head railway track. The path along the Elbe begins here and runs down river towards Blankenese; up on the Geest, the 'dream road' of the Elbchaussee follows the same route. The first span of the waterside is fringed by part of the "sumptuously woven garland of the Elbe park".[2]

It was this exposed situation within the abandoned port complex that persuaded urban development authorities to integrate this strip of the riverbank into its overall concept for the north bank of the Elbe. Along a stretch of five kilometres from Neumühlen to Kehrwiederspitze, including the new Hafen City, the implementation of this plan will create a radically transformed view of Hamburg towards the Elbe.

Former building director Egbert Kossak is attributed with the Neumühlen 'string of pearls' – a development now in place following an international competition in 1996. The row of four office buildings, generously spaced from one another and yet giving shape to the overall form of the riverbank, certainly deserves this metaphor. The U-shaped buildings are all of the same type, and all of the same height (five storeys). Yet the architectural brilliance of these 'pearls' differs in intensity.[3]

An elongated, angular loft house by KSP Engel and Zimmermann is currently being built on the west flank of this riverbank ensemble. The extensive quay behind it affords views of the high and massive Augustinum old-age-home that dominates the entire architectural array, built on the site of the former Union cold store, which was demolished in 1991.

Calls for improved floodwater protection resulted from a subsequent survey. As a result, the entire ensemble had to be saddled on a 3.5-metre high dyke at the level of the quay. The new 'garage base' has now altered the original building proportions to a considerable degree. The slope of the dyke, with rough-hewn stones and rubble running below the side wing of the building, now creates a second 'amphibian' front on the other side of the promenade alongside the quay wall – and unfortunately also forms a distinct barrier. Typologically, the four buildings are reminiscent of aristocratic town houses, whereby the building by Grüntuch Ernst plays down any hint of

Architekten Architects Grüntuch Ernst Architekten BDA, Berlin, www.gea-berlin.de; Armand Grüntuch, Almut Ernst; Team: Kai Hansen & Olaf Menk, Volker Raatz, Jacob van Ommen | **Bauherr** Client Hermann Ebel + Frank Leonhardt, Vermögensverwaltung Schifffahrtskontor Elbe GbR | **Tragwerk** Structural Ingenieurbüro Dr. Binnewies GmbH, Hamburg | **HL-Technik** Technical Amstein Walthert Beratende Ingenieure AG, Zürich; Ansorg + Horn, Berlin/Hamburg | **Projektsteuerung** Project Management Hansa Projektmanagement GmbH, Hamburg | **Wettbewerb** Competition 1996 | **Ausführung** Construction 2001/02 | **Standort** Location Neumühlen 13–15, Hamburg

nade eine zweite ›amphibische‹ Front – und leider auch eine spürbare Barriere. Typologisch rücken die vier Bauten in die Nähe von veritablen Stadtpalais, und dasjenige von Grüntuch Ernst kommt der noblen Repräsentation einer ›ersten Adresse‹ am nächsten. Die brüstungslose Ganzglasfassade spannt sich straff und in geradezu ›klassischen‹ Proportionen über das Gebäude, sichtbar durchtrennt nur von minimierten Deckenhorizontalen. Die landseitige Front zeigt zwischen den übereck gezogenen Seitenfassaden eine Art ›Stadtfenster‹. Drei wuchtige, textilverhüllte und nachts farbig durchleuchtete Vertikalen durchschneiden den gebäudehohen Luftraum der eher knapp bemessenen Eingangshalle; an Verbindungsbrücken gelehnt, nehmen sie Treppenhäuser und Lifts auf. Als sensibles Detail lässt das zurückgesetzte Erdgeschoss für einen kurzen Moment die amöbenhaften Formen der Treppenhäuser frei, die flankierend auf den Eingang hinweisen. Das Licht- und Schattenspiel, das die die Eingangshalle durchstrahlende Südsonne hier inszeniert, macht das Gebäude höchst lebendig und lockert die eher strenge Fassade auf. Ein Blick von den dahinter liegenden Höhen des Rosengartens oder von Donners Park aus macht das wirkungsvoll deutlich.

Das System des Tragwerks offenbart sich im Blick durch die Doppelfassade. Siegfried Giedions einleuchtende Definition von »der Konstruktion als dem Unterbewußtsein der Architektur«[4] dürfte kaum besser illustriert werden können. Eine outrierende, sich an maritimen Hafendetails abarbeitende Außenwirkung wird vermieden. Erst beim zweiten Blick sichert die kraftvolle Statik das elegante Schwebegleichgewicht. Die flexibel nutzbaren Bürozonen im Inneren werden inspiriert von dem außergewöhnlichen Panorama des betriebsamen Hafens. Diesen Genius Loci hat das Haus eingefangen und in sich versammelt; selbst eine gläserne Bühne, gibt sie ihn zurück.

Düsseldorf hat mit dem Neuen Zollhof am alten Rheinhafen und den dort versammelten höchst individuellen Schaustücken der internationalen Architekturprominenz für Furore gesorgt. Der ungleich schwierigere Weg ist es, die Balance von Einheitlichkeit und Vielfalt in einer architektonischen Gesamtkonzeption zu finden. Das ist in Hamburg versucht worden und grosso modo auch gelungen.

Dietmar Brandenburger

prestigious ostentation. The fully glazed facade without a parapet spans the entire building in 'classical' proportions visibly divided only by minimal ceiling horizontals. On the leeward side, the angled corner facades form a kind of 'urban window'. Three massive, textile-covered verticals, illuminated and coloured at night, penetrate the full-length air space of the compact entrance hall, accommodating stairwells and lifts in the manner of link bridges. A sensitive detail is the way in which the ground floor briefly reveals the amoebic forms of the stairwells flanking the entrance. The play of light and shadow created here by the sun streaming into the entrance hall from the south lends the building enormous vitality, and heightens the stringency of the facade. A view from the slopes of the Rosengarten behind it or from Donners Park makes this particularly clear.

The load-bearing system can be seen on looking through the double facade. Siegfried Giedion's succinct definition of "the structure as the subconscious of architecture" could hardly be better illustrated.[4] No attempt has been made here to fabricate a themed appearance based on maritime details. Only at second glance does the powerful structure reveal its elegantly balanced lightness. The versatile office areas of the interior are inspired by the extraordinary panorama of the busy port. This *genius loci* pervades the building, and like a glass stage, the house reflects it back.

Düsseldorf has caused a sensation with the Neuer Zollhof on the old Rhine river port, featuring an illustrious collection of highly individual showpieces by internationally renowned architects. It was undoubtedly a far greater challenge to strike the balance between uniformity and diversity within an overall architectural concept. This has been attempted in Hamburg and, by and large, it has proved successful.

Dietmar Brandenburger

1 Peter Rühmkorf, *TABU 1. Tagebücher* 1989–1991, Hamburg, 1997, p. 202.
2 Manfred Sack, "Die Elbchaussee", in: *Die Hamburger Elbchaussee. Die Schönste Strasse der Welt*, Berlin, 1992, p. 8.
3 Apart from architect Grüntuch Ernst, the architects Antonio Citterio, Bothe Richter Teherani and von Bassewitz, Hupertz, Limbrock were also involved.
4 Siegfried Giedion, *Raum Zeit Architektur*, Ravensburg, 1965, p. 46.

1 Peter Rühmkorf, *TABU I, Tagebücher 1989–1991*, Hamburg 1997, S. 202.
2 Manfred Sack, *Die Elbchaussee*, in: *Die Hamburger Elbchaussee. Die schönste Straße der Welt*, Berlin 1992, S. 8.
3 Beteiligte sind neben den Architekten Grüntuch Ernst die Architekten Antonio Citterio, Bothe Richter Teherani und von Bassewitz, Hupertz, Limbrock.
4 Siegfried Giedion, *Raum Zeit Architektur*, Ravensburg 1965, S. 46.

Seiten 132/133 **pages 132–133**
Blick auf den Hafen
View of the harbour

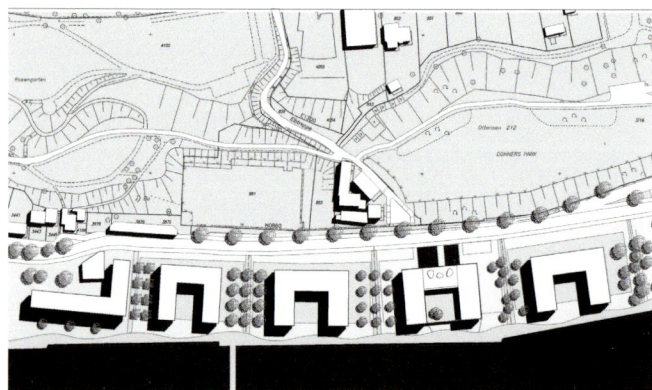

Lageplan **Site plan**

Ansicht von Südwesten **View from the south-west**

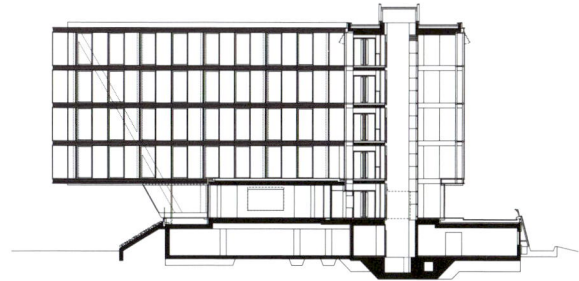

Schnitt **Section**

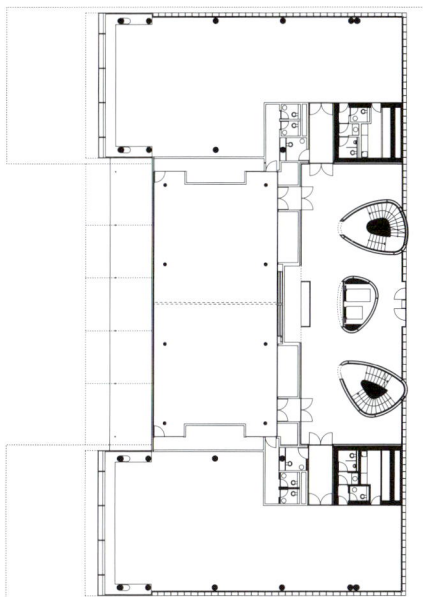

Grundriss Ebene 0 **Ground-plan level 0**

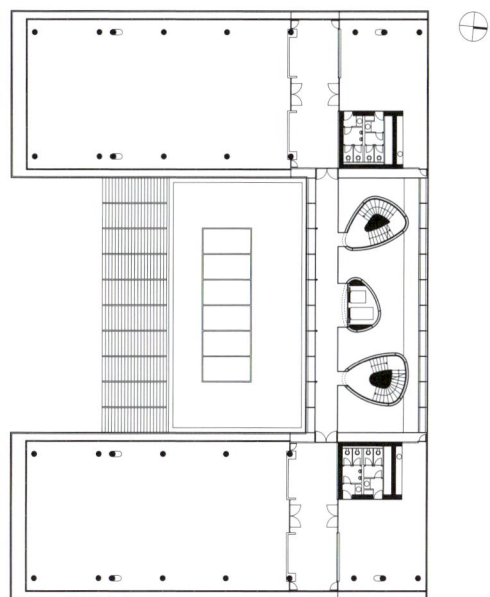

Grundriss Ebene +1 **Ground-plan level +1**

Ansicht von Norden **View from the north**

Foyer **Foyer**

Büro **Office**

Terrasse **Terrace**

Werner-Otto-Saal im Konzerthaus Berlin
Werner-Otto-Saal, Konzerthaus Berlin

Peter Kulka

■ Der Bombenhagel des Zweiten Weltkriegs hat vom Berliner Schauspielhaus nur die Steine der Fassaden stehen gelassen, das Innere ist verbrannt. Die Fassaden von Karl Friedrich Schinkel scheinen – jenseits aller gängigen klassizistischen Muster – wie ein radikales Modell von Repetition und Reihung, bei dem Säulen zu Pfeilern reduziert werden, ohne Basen und Kapitelle, und zu horizontalen Fensterreihen addiert, wie eine Frühform des ›fenêtre à longeur‹. Dieser Radikalität im Äußeren steht die nachempfundene Neuschöpfung der achtziger Jahre im Inneren gegenüber, mit einem vollkommen veränderten Konzertsaal im Zentrum. Unübersehbar ist der aufdringlich hohe Aufwand, doch bleibt das Ganze ohne Esprit, manche sprechen von Kitsch. Dieser Widerspruch bleibt vielen verborgen, da sie meinen, es sei noch der alte Guss.

Jetzt darf man über einen neuen Gegensatz, oder besser: eine Antithese zum totgestrickten Schinkel, staunen. Oder noch anders gesagt, Peter Kulka formulierte sein Konzept zum neu implantierten Konzertsaal im zweiten Geschoss des Nordflügels mit der gleichen Radikalität, mit der Schinkel die Fassaden schuf. Kulka entwickelte eine Antithese aus demselben Geist.

Inmitten des Stilgewirrs aus Original und Fälschung finden wir jetzt einen Konzertsaal, der in seiner Reduktion nicht mehr zu übertreffen ist – eine Black Box im Goldrahmen, ein minimalistisches Raumkonzept im ornamentierten Passepartout der Rekonstrukteure. Es ist das Ergebnis konsequenten Nachdenkens über die Aufgabe, einen Saal für neue Musik in einem Gebäude mit Tradition zu schaffen. Die Verpflichtungen und Rücksichtnahmen führten zu einem einfachen Raum von großer Sinnlichkeit, zu einem Instrumentenkorpus, der schon ohne Musik vibriert, allein seiner emotionalen Tiefe wegen.

›Black Box‹ trifft den Charakter nur oberflächlich, denn eine Black Box ist ein ›Unraum‹. Kulkas Konzertsaal aber ist das Gegenteil, denn er zelebriert nicht die Abwesenheit von Raum. Seine Erscheinung ist zwar wandelbar, doch seine Proportion bleibt harmonisch. In seiner strengsten Form erscheint er als Gehäuse von 24 x 14 x 4 Metern Kantenlänge, bestehend aus schwarzen Wänden, einem schwarz-braunen Boden und einer durchscheinenden leuchtenden Decke. Die Wandpaneele sind horizontal geriffelte lackierte Holz-Akustikplatten, der Fußboden besteht aus geräuchertem Eichenparkett und die Decke aus verzinkten Streckmetall-Kassetten.

So weit wäre alles simpel, doch ist dieser Raum kein starrer Klangkörper, der wie ein Musikinstrument eingespielt werden müsste; er ist vielmehr eine perfekte Maschine im Dienst der Multifunktionalität. Der gesamte Fußboden besteht aus 132 ein mal zwei Meter großen Hebebühnen, die zusammen die größte Hubbühne Europas bilden. Mit ihrer Maschinerie kann die Flachlandschaft zu Bergen und Tälern geformt werden – der Raumgestaltung und Nutzung sind keine Grenzen gesetzt. Jedes Wandpaneel ist um 180 Grad klappbar, sodass zwei Oberflächen zur Verfügung stehen, die unterschiedlich akustisch wirksam sind. Gleichzeitig können diese Paneele zwei Fensterreihen übereck freilegen und dem Raum so Tageslicht geben und

■ The bombs of World War Two left only the facade stones of the Berlin Schauspielhaus standing. The interior was completely gutted by fire. The facades by Karl Friedrich Schinkel appear as a radical model of repetition and rows, in which columns are reduced to pillars with neither base nor capital and added into horizontal rows of windows like some early form of *fenêtre à longeur* – a far cry from conventional neoclassicist patterns. This radical exterior now contrasts with the new interior created in the 1980s, with a completely transformed auditorium at its heart. Though it is clear that neither expense nor effort has been spared, the overall impression is one of soullessness, and even of kitsch. This contradiction in terms is not evident to all, for many still believe that it is all of the same mould.

Now there is a new contrast, or rather, an antithesis to Schinkel. In other words, Peter Kulka has formulated his concept for the new auditorium on the second floor of the north wing with the same radical approach that Schinkel adopted in creating the facades. Kulka developed an antithesis in the same spirit.

In the midst of the stylistic confusion between original and copy, we now find an auditorium that could hardly be more radically reduced – a black box in a golden frame, a minimalist spatial concept set in the ornamental passe-partout of the reconstructors. It is the result of solid thinking on the task of creating a venue for new music within a building of long-standing tradition. Obligation and sensitive reflection have resulted in a simple room of enormous sensuality, like the body of an instrument, vibrant with emotional depth even before the first note is played.

The term 'black box' is not entirely appropriate, for a black box is a 'non place'. Kulka's auditorium is the very opposite, for it does not celebrate the absence of space. Its appearance may be transmutable, but its proportions remain harmonious. In its most stringent form, it appears as a shell measuring 24 x 14 x 4 metres, consisting of black walls, a blackish brown floor and a translucently shimmering ceiling. The wall panelling is made of varnished, horizontally ribbed wooden acoustic panels, the flooring of smoked oak parquet and the ceiling of galvanised rib mesh coffering.

So far, so simple. Yet this space is no rigid resonator that has to be played like a musical instrument. Instead, it is a perfect machine in the service of multi-functionality. The entire floor consists of 132 one-by-two metre lifting platforms which together form Europe's biggest adjustable stage. The machinery allows this flat area to be transformed into a veritable landscape of mountains and valleys – the versatility and functionality of the room knows no bounds. Each wall panel can be swivelled 180 degrees, providing two surfaces with different acoustic effects. At the same time, these panels can be opened to reveal two rows of windows at right angles to one another, providing natural daylight and a view of the outdoors. Above the ceiling there are two concealed levels of adjustable lighting and a seven-metre high concealed attic room with sound insulation for painstakingly calculated acoustic reflections.

Architekten Architects Peter Kulka Architekt, Köln/Dresden; Peter Kulka, Henryk Urbanietz; Team: Jürgen Lindner & Sophia Pachiadakis, Monika Stallmann, Axel Möser | **Bauherr** Client Konzerthaus Berlin, vertreten durch ECE Projektmanagement, Berlin/Hamburg | **Bühnentechnik** Stage Technology Ingenieurbüro Heinrich Wiczkowiak VDE, Recklinghausen | **Licht** Lighting Lichtplanung Dipl.-Ing. Annette Hartung, Köln | **Akustik** Acoustics Graner + Partner, Bergisch Gladbach | **Ausführung** Construction 2002/03 | **Standort** Location Gendarmenmarkt, Berlin

Aussicht ins Freie bieten. Über der Decke verbergen sich zwei Ebenen von Leuchtkörpern mit unterschiedlich schaltbaren Lichtstimmungen und ein sieben Meter hoher, nicht einsehbarer Dachraum mit Schalldeckeln für die kompliziert kalkulierten akustischen Reflexionen.

Somit verfügt der Saal in seiner einfachen Form über eine unsichtbare Hochleistungstechnik. Über Knopfdruck kann die Stimmung verändert werden, optisch wie akustisch. Aus dem hermetischen Raum kann ein nach außen gerichteter werden, aus dem zentrierten einer, der den Gendarmenmarkt hereinholt und in seiner puren Abstraktion die Außenwelt wie aus grellbunten Märchenbildern aufnimmt. Aus dem weich und tief klingenden Schallraum wird ein härterer, reflektierender, abgegrenzter Ort. Aus dem konzentrierten, reduzierten Licht bei Kammerkonzerten wird die Festbeleuchtung des Ballsaals und aus dem klassischen ansteigenden Orchestersaal ein flacher Raum für den Stehempfang.

Die Bewegung, welche die Zustände verändern kann, ist selber nicht Gegenstand der Dramaturgie; sie bleibt dem Besucher verborgen, wie beim Kulissenumbau im Theater. Ihr gehören die Zeitzwischenräume, in denen die Techniker regieren. Der Maschinerie gehören die doppelten Böden und Wände, von denen der Besucher nichts ahnt. Dieser erfährt immer nur einen in sich ruhenden Raum.

Der Hamburger Unternehmer und Musikliebhaber Werner Otto hat diesen Saal der Musikwelt und der Stadt geschenkt, und so trägt dieser seinen Namen. Der Saal soll in Kürze, nach einem korrespondierenden Entwurf Kulkas, im Erdgeschoss um ein Foyer für Kartenverkauf mit Café und Platz für Veranstaltungen ergänzt werden.

Das Schauspielhaus ist schon mehrfach ›vollendet‹ worden. Doch von Eingriffen wie denen Kulkas werden diese Vollendungen immer wieder überraschend in Frage gestellt. Die Antwort für diesen Ort ist das geistreiche Ensemble eines Raums, der ab jetzt zu den schönsten Berlins gehört.

Konrad Wohlhage

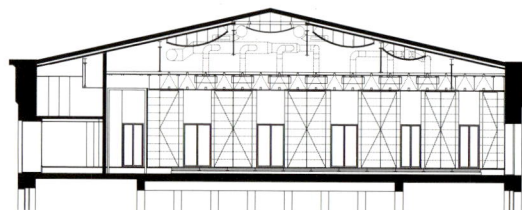

Thus, for all its formal simplicity, this auditorium possesses an invisible array of cutting-edge technology. At the press of a button, the entire atmosphere can be transformed, both optically and acoustically. The self-contained space can be turned into one that looks outwards, turning an inwardly centred room into a space that responds in dialogue with the Gendarmenmarkt, a composition whose pure abstraction absorbs the outer world like so many brightly coloured fairytale pictures. The deep, soft tones of this acoustic space can become a much harsher, reflecting, enclosed space. The concentrated, reduced light of a chamber concert can give way to the ostentatious lighting of a ballroom, while the classical incline of the auditorium can be made into an even-floored reception room.

The movement that results in changing states is not in itself the focus of the setting; it remains hidden from the visitor, like the set changes in a theatre. It is here that we find the intervals in which the technicians work. The machinery is housed in double floors and walls of which the visitor knows nothing. All the visitor perceives is a calm space.

The Hamburg entrepreneur and music lover Werner Otto has donated this room to the city and the world of music, which is why it bears his name. In the near future, a ground-floor foyer for ticket sales, with café and functions area, is to be added – also to a design by Kulka.

The Schauspielhaus in Berlin has already been 'completed' several times. Yet such designs as Kulka's repeatedly call its completion into question in the most surprising ways. The response is a highly intelligent spatial ensemble that is now one of the most beautiful in Berlin.

Konrad Wohlhage

Schnitt **Section**

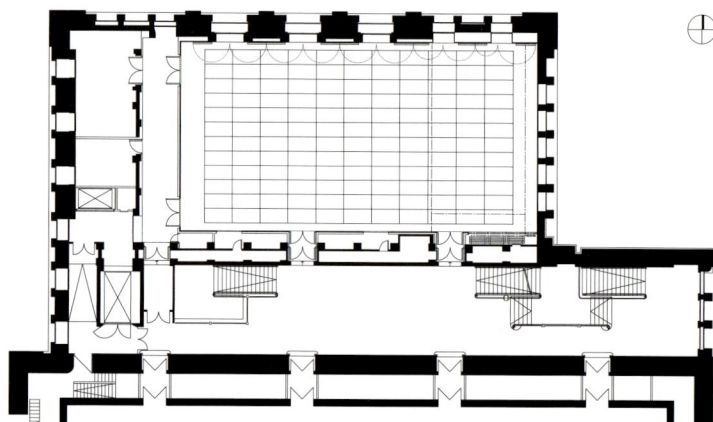

Grundriss **Ground plan**

Arenabühne **Arena stage**

Karl Friedrich Schinkel, ehemaliges Schauspielhaus, Berlin, 1821
Karl Friedrich Schinkel, former playhouse, Berlin, 1821

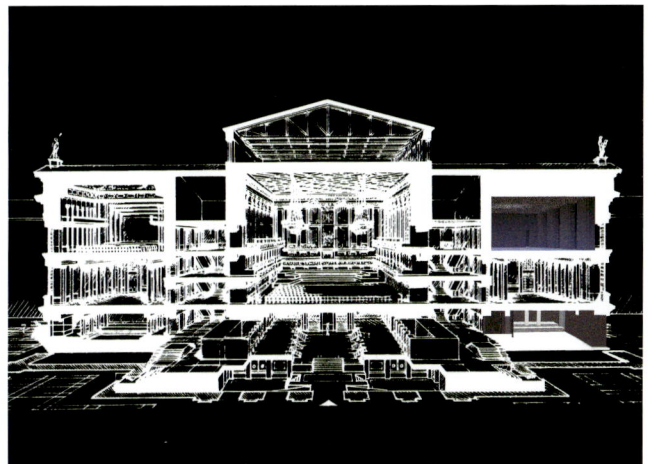

Lage im Gebäude
Location in the building

Geschlossene Wandflügel   **Closed wall-panel shutters**

Geöffnete Wandflügel
Open wall-panel shutters

Sächsische Landesbibliothek – Staats- und Universitätsbibliothek, Dresden
Saxon State and University Library, Dresden

Ortner & Ortner

■ Der Zellescher Weg ist nicht gerade eine Straße, die einen Campus in der Nähe vermuten lässt. Unwirtlichkeit empfindet der Passant, wenn die Autos an ihm vorbeirauschen und der Maßstab des Straßenraums ihn eher verschlingt als aufnimmt. Gern nutzt er die Öffnung im begrünten Wall, um zu entkommen. Über einen geschützten Hof gelangt er so zum Haupteingang der Staats- und Universitäts- und Landesbibliothek.

Nach außen zeigt sich diese in zwei gleichartigen Gebäudekuben, die mit ihrer Gestaltung das Thema ›Bücherregal‹ abstrahieren. Sie spannen zwischen sich ein grünes Feld, welches von einem dichten Wegenetz durchzogen wird. Die den Kuben vorgelagerten gerundeten Höfe im Norden und Süden erinnern an das Rund des ehemaligen Sportplatzes.

Im Haupteingang empfängt den Besucher ein offenes, großzügiges und helles Entree, das einen weiten Blick in die Bibliothek erlaubt. Von der unkomplizierten, angenehmen Arbeitsatmosphäre wird man sofort aufgenommen. Die warmen Rotbrauntöne der Wände und Böden beherrschen das Bild. Im Kontrast dazu steht das Grau des Sichtbetons und der Metalloberflächen für Geländer und Leuchten. Die offenen Freihandbereiche mit den eingestreuten Leseplätzen sind übersichtlich angeordnet, man kann sich gut orientieren. Eingeschnittene Lichthöfe sorgen für natürlichen Lichteinfall und ermöglichen den Kontakt zur Außenwelt, wenn man über den Büchern den Tageslauf vergessen hat. Das bewusste Hineinlenken des Tageslichts bis in die unteren Ebenen der Bibliothek ist Bestandteil eines durchdachten Lichtkonzepts im gesamten Haus. Die Allgemeinbeleuchtung ist eher sparsam, dafür wird dort Lichtintensität erzeugt, wo sie auch benötigt wird: unmittelbar an den Bücherregalen oder über den Arbeitsplätzen. Gemeinschaftsflächen wie zum Beispiel Infostände werden durch ›Lichtinseln‹ hervorgehoben.

In einer Fuge, die sich über alle Ebenen erstreckt, kann man die Buchförderanlage sehen: In kleinen Containern werden die Bücher aus den Tiefen der Magazine zur Ausleihe und zurück transportiert.

Anziehungspunkt ist der zentrale Lesesaal. Hohe Säulenreihen inszenieren diesen besonderen Ort auf allen Ebenen. Seine Gestaltung bedient sich der klassischen Struktur eines Lesesaals. Ein helles Segel unter dem Glasdach sorgt für diffuses Licht. Hell gebeizte Holzbinder tragen die Glaskonstruktion. Breite, verschiedenfarbige Holzstäbe fügen sich zu den Bändern des Holzbodens. Es sind sparsame, aber wirkungsvolle Mittel, die eingesetzt wurden, diesem Saal Ausdruck zu verleihen. Die warmen Töne im Raum und die helle, leichte Decke schaffen eine gute Stimmung. Man kann in alle Ebenen der Bibliothek sehen und hat somit den Bezug zum Gesamtgebäude.

Um den Lesesaal gruppieren sich diverse Arbeitsplätze, von Schreibtischgruppen über Stehtische bis zu klausurartigen Zellen, in denen man ungestört arbeiten kann. Auf gemütlich gepolsterten Bänken darf man es sich bequem machen. Alle Arbeitsplätze stehen trotz ihres unterschiedlichen Charakters in unmittelbarem Sichtbezug zur Umgebung.

■ Zellerscher Weg is hardly the kind of street one expects to lead to a campus. Passers-by have a sense of unease as the traffic rushes past and the sheer scale of the urban fabric seems more all-devouring than welcoming. The opening in the wall of greenery offers a welcome escape – across a sheltered courtyard leading to the main entrance of the Saxon State and University Library.

Outwardly, the library takes the form of two identical cubic structures whose design is an abstraction of the 'bookshelf' theme. Between them lies a green area crisscrossed by pathways. The rounded courtyards to the north and south in front of the cubes recall the sweeping arena of the former sports field.

The main entrance leads to an open, spacious and light foyer that provides a broad view into the library itself. The uncomplicated and pleasant working atmosphere feels immediately welcoming. The warm, reddish brown hues of the walls and flooring predominate, contrasted by the grey of the exposed concrete and the metal surfaces of the railings and lighting. The open access library area with its scattered reading places is well structured for easy orientation. Patios have been inserted to provide natural daylight and contact with the outside world for those engrossed in reading. The deliberate channelling of natural light all the way down to the lower levels of the library is part of a carefully orchestrated lighting concept throughout the building. The general lighting is kept to a minimum, using direct lighting wherever it is needed: at the bookshelves or above the work spaces. Areas for general usage, such as the information stands, are pinpointed by 'islets of light'.

A gap running through all the levels allows a view of the book conveyor system that transports the volumes from the basement magazines to the lending points and back again in small containers.

The focal point is the central reading room with tall rows of pillars that set it apart at every level. The design of the room makes reference to the classical structure of the reading room. A bright sail beneath the glazed roof diffuses the light. The glass structure itself is supported by pale wooden roof timbers, and broad wooden bars of different colours reiterate the stripes of the wooden flooring. These are a sparse but highly effective means of lending expression to this room. The warm hues and the pale, light ceiling create a fine atmosphere. There are views into all levels of the library so that one can relate to the building as a whole.

Arranged around the reading room are various work spaces consisting of groups of desks, from lecterns to cell-like areas where it is possible to work undisturbed. There are comfortably upholstered benches. Although they are different in character, all the work spaces have a direct visual relationship to their surroundings.

The sense of openness within the building has been achieved by means of galleries and patios, with transparent wall elements separating the different work spaces or special reading rooms with valuable stocks. Most users are surprised at the fact that, in spite of the sense of space and openness throughout the building, it never-

Architekten Architects Ortner & Ortner Baukunst, Berlin/Wien, www.ortner.at; Laurids Ortner, Manfred Ortner; seit 1999: Planungsarge S.L.U.B. Ortner & Ortner Baukunst und ATP Achammer-Tritthart & Partner, München; Team: Christian Lichtenwagner, Ekkehart Krainer, Ulrich Wedel, Rudi Finsterwalder, Michael Ewerhardt & Michael Adelkofer, Maria Baptista, Roland Duda, Bernhard Eichinger, Michael Franke, Berit Großmann, Thomas Großmann, Thorsten Heine, Thomas Heydenreich, Georgia Prätorius, Ralf Prätorius, Heike Simon, Robert Westphal, Hans Witschurke, Dirk Zimmermann | **Bauherr** Client Freistaat Sachsen, vertreten durch das Staatshochbauamt Dresden | **Tragwerk** Structural Gmeiner Haferl Tragwerksplanung KEG, Wien | **HL-Technik** Technical Zibell Willner & Partner, Dresden | **Freianlagen** Landscape Burger + Tischer, Berlin, mit Jörg Coqui, Berlin | **Wettbewerb** Competition 1996 | **Ausführung** Construction 1999–2002 | **Standort** Location Zellescher Weg 18–20, Dresden

Die Offenheit innerhalb des Gebäudes wird bewusst organisiert, durch eingeschnittene Galerien und Lichthöfe, mit transparenten Wandelementen zu Arbeitsräumen oder Sonderlesesälen mit wertvollen Buchbeständen. Verblüffend für den Nutzer ist die Tatsache, dass trotz dieser großzügigen Offenheit im ganzen Haus die notwendige Ruhe zur wissenschaftlichen Arbeit gewahrt bleibt. Das zeugt von einer gelungenen Umsetzung des Entwurfskonzepts. Konzentration und Stille nehmen zu, je tiefer man in das Innere, das Herzstück des Hauses eintaucht: den Lesesaal auf der untersten Ebene.

Die Reduktion der Themen und Gestaltungsmittel macht das besondere Erscheinungsbild der Bibliothek aus. Das unregelmäßige Raster eines Bücherregals wird zum bestimmenden Architekturthema. Wie eine feine Textur durchzieht es das Haus und wird variiert in der Verschiedenartigkeit der Materialien: in der Profilierung der Fassadenelemente aus Travertin genauso wie in den Schlitzen der Wandverkleidungen, in den Positiv-/Negativ-Formen der Sichtbetondecken, selbst im gebänderten Parkettboden des Lesesaals.

Mit der kühnen Entscheidung, das Hauptvolumen des Bibliotheksneubaus unter die Erde zu verbannen, war man sich bewusst, einer kostenintensiveren Lösung den Vorzug zu geben. Aber nur so war es möglich, sehr behutsam mit dem vorhandenen Freiraum umzugehen und einen Lesegarten für die Nutzer anzulegen.

Die neue Bibliothek, die aus der Zusammenlegung der 450 Jahre alten Landesbibliothek mit der wesentlich jüngeren Staats- und Universitätsbibliothek entstanden ist, hat mit dem Entwurf von Laurids und Manfred Ortner einen bemerkenswerten und in seiner inneren Konzeption zukunftsorientierten Neubau erhalten, den die Nutzer sich mit Freude aneignen können. Das Thema ›Bücher‹ wurde auf neue spielerische Weise in Architektur gefasst.

Angela Wandelt

theless provides the calm atmosphere that is necessary for academic work. This in itself is proof of a successful design concept. The further one enters into the interior of the building, to its very heart, as it were – the reading room on the lower level – the more the sense of concentration and calm increases.

It is the reduction of themes and design elements that gives the library its distinctive appearance. The irregular grid of a bookshelf becomes a determining architectural motif running throughout the entire building like a fine texture, varying only in the use of different materials: the profiled travertine facade elements, the slits in the wall cladding, the positive-negative forms of the exposed concrete ceilings, and even the striped wooden flooring of the reading room.

The bold decision to place the main body of the new library below ground meant consciously choosing a more costly solution. However, it was precisely this that allowed such a sensitive approach to the existing open spaces and permitted the creation of a reading garden for the library's users.

The new library, created by combining the 450-year-old State Library with the much newer University Library, now has a remarkable and future-oriented building designed by Laurids and Manfred Ortner which will give great pleasure to those who use it. The theme of 'books' has been addressed in architecture in a new and spirited way.

Angela Wandelt

Seiten 146/147 **Pages 146–147**
Blick über das Glasdach des Lesesaals auf den nördlichen Baukörper
Northern block as seen across the glass roof of the reading room

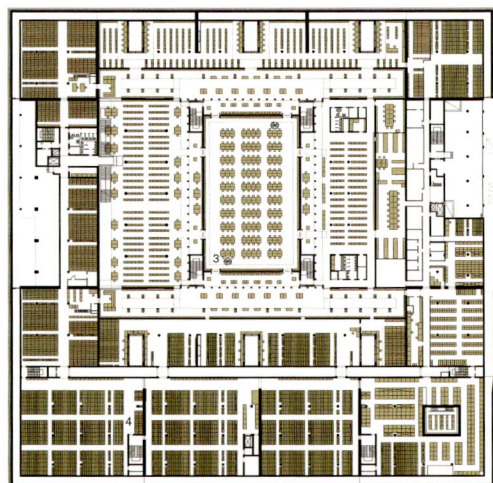

Grundriss Ebene -2 **Ground-plan level -2**

Blick von Westen **View from the west**

1 Eingang **Entrance**
2 Foyer **Foyer**
3 Lesesaal **Reading room**
4 Magazin **Depot**
5 Verwaltung **Administration**
6 Vortragssaal **Lecture hall**
7 Cafeteria **Cafeteria**

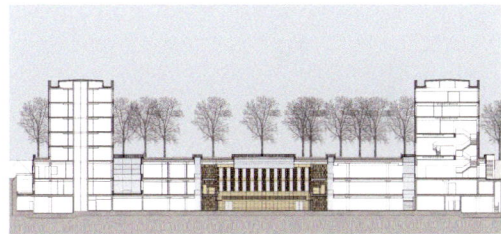

Schnitt **Section**

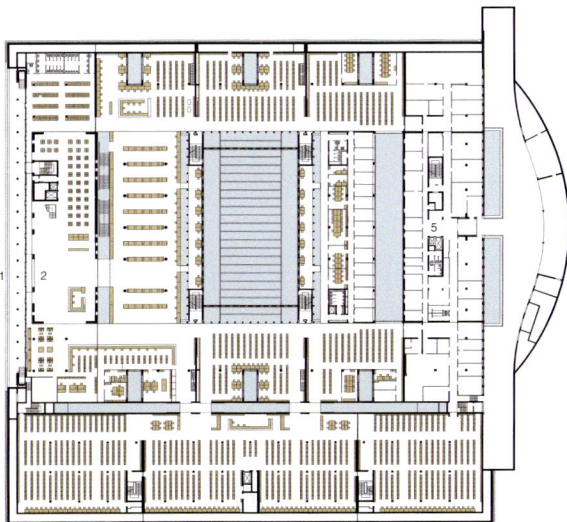

Grundriss Ebene 0 **Ground-plan level 0**

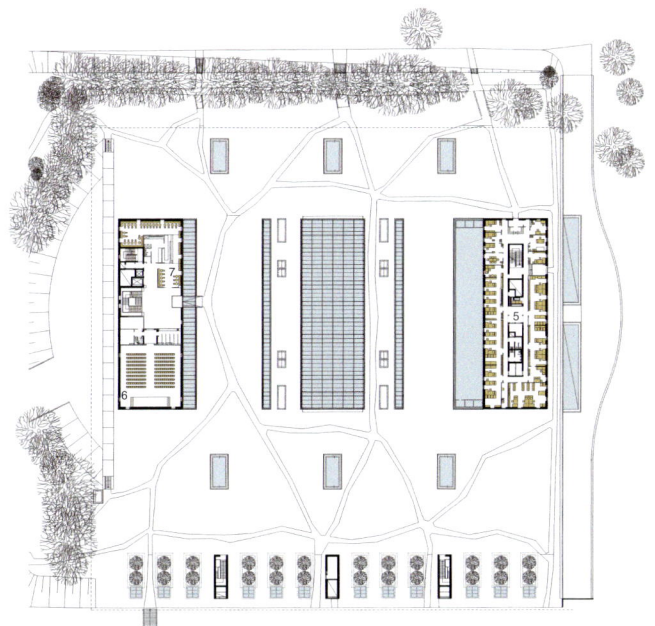

Grundriss Ebene +1 **Ground-plan level +1**

Sächsische Landesbibliothek – Staats- und Universitätsbibliothek, Dresden
Saxon State and University Library, Dresden

149

Foyer **Foyer**

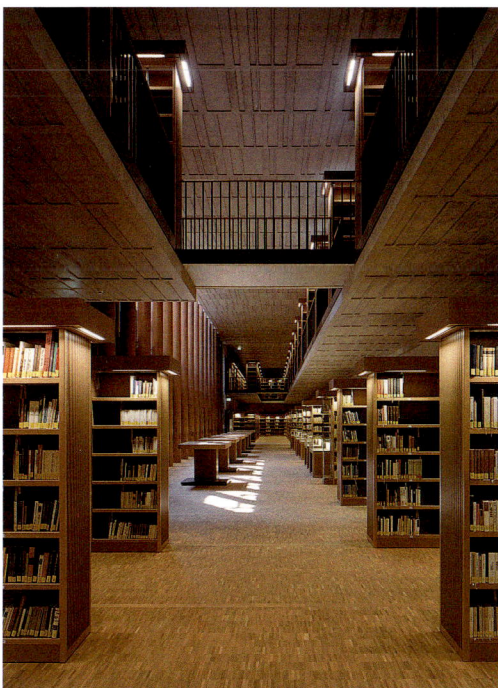

Freihandbereich **Open-shelf area**

Treppe **Staircase**

Galerie **Gallery**

Seiten 150/151 **Pages 150–151**
Lesesaal **Reading room**

Bäckereikette Dat Backhus, Hamburg
'Dat Backhus' Bakery Chain Outlet, Hamburg

André Poitiers

■ Das Gebiet zwischen Hamburger Rathaus und Gänsemarkt ist vielleicht die einzige urbane Topografie Deutschlands, die in ihrer baulichen Präsenz und Dichte den Vergleich mit europäischen Zentren wie Mailand und Barcelona wagen kann. Umso frappierender ist es, dass ausgerechnet auf der Identitätsmeile Jungfernstieg zwei benachbarte Grundstücke nur mit ein- und zweigeschossigen Flachbauten besetzt sind, welche die gebietsprägende Sechsgeschossigkeit unterbrechen und tiefe Blicke in das ungeordnete Blockinnere zulassen. Was andernorts eher mit einem Schulterzucken abzutun ist, wirkt als Bruch hier in seiner unvermittelten Banalität obszön.

Während der rechte, eingeschossige Ladenbau von einer Textilkette genutzt wird, gehört der linke Zweigeschosser zur Bäckereikette Dat Backhus und wurde von dem Hamburger Architekten André Poitiers entworfen. Dieser hat in den vergangenen Jahren bereits mehrere firmenzugehörige Ladenlokale gestaltet, wobei ihm nicht nur hervorragende Innenraumgestaltungen gelungen sind, sondern auch deren Transformation in überaus öffentliche Orte und leistungsfähige Stadtbausteine. Als solche interpretieren die biedere Bauaufgabe ›Backwarengeschäft mit Schnellcafé‹ trotz des hanseatischen Naturells und Klimas quasi italienisch, als architektonische Erweiterung des Straßenraums samt voyeuristisch-theatralischer Inszenierung. Unmittelbar hinter den straßenseitigen Vollverglasungen werden die Cafékunden in idealer Beobachtungsposition platziert und verwandeln sich ihrerseits in Schauspieler auf der städtischen Guckkastenbühne. Eine straßenparallele Staffelung des Ausbausystems und der mittels Wiederholung und Schichtung raumplastisch eingesetzte Schriftzug ›Dat Backhus‹ unterstützen dieses Konzept.

Bei einer am Saseler Markt im Nordosten Hamburgs gelegenen Filiale gelingt Poitiers eine sogar weit über das engere Ladenumfeld hinausreichende städtebauliche Wirkung. Ein fein detaillierter, verglaster Vorbau erweitert hier die in einem kleinen Ziegelbau mit Giebeldach untergebrachte Bäckerei um den Caféraum. Doch handelt es sich nicht um eine der üblichen Pavillonformen, sondern ausgerechnet um den ›Verbinder‹. Als präzise gewählter Anti-Typus deutscher Nachkriegsarchitektur greift dieser die den Saseler Markt prägenden Versatzstücke wie Runderker, geneigte Vitrinen und Wintergärten thematisch auf und macht sie erst durch die zeitgenössische Fortschreibung als historische Schicht lesbar. Es ist zudem wirklich beeindruckend, wie dieser kleine Bäckerladen das bedrückend nichtssagende Zwischen- und Nachkriegsmilieu dieses Vorstadtplatzes aufwertet und seine abendlich erleuchtete Glasarchitektur urbane Präsenz behauptet.

Solche Brillanz in der kontextuellen Bezugnahme hat Poitiers am Jungfernstieg offensichtlich nicht entwickeln wollen. Vielmehr scheint er die Baulückensituation als Chance verstanden zu haben, seiner Vorliebe für die bereits prominent publizierten ›objects in the territory‹[1] entwurflich Raum geben zu können. Diese plastischen, durch Abrundung und Böschung gekennzeichneten Volumen und Hohlformen bieten in der Tat eine Möglichkeit, dem am Standort unterbrochenen

■ The area between Hamburg City Hall and the Gänsemarkt is the only urban topography in Germany whose architectural presence and density can compare with such European centres as Milan or Barcelona. It is therefore all the more remarkable that such a prime boulevard as Hamburg's identity-shaping Jungfernstieg should have two adjacent sites occupied by only one- and two-storey buildings which interrupt the six-storey urban fabric, allowing views far into the informal interior block structure. While it might be shrugged off casually anywhere else, here the immediacy of the break possesses a banality that seems veritably obscene.

The one-storey retail outlet on the right is occupied by a clothing chain. The two-storey building on the left, designed by Hamburg-based architect André Poitiers, houses a branch of 'Dat Backhus' bakery chain. In recent years, Poitiers has created a number of retail outlets, some of which are not only outstanding examples of interior design, but also of public accessibility and dynamic urban spaces. What might otherwise have been a run-of-the-mill task of building a fast food bakery-cum-coffee outlet succeeds in defying the hanseatic mindset and the northern European climate by creating an almost Italian ambience with a dramatically voyeuristic setting that is an architectural enhancement of the street. Customers find themselves perched directly behind the glazed facade, perfectly poised to watch the world go by, while at the same time becoming actors on an urban stage. The shop fittings are aligned parallel with the street and the lettering 'Dat Backhus' is repeated and layered at staggered intervals, forming a sculptural sense of space that further underpins this concept.

For another branch of the same chain at Saseler Markt in the north-east of Hamburg, Poitiers has gone even further: The bakery shop, housed in a small brick building with a pitched roof, has been given a finely detailed glass frontage which creates an extension for the cafe area. Yet instead of choosing a conventional pavilion form, he has fashioned a 'link' that stands in deliberately stark contrast to the post-war architecture of the surrounding area, yet at the same time echoes the bay windows and conservatories of Saseler Markt in a contemporary mode that actually renders them more clearly legible in terms of historic continuity. What is more, the little bakery shop is impressive in the way it lifts the stultifyingly faceless interwar and post-war ambience of this suburban square, its illuminated glass structure asserting a distinctly urban presence.

Poitiers clearly did not want to develop such scintillating contextual references on the Jungfernstieg. Instead, he seems to have seized the opportunity offered by the undeveloped site as a chance to lend expression to his already much-cited concept of 'objects in the territory'.[1] These sculptural volumes and hollow forms, characterised by rounded edges and inclines, do indeed provide a means of countering this hiatus in the urban context by placing a formally autonomous architecture at precisely the point where the break occurs. The shop frontage reflects this approach with its two-storey

Architekten Architects André Poitiers Architekt BDA, Hamburg, www.poitiers.de; Design **Interior Design:** Ulrich Engel, Martin Michel, André Poitiers; Team: Ulrich Engel, Thomas Ladehoff & Zerrin Alkan, Sigrun Esser, Klaus Junge, Ken Kuroda, Oliver von der Lippe, Julia Roth, Tarkan Tarbasar, Jens Winter | **Bauherr Client** Dat Backhus, Heinz Bräuer, Hamburg | **Licht Lighting** ERCO, Hamburg (Rothenbaumchaussee, Saseler Markt, Wandsbeker Chaussee); Prediger Lichtberater, Hamburg (Jungfernstieg, Lange Reihe) | **Tragwerk Structural** Wetzel & von Seht, Hamburg (Jungfernstieg, Saseler Markt) | **Ausführung Construction** 1999–2002 | **Standort Location** Jungfernstieg 45, Lange Reihe 29, Rothenbaumchaussee 78, Saseler Markt 13, Wandsbeker Chaussee 177, Hamburg

großstädtischen Kontext exakt an der Störstelle eine formal autonome Architektur entgegenzustellen. Die Ladenfront reflektiert diesen Ansatz mittels einer zweigeschossigen Verglasung im Softline-Design der siebziger Jahre, die dank einer minimierten Konstruktion teilungs- und sprossenlos wirkt und deren umlaufende weiße Metallrahmung das Entree als Karosserie erscheinen lässt. Konsequent entwickeln sich der erdgeschossige Verkaufsraum und das im Obergeschoss befindliche Bistro, deren Ausbauelemente und -materialien in einem einheitlichen, in Rundungen durchformten Objektdesign zusammengefasst werden.

Ungünstig wirkt sich hingegen die schmale, tief in den Block schneidende Parzellenform aus, die das Aufgeben der bewährten Straßenparallelität der Thekenbereiche zur Folge hat und deren Verdrehung um 90 Grad bedingt. Dies und die Zweigeschossigkeit bedeuten einen erheblichen Öffentlichkeitsverlust im räumlichen wie im sozialen Sinne, der innenarchitektonisch kaum aufgefangen werden kann. Zwar sitzen zumindest im Obergeschoss einige Bistro-Kunden wieder in unmittelbarer Zuordnung zur straßenseitigen Glasfront, doch beschränkt sich dies nur auf die erste Reihe, während die Raumtiefe visuell isoliert und somit im städtischen Sinne inaktiv bleibt.

Das kleine Wunder, aus der Gestaltung einer Bäckerei die für Hamburg gleichermaßen seltene wie wichtige Weitung des öffentlichen Raums als Voraussetzung urbaner Teilhabe zu gewinnen, hat Poitiers gleich an mehreren Orten vollbracht. Sein ambitionierter Entwurf für den Jungfernstieg schafft dies nicht, bleibt aber eine im gestalterischen Ansatz plausible und funktional überzeugende Lösung, deren wesentliche stadträumliche Mängel dem Laisser-faire der Hamburger Stadtplanung anzulasten sind.

Ingo Andreas Wolf

1 Kristin Feireiss (Hrsg.), *André Poitiers, Objects in the Territory,* Basel 2002.

glazed facade in a 1970s retro softline design, whose minimalist structure creates an impression of uninterrupted smoothness with an entrance framed in white metal, reminiscent of a chassis. In a consistent development of the overall appearance, the fittings and materials of the ground floor sales area and the upper level bistro are of uniformly sculptural plasticity.

A less successful feature is the long, narrow floor plan running deep into the interior of the block. It works against the layout of the counter area, which runs parallel to the street, causing a 90-degree turn. This, and the fact that it is split into two levels, detracts considerably from the public aspect of the building – both spatially and socially – in a way that the interior design cannot fully alleviate. Although some bistro customers sit right up at the glass front overlooking the street on the upper level, only those in the first row of seats can do so, while the depth of the room is visually isolating and, in urban terms, inactive.

The minor miracle of designing a bakery that opens up the public space as a means of increasing participation in urban life is as rare in Hamburg as it is important. It is a miracle Poitiers has pulled off successfully on several occasions. His ambitious design for the Jungfernstieg does not quite come up to the mark, but its design approach is nevertheless a plausible and functionally persuasive solution whose shortcomings are mainly a result of Hamburg's laissez-faire urban planning.

Ingo Andreas Wolf

1 Kristin Feireiss (ed.), *André Poitiers, Objetcts in the Territory, Basle, 2002.*

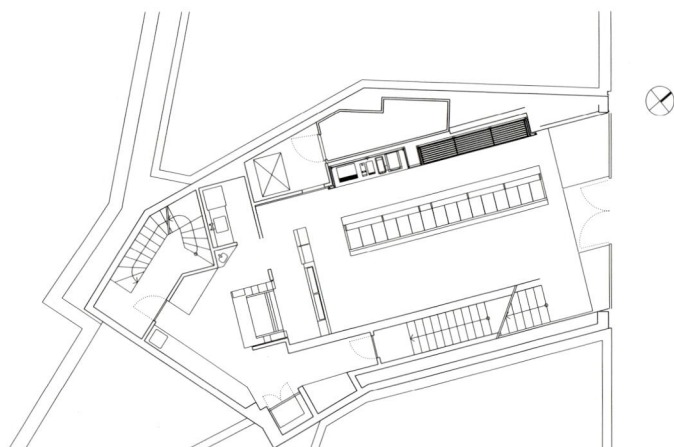

Grundriss Jungfernstieg **Ground plan, Jungfernstieg**

Filiale am Jungfernstieg
Branch on Jungfernstieg

Café 1. Obergeschoss, Jungfernstieg   **Café, first floor, Jungfernstieg**

Verkauf, Jungfernstieg **Shop, Jungfernstieg**

Filiale am Saseler Markt **Branch on Saseler Markt**

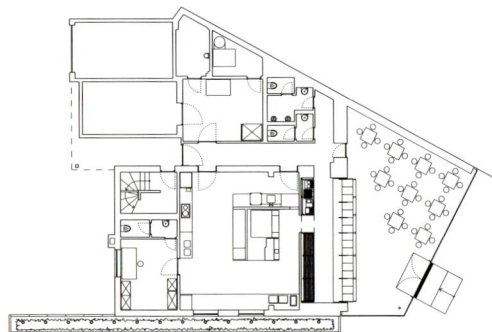

Grundriss Saseler Markt
Ground plan, Saseler Markt

Bäckereikette Dat Backhus, Hamburg
'Dat Backhus' Bakery Chain Outlet, Hamburg

Filiale im Multimedia Centre Rothenbaum
Branch in the Rothenbaum Multimedia Centre

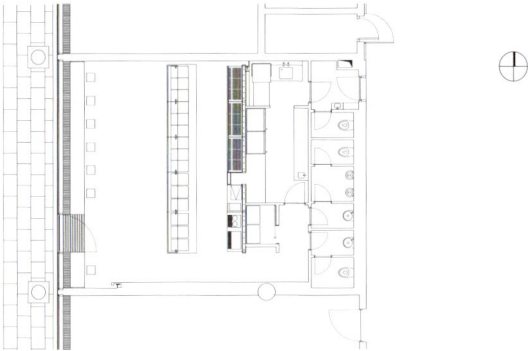

Grundriss Multimedia Centre Rothenbaum
Ground plan, Rothenbaum Multimedia Centre

Filiale in der Wandsbeker Chaussee
Branch on Wandsbeker Chaussee

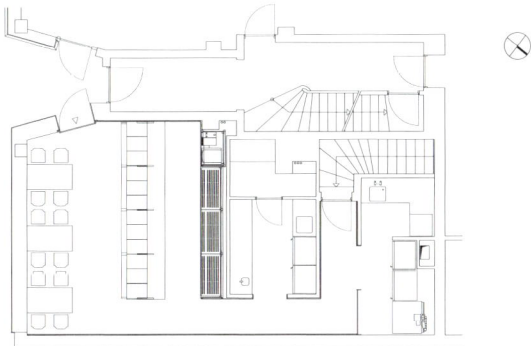

Grundriss Wandsbeker Chaussee
Ground plan, Wandsbeker Chaussee

Filiale in der Langen Reihe
Branch on Lange Reihe

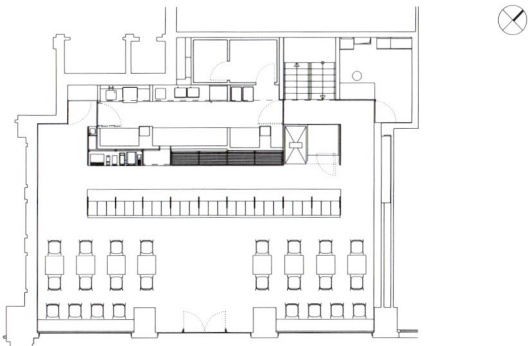

Grundriss Lange Reihe
Ground plan, Lange Reihe

Neues Stadtquartier Westhafen, Frankfurt am Main
New City Quarter, Westhafen, Frankfurt/Main

schneider + schumacher

■ Das Westhafen-Gebiet in Frankfurt mit Schleusen- und Gutleut-straße ist ein verlassenes Hafen- und Lagerhausquartier, das wegen seiner zentralen und reizvollen landschaftlichen Lage am Ufer des Mains zu Entwicklungsmodellen geradezu herausfordert. Das mit der Erschließung des Gebiets befasste Investorengremium beauftragte die Architekten Till Schneider und Michael Schumacher mit einer Studie zur Bebauung des östlichen Hafenzugangs, in der bereits an der heutigen Stelle das Trio Westhafen-Tower, Brückengebäude und Westhafen-Haus skizziert wurde. Diese Idee führte in dem nachfolgenden Realisierungswettbewerb zum Erfolg.

Das Ensemble dieser drei Solitäre am Landeingang zum Hafen ist ein Zusammenspiel architektonischer Individuen, nicht das stadt-raumergänzender Baukanten. Daraus ergeben sich unterschiedliche Aufgaben: Der Westhafen-Tower ist die Landmarke in der Skyline am Ende der Grünzone des Mainufers. Sein Mittelpunkt, exakt auf Achse der Innenkante des Hafenbeckens, signalisiert ›Zukunft des Ge-biets‹. Das Brückengebäude erinnert an die ehemalige Einfahrt zur Schleuse, mit einer entschlossenen Geste über den Fluss in die süd-liche Stadtlandschaft. Das Westhafen-Haus bildet den Kopf des kammartigen Baublocks, der sich westlich davon am landseitigen Ufer des Hafenbeckens entwickelt.

Dieses Konzept unabhängiger Bauwerke macht aus dem da-zwischen liegenden Westhafenplatz natürlich keinen städtischen Platz, aber – und das war den Architekten wichtiger – es öffnet Blick-schneisen in die landschaftlich wichtigen Richtungen, ohne den Soli-tären ihren Auftritt zu nehmen. Ob der Platz von dem Wind beein-trächtigt wird, der um den Tower und unter der ›Brücke‹ durchblasen wird, muss sich zeigen.

Die Verkehrserschließung hat nicht viele Reserven, wie es solche Standorte unvermeidlich mit sich bringen. Dies aber kann kein Argu-ment gegen die Entwicklung solcher Standorte sein.

Als Bonsai-Gigant hat sich der Tower in der inzwischen eindrucks-vollen Mainhattan-Party eine auffällige Garderobe ausgedacht. Die schlanken, gleichschenkligen Dreiecke, deren durchlaufende Kanten sich kreuzend gegenläufig nach oben schrauben, erzeugen eine ›Schuppenhaut‹, die dem Zylinder mehr schmeichelt, als es eine orthogonale Teilung täte. Glitzerndes Sonnenlicht und die geöffneten Lüftungsflügel verstärken diese Struktur, die – von den Architekten selbst als ›Apfelweinglas‹ karikiert – bereits im Vorentwurf vorge-sehen war. In der Skyline gebärdet sich der Turm so, als wolle er den penetranten Chefetagenhabitus seiner Kollegen ein wenig auf den Arm nehmen, und dies ohne den heute üblichen architektonischen Kopfschmuck aus ›Nadeln‹ und Auslegern, die sinnlos in den Him-mel stechen.

In die Hüllfigur sind quaderförmige Etagen eingepasst. Durch die Überlagerung von Kreis und Quadrat entstehen Lufträume, die sich entsprechend der geschossweisen Rotation um jeweils 90 Grad zu viergeschossigen Wintergärten addieren. Diese etwa 14 Meter hohen Lufträume als Kreissegmente zwischen innerer und äußerer Fassade

■ The streets of Schleusenstrasse and Gutleutstrasse traverse the Westhafen district of Frankfurt, a derelict river port and warehous-ing area. The central, scenic location on the banks of the River Main positively cries out for redevelopment. A panel of investors is look-ing into ways of developing the area, and has commissioned archi-tects Till Schneider and Michael Schumacher to draw up a study for the eastern approach to the river port that incorporates plans for the Westhafen-Tower, the Brückengebäude, or 'bridge building', and the Westhafen-Haus. The concept proved a success in the subsequent architectural competition.

The ensemble of these three buildings at the entrance to the river port forms an interesting interplay of individual architectural works rather than the mere delineation of urban expansion. The re-sulting challenges could hardly be more varied: The Westhafen-Tower is a landmark on the skyline at the end of the green belt run-ning along the river bank. Its centre, axially aligned with the inner edge of the harbour basin, sends out a clear signal that this district has a future. The Brückengebäude recalls the former entrance to the lock, making a distinctive gesture across the river towards the southern part of town. The Westhafen-Haus forms the head of the comb-like block that is developing to the west by the harbour basin.

Needless to say, this concept of independent structures does not turn the Westhafen-Platz between them into an urban square, but – and this was more important to the architects – it does open up vistas towards the surrounding landscape without diminishing the impact of individual buildings. Whether the square will be affected by winds that blow round the tower and under the 'bridge' remains to be seen.

As is so often the case with locations like these, there is little lee-way to extend the traffic and transport infrastructure. Still, this hard-ly constitutes an argument against developing such areas.

The Westhafen-Tower makes a distinctive mark among the im-pressive high-rise buildings that have earned Frankfurt the nick-name 'Mainhattan'. The slender triangles whose edges cross and spiral upwards create a 'scaly skin' that is far more flattering to the cylindrical form of the building than an orthogonal design would have been. The glint of sunlight and the open ventilation slats fur-ther emphasise this pattern, which, as the architects themselves have observed, resembles a traditional Frankfurt cider glass. De-void of any functionally meaningless architectonic crown or wreath, the tower almost seems to make fun of the blue-chip pomposity of its neighbours on the skyline.

Block-like floors inserted into the shell of the building cause a superimposition of circle and square to create air spaces, rotated by 90 degrees on each floor, that combine to form four-storey winter gardens. These fourteen-metre high air spaces between the inner and outer facades make an important contribution to the air condi-tioning within the building, while at the same time accommodating stairways that link the various levels. All manner of workspaces are

Architekten Architects schneider + schumacher, Frankfurt am Main, www.schneider-schumacher.de; Till Schneider, Michael Schumacher; Team: Henry Hess & Beate Bendel, Kerstin Bräuer, Harald Brutscher, Nina Delius, Stefan Goeddertz, Nadja Hellenthal, Sebastian Krehn, Michaela Kroll, Bernward Krone, Michael Schumacher | **Bauherr** Client Westhafen Tower GmbH & Co Projektentwicklungs KG, Frankfurt am Main | **Projektsteuerung** Project Management STRUKTUR GmbH, Dortmund | **Tragwerk** Structural SPI Schüßler-Plan Ingenieurgesellschaft, Frankfurt am Main | **HL-Technik** Technical HL-Technik AG, Frankfurt am Main | **Wettbewerb** Competition 1996 | **Ausführung** Construction 2000–2003 | **Standort** Location Westhafenplatz 1, Frankfurt am Main

tragen zur Klimadämpfung bei und erlauben für etagenübergreifende Nutzungen interne Verbindungstreppen. Vom Zellen- bis zum Großraumbüro sind alle Ausbauvarianten möglich, der prächtige Ausblick in jede Richtung bestätigt die Standortqualität. Für nicht schwindelfreie Gemüter übrigens erscheint die trianguläre Teilung weniger beängstigend als die normale innere Fassade, durch die man in den Luftraum hinunterschaut.

Das Foyer wirkt räumlich ein wenig beengt. Michael Schumacher begründet diese Entscheidung mit dem noch unterprivilegierten Standort, der keine verschwenderischen Entrees akzeptiere. Die Anschlüsse der Foyer-Innenwand an die Dreiecksfassade erzeugen ein kleines Lehrstück sphärischer Trigonometrie, das zusammen mit dem Spiel von Durchlässen und Galerien den Eindruck der Enge überspielen wird.

Im Brückengebäude wird das Dreiecksmotiv in den Längswänden wiederholt, so als wären die Betonscheiben stählerne Fachwerkträger. Trotzdem gelingt diese Anknüpfung, weil auch im Tower das Dreieck nicht eine Form der Konstruktion, sondern der Fassade ist. Zusammen mit den schrägen Front- und Heckfassaden gelingt eine dynamische Geste, die über das Ufer in den Fluss hineinzuragen scheint. Der Innenraum nutzt diese Gebärde zu einer großartigen mehrgeschossigen Öffnung nach Süden zum Licht und zum Wasser. Das Haus steht landseitig auf einem verglasten Café-Pavillon und vorn am Wasser auf dem Hauptzugang mit dem Treppenhaus. Die ehemalige Schleuse bleibt frei als Durchlass zum Hafenbecken.

Das Westhafen-Haus füllt das im Bebauungsplan angebotene Baufeld bewusst nicht vollständig aus; dies hätte den Westhafenplatz dramatisch beschnitten. Der schlanke, keilförmige Baukörper kommt dem Platz ebenso zugute wie die über einen Teil der Höhe eingezogene Südkante mit einer ›Loggia‹, die dem Platz ein wenig schmeicheln soll. Ob dies gelingt, muss die Akzeptanz des Alltags zeigen. Zumindest der Tower und die Brücke sind für jede Firma eine attraktive Adresse, weil sie die Erwartungen an das neue Quartier erfüllen.

Jochen Boskamp

possible here, from small cells to huge open-plan offices, and the magnificent views to all sides simply confirm the quality of the location. Incidentally, for those who are not particularly fond of heights, the triangular layout is far less intimidating than the normal interior facade with its downward views into the clear space.

The foyer seems a little cramped. Michael Schumacher explains that this was a conscious decision for an underprivileged location where a lavish entrance area would have been out of place. The way the foyer's inner wall joins the triangular facade is a superb example of spheric trigonometry, which, together with the apertures and galleries, tempers the impression of narrowness.

The triangular motif is reiterated in the longitudinal walls of the Brückengebäude, making the concrete panels appear as steel girders. This reiteration works well, since the Tower has the triangle as part of the facade and not as part of the structure. Together with the tilted front and side facades, the overall result is a dynamic gesture that seems to jut across the river bank and into the river. The interior uses this feature to create a superb southerly aspect that opens over several storeys towards the light and the water. On the leeward side, the house stands upon a glazed café pavilion, and on the waterfront it stands upon the main entrance with stairwell. The former lock remains as an open entrance to the harbour basin.

The Westhafen-Haus has been deliberately designed so that it does not take up the entire site provided by the development plan. To have done so would have dramatically infringed upon the Westhafenplatz. The slender, wedge-shaped building is intended to enhance the square, as is the 'loggia' built into part of the southern edge. Only through everyday use will the effectiveness of this approach become apparent. Both the Westhafen-Tower and the Brückengebäude are appealing locations for any company, and measure up to all of the expectations of the new quarter.

Jochen Boskamp

Blick von Südosten **View from the south-east**

Lageplan **Site plan**

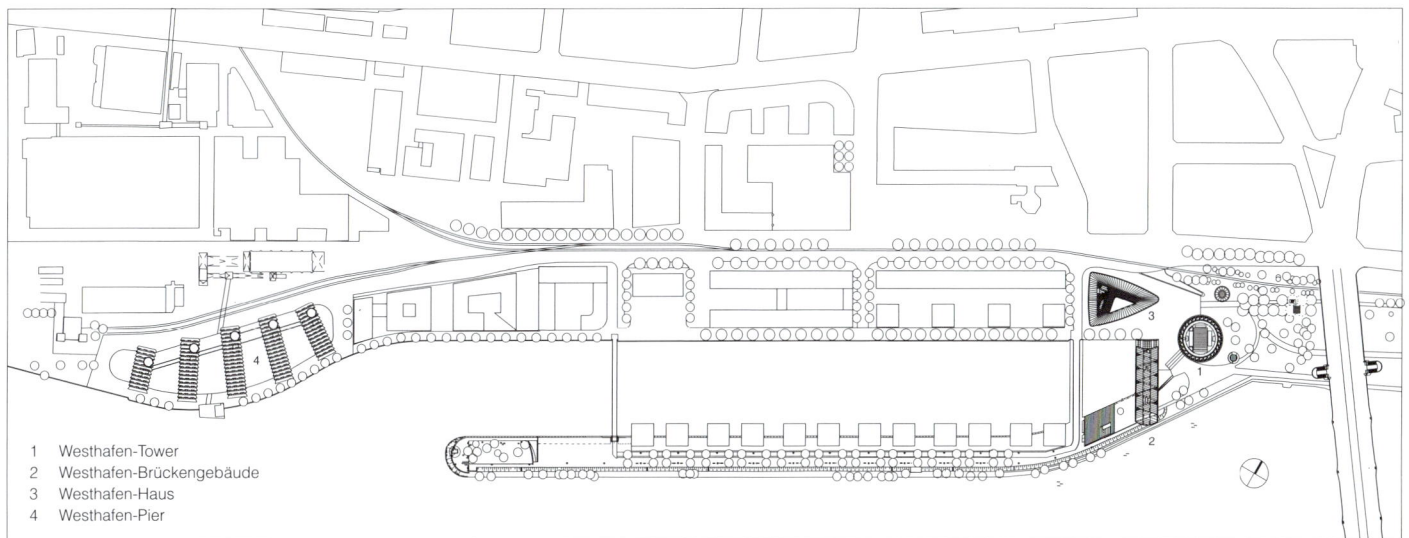

1 Westhafen-Tower
2 Westhafen-Brückengebäude
3 Westhafen-Haus
4 Westhafen-Pier

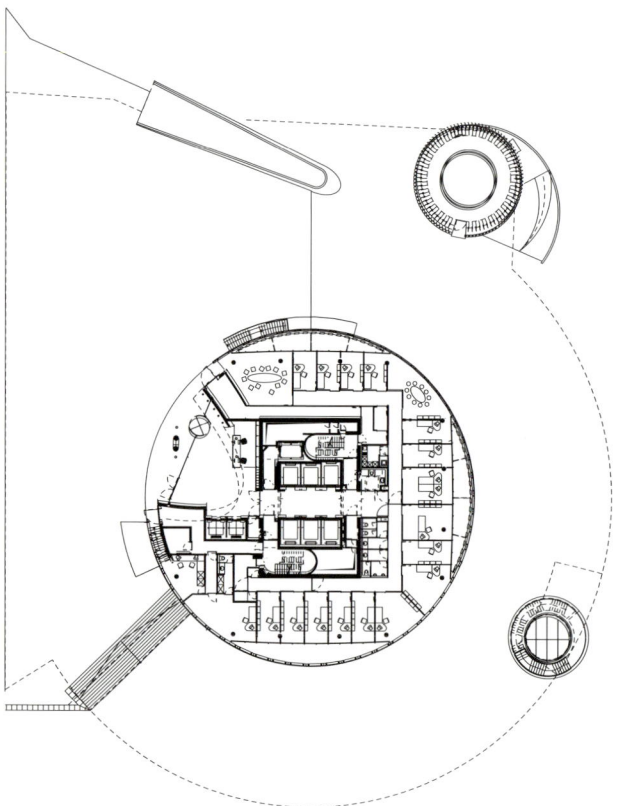

Grundriss Erdgeschoss Westhafen-Tower
Ground-floor plan Westhafen-Tower

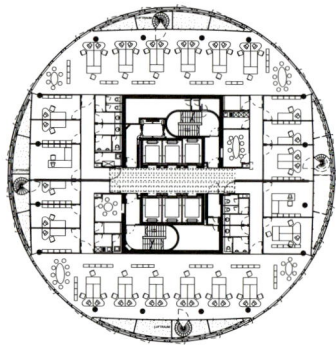

Grundriss Großraumbüros
Ground plan, open-plan offices

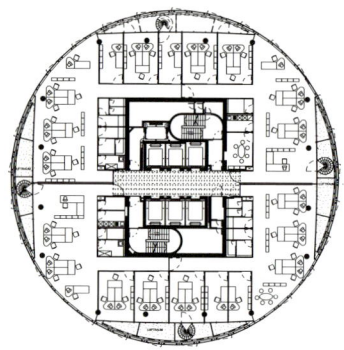

Grundriss Kombibüros
Ground plan, modular offices

Detail der Fassade im Wintergarten des Towers
Facade detail of the winter garden in the Tower

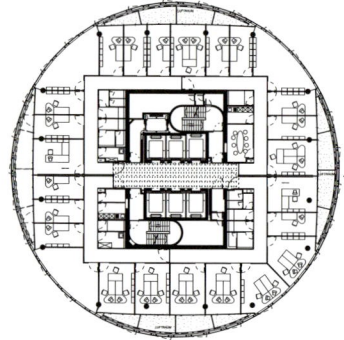

Grundriss Zellenbüros
Ground plan, office cells

Wintergarten im Tower
Winter garden in the Tower

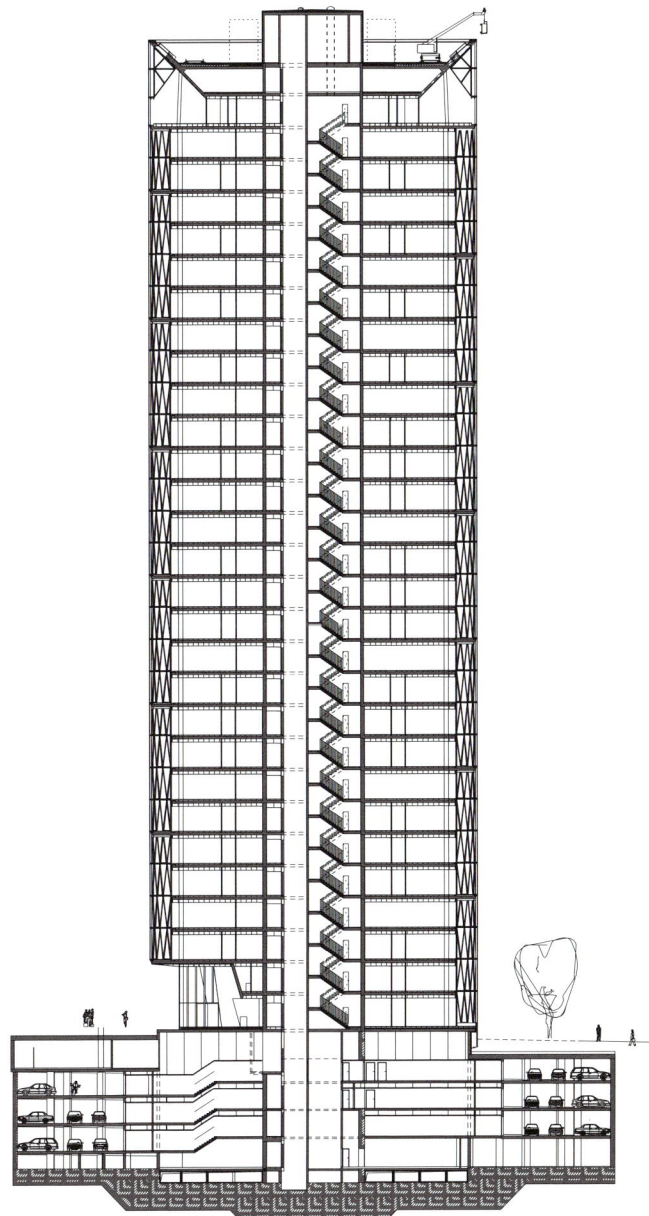

Schnitt Westhafen-Tower
Section Westhafen-Tower

Innenraum im Brückengebäude **Interior of the Brückengebäude**

Arbeitsplatz im Brückengebäude
Workspace in the Brückengebäude

Kindertagesstätte, Berlin
Day-Care Centre, Berlin

Volker Staab

■ Die neue Kindertagesstätte in Berlin Mitte liegt auf einem spitzwinkligen Grundstück zwischen zehngeschossigen Wohnzeilen des DDR-Städtebaus und Resten einer Blockrandbebauung aus dem 19. Jahrhundert. Genauer betrachtet ist das Grundstück Ergebnis einer Grundstücksaktion in der inzwischen hochwertigen Innenstadtlage. Zugunsten von Büroneubauten zur gefälligen Arrondierung des Hausvogteiplatzes wurde der Vorgängerbau dieser Kindertagesstätte auf seinem weiträumigen Grundstück abgerissen und das Grundstück geteilt. Das entsprach dem Ansatz der ›Kritischen Rekonstruktion‹, sich der städtebaulichen und architektonischen ›Sünden‹ der DDR-Zeit zu entledigen, um eine Geschlossenheit im Stadtraum wiederherzustellen und darüber hinaus neue Grundstücke zu erschließen. Der dreigeschossige Fertigbau aus den siebziger Jahren genüge heutigen Anforderungen nicht mehr und solle deswegen ›rückgebaut‹ werden, so die Wettbewerbserläuterungen. Nunmehr lieferte die Restfläche das Ersatzgrundstück für die abgebrochene Kindertagesstätte. Dennoch oder gerade deswegen war die Aufgabe eine besondere Herausforderung für die Teilnehmer des Wettbewerbs.

Volker Staab hat das Problem wunderbar leichtfüßig gelöst und für sein Projekt zu Recht den ersten Preis erhalten. Er setzte an die Straßenkante eine scheinbar einfache Figur: Welche wäre besser geeignet als ein Kubus mit quadratischem Grundriss, ein lagernder Körper, richtungslos, in sich ruhend, Bezüge verweigernd, den Freiraum in seiner tiefen spitzen Ausdehnung belassend? Das Besondere ist die Klarheit des Gebäudes, das präzise in den Ort eingemessen wurde. Es wirkt wie ein Schlussstein im Gewölbe. So kann sich dieses kleine Gebäude neben den mächtigen Nachbarbauten behaupten, ja geradezu versöhnlich wird diese städtebauliche Schnittstelle im Sinne einer Stadtreparatur geschlossen. Nur ist es eine, die auf der Logik des Zusammenspiels einzelner in sich divergierender Teile basiert und nicht auf dem Primat von geschlossenen Straßenfluchten und gleichen Gebäudehöhen, entsprechend einer reduzierten Vorstellung der Stadt des 19. Jahrhunderts. Gerade die Ambivalenz und Widersprüchlichkeit lässt diesen Ort vibrieren und die vielschichtige Geschichte spüren. Das Gebäude von Volker Staab ist damit eine kreative Umsetzung der ›Kritischen Rekonstruktion‹ der Stadt. Wie schon Frank O. Gehry bei der Deutschen Genossenschafts Bank am Pariser Platz in Berlin bewiesen hat, können enge Grenzen Ideen beflügeln, wenn man die Regeln anerkennt, ausreizt und letztendlich sprengt. Das Neue im Bekannten zu finden ist eine gute Voraussetzung für Architektur, gerade wenn sie in Übereinstimmung mit einem sozialen Thema realisiert wurde. An dem Werk von Volker Staab lässt sich das überzeugend nachvollziehen.

Das Gebäude nimmt die archaische Typologie des Hofhauses auf, seine architektonische Interpretation zeigt sich als Raumskulptur, bei der das zentral gelegene Atrium nach unten zu einer Loggia mutiert und sich nach oben zu einer Dachterrasse verschiebt. So erreicht Staab eine direkte und elegante Verschränkung von Außen-

■ The new child day-care centre in central Berlin is located on an angular section of real estate between ten-storey residential blocks typical of Communist planning in former East Germany, and the remains of blocks built in the 19th century. On closer inspection, the site is the result of changes to real-estate lines in what is now the upgraded central business district. In order to build new office blocks that pleasantly set the boundaries to Hausvogteiplatz, the previous day-care centre was torn down and its spacious site was sub-divided. This undertaking was fully in line with the spirit of 'critical reconstruction', whereby the vestiges of urban planning and architectural 'sins' dating from East German days were shed in order to restore unity to the city's fabric and, in addition, to develop new building sites. The statement explaining the architectural competition declared that the three-storey prefabricated centre built in the 1970s no longer met current requirements and therefore had to be 'taken down'. A remaining area was chosen as the new site for the demolished child care centre. In spite of this, or precisely because of this, the task of designing a new centre was a special challenge to the participants of the competition.

Volker Staab found a marvellously uncontrived solution and justifiably won first prize for his project. He placed a seemingly simple form at the edge abutting the road: What could have been more suitable than a cube, with its square footprint, a body sitting heavily without direction this way or that, self-composed, refusing to reference anything, leaving the surrounding space untouched with its deep, angled extension? The clarity is exceptional. The structure was precisely fitted into the available space, as seamlessly as if it were the keystone in a vault. As a consequence, this relatively small building is able to assert itself in the face of mighty neighbours. Indeed, Staab has thus created an interface that reconciles its flanks, repairing the urban setting, as it were. The interface is one based on the logic of the interplay of individual and divergent parts, and not on the primacy of uninterrupted rows of streets on which every building is the same height as once dictated by the conceptual constraints of the 19th century. It is precisely this ambivalence and contradiction which make this place vibrate, and which allow many layers of history to be experienced at once. The building is thus a creative example of the 'critical reconstruction' of the city. As Frank O. Gehry proved with the Deutsche Genossenschafts Bank on Pariser Platz in Berlin, tight borders can inspire ideas when one recognises, provokes and finally disregards the rules. Finding the new within the familiar is a good basis for architecture, especially when it occurs in concordance with a social theme. This is persuasively accomplished by Volker Staab's building.

The day-care centre reflects the archaic typology of a courtyard house; it can be architecturally interpreted as a three-dimensional sculpture in which the central atrium mutates into a loggia in the lower section, and into a roof terrace in the upper section. In this way, Staab dovetails the inside and the outside directly and ele-

Architekten Architects Volker Staab Architekten, Berlin, www.staab-architekten.com; Volker Staab | **Projektpartner** Project partner Alfred Nieuwenhuizen; Team: Madina von Arnim, Birgit Knicker & Alexander Böhme, Nicole Braune, Manuela Jochheim, Saskia Hoffmann, Per Pedersen, Thomas Schmidt, Hanns Ziegler | **Bauherr** Client DSK, Deutsche Stadt- und Grundstücksgesellschaft mbH, Berlin | **Tragwerk** Structural BIG, Beratende Ingenieure für das Bauwesen GmbH, Berlin | **Freianlagen** Landscape LML, Levin Monsigny Landschaftsarchitekten, Berlin | **Wettbewerb** Competition 2000 | **Ausführung** Construction 2001/02 | **Standort** Location Jerusalemer Straße 10, Berlin

und Innenraum bis ins oberste Geschoss. Jede Kindergruppe hat von ihrer Ebene aus einen direkten Zugang zum Garten, und damit ist eine der Anforderungen an mehrgeschossige Kindertagesstätten erfüllt. Die Organisation der Räume ist überschaubar und in nahezu trockener Unerschütterlichkeit stimmig. Das geringe Baubudget ist in seiner sparsamen Umsetzung auf angenehme Weise spürbar, sodass jede gestalterische Feinheit eine besondere Wertschätzung erfährt. Deutlich zeigt sich das Zusammenspiel der begrenzten Mittel und deren bewusster Einsatz beispielsweise bei den sorgfältig geplanten, leicht aufgehellten Sichtbetonwänden. Sie durchbrechen die farbige Hülle aus einfachem Wärmedämmverbundsystem an den großen Öffnungen des Hauses, dem Eingang, der Loggia und der Dachterrasse. Ein ähnlicher Ansatz lässt sich beim äußeren Erscheinungsbild verfolgen: Die horizontal gleichmäßig gegliederte Fassade gewinnt durch das heitere Spiel der Erker mit ihren irritierenden Proportionen eine besondere Aufmerksamkeit. Diese Erker könnten architektonische Spielerei sein, ahnte der Betrachter nicht bereits von außen, was sich im Innern bestätigt: Als ›Glasnester‹ sind sie besondere Orte, die aufgrund ihrer niedrigen Höhe für Erwachsene ungeeignet sind, Kindern aber wunderbare Rückzugsorte bieten mit freiem Blick auf die Stadt. Weil die Akzente insgesamt sparsam gesetzt sind, erhalten sie eine besondere Betonung in einem Projekt, dessen Gesamtkonzept, von der räumlichen Gliederung bis in die Details der Lichtführung, Einbauten und gezielten Farbsetzungen, sorgfältig und diszipliniert ist.

Aus einer vernachlässigten Fläche in der Stadt ist so ein öffentlicher Ort entstanden. Architektur könnte erstaunlich einfach und überzeugend erscheinen, wenn man nicht wüsste, wie viel Kraft, Durchhaltevermögen und inhaltliche Stringenz dazu gehören, sie so klar und so poetisch zur Wirkung zu bringen.

Hilde Léon

gantly, all the way through to the top floor. The groups of children on each floor have direct access to the garden, thus fulfilling a requirement of multi-storey child day-care centres. The inner space of the building has been logically structured and its organisation is almost unshakeably coherent. One can sense the cautious yet pleasant way in which the small budget was brought to bear. Each detail in the plan is thus accorded a special significance. The interaction of limited financial resources and their conscious use is exemplified by the carefully planned, fair-faced concrete walls, which have been given a slightly lighter colour. At the major openings to the building – the entrance, the loggia, and the roof terrace – they break through the colourful outer shell with its simple compound heat-insulating system. A similar approach is to be seen on the exterior. The regular horizontal subdivisions of the facade are enhanced by cheerful bay windows, eye-catching in their unsettling proportions. These bays could be viewed as playfulness on the part of the architect, were the view inside the building not to confirm a suspicion aroused by the outside: These 'glass nests' are special places that were built not with adults in mind – the ceilings are too low – but for children, as wonderful retreats with unobstructed views of the city. The building stands out for its sparing use of highlights, which are thus lent special emphasis. From the sub-division of the available space through to the details of light, furnishings and the deliberate colour choices, the entire concept underlying the project is disciplined and carefully planned.

A neglected area of the city has been transformed into a living, public place. And the architecture would seem amazingly simple and satisfying if one did not know how much strength, perseverance and stringency of purpose were invested in creating a poetic object of such clarity.

Hilde Léon

1 Foyer **Foyer**
2 Gruppenraum **Group room**
3 Terrasse **Terrace**
4 Therapieraum **Therapy room**
5 Büro **Office**
6 Personalraum **Staff room**
7 Küche **Kitchen**

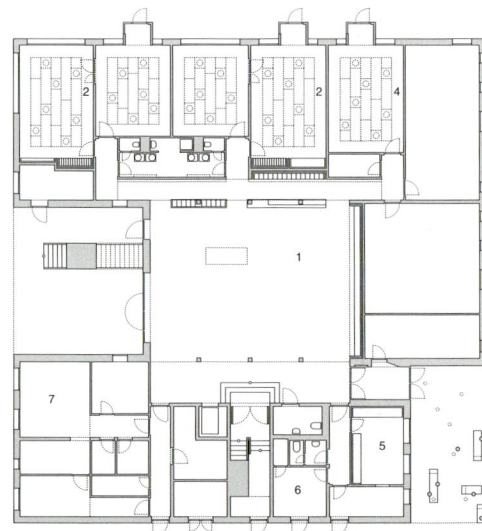

Grundriss Erdgeschoss **Ground-floor plan**

Blick von Südosten **View from the south-east**

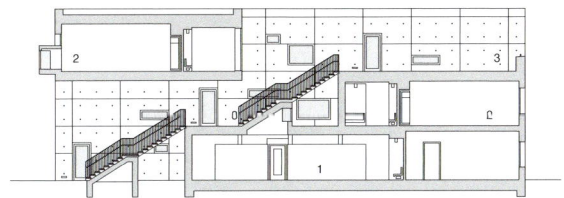

Schnitt **Section**

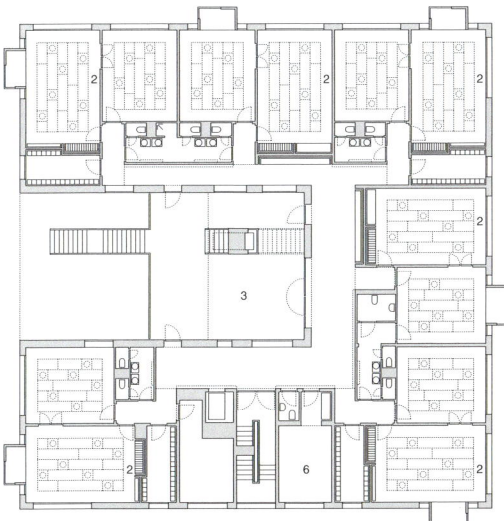

Grundriss 1. Obergeschoss **First-floor plan**

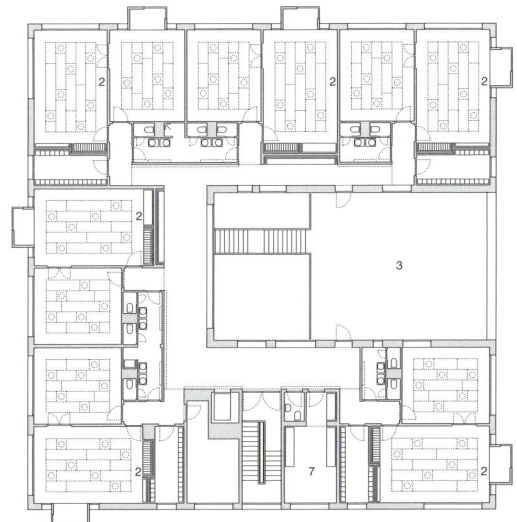

Grundriss 2. Obergeschoss **Second-floor plan**

Terrasse 1. Obergeschoss   **Terrace, first floor**

Gang 2. Obergeschoss   **Corridor, second floor**

Südfassade
South facade

Spielerker   **Playing bay**

" ... PREISET DEN HERRN, SONNE UND MOND;
PREISET DEN HERRN DES HIMMELS STERNE, ... "

(BENEDICITE)

2

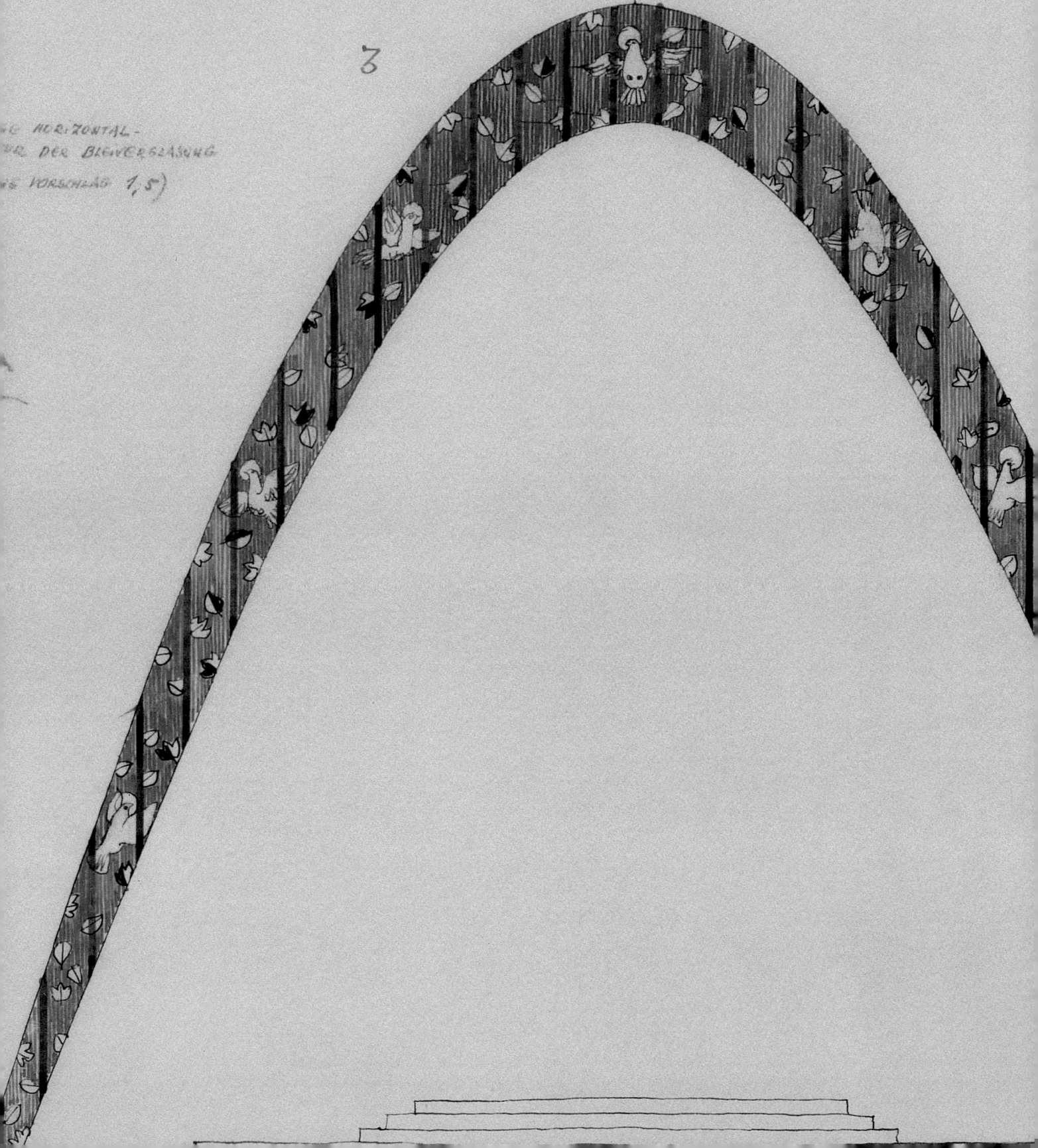

Sakrale Orte – Kirchenbauten von Emil Steffann (1899–1968)
Sacred Places – the Religious Architecture of Emil Steffann (1899–1968)

Inge Wolf

Scheunenkirche, Boust, Lothringen, Frankreich, 1943 **Barn Church, Boust, Lorraine, France, 1943**

■ Kirchen, Klöster und Gemeindezentren – es sind sakrale Orte, die das Werk von Emil Steffann prägen. Und so kommt man an ihm nicht vorbei, wenn man mit Blick auf das aktuelle Thema des Jahrbuchs aus der Sammlung des Deutschen Architektur Museums berichten möchte. Wie der Weggenosse und von ihm selbst als Lehrer bezeichnete Rudolf Schwarz (1897–1961) steht auch Emil Steffann in der Reihe der Architekten, deren Namen mit wegweisenden Kirchenbauten verbunden sind. Als es nach 1945 um die Beseitigung der Kriegsschäden ging, gehörte auch der Kirchenbau zu den anstehenden Bauaufgaben. In den Nachkriegsjahren bis 1960 wurden in Deutschland mehr Kirchen errichtet als jemals zuvor in vergleichbarer Zeitspanne.

Glaube und Liturgie sowie Armut und Einfachheit sind Begriffe, die fallen, wenn man sich mit Steffann auseinander setzt.[1] Assisi und die Begegnung mit Rudolf Schwarz sind zu nennen. Die Stadt des heiligen Franziskus wurde 1926 zum Wendepunkt in Steffanns Leben. Während seines Aufenthalts in Umbrien konvertierte er zum katholischen Glauben. Hier wurde er sich darüber klar, dass er als

■ Churches, monasteries and parish community centres – the œuvre of Emil Steffann is marked by sacred places. And so, given the topic theme of this year's publication on the collection of the Deutsches Architektur Museum, we take a closer look at this architect's work. Like his contemporary Rudolf Schwarz (1897–1961), described by Steffann himself as his mentor, Emil Steffann ranks among those whose names are associated with the creation of ground-breaking religious architecture. In 1945, the task of rebuilding in the wake of wartime destruction included the construction of churches. During no other period in history did Germany see so many churches built within such a short space of time as in the post-war years up to 1960.

Faith and liturgy, poverty and simplicity – these are the words that spring to mind when considering the work of Emil Steffann.[1] The town of Assisi and the architect Rudolf Schwarz were both important influences. In 1926, the city of St Francis marked a turning point in Steffann's life. It was while he was staying in Umbria that he converted to the Catholic faith, and it was here, too, that he realised

Architekt arbeiten wollte. Zurück in Lübeck, absolvierte er eine private Ausbildung, danach folgten Volontariat und erste bescheidene Bauaufgaben.

Mit Rudolf Schwarz trat er 1931 nach Besuch von dessen Fronleichnamskirche in Aachen (siehe S. 24) in Kontakt. Schwarz führte Steffann in den Rothenfelser Kreis der katholischen Jugend ein. Durch ihn lernte er den Theologen Romano Guardini kennen, der zu den bedeutenden Vertretern der Liturgischen Bewegung zählt. Die um den Altar versammelte Gemeinschaft der Gläubigen, die bewusste und tätige Teilnahme des ganzen Volkes an liturgischen Feiern, war eine Forderung, zu deren Durchsetzung Guardini beim Zweiten Vatikanischen Konzil (1961–1965) beitragen sollte. Steffann blieb nicht unbeeinflusst. Spätere Kirchenbauten zeigen dies.

Schwarz war es auch, der dafür sorgte, dass Steffann während des Zweiten Weltkriegs beim Wiederaufbau in Lothringen zum Einsatz kam. In der regionalen Architektur, in den Häusern, gemauert aus dem ortstypischen graugelben Sandstein, sah Steffann »die zeitlose Urform des Bauens in Stein«[2] bewahrt. Zu den Aufgaben in Lothringen zählte der Wiederaufbau des zu 80 Prozent zerstörten Dorfes Boust. Die große Gemeinschaftsscheune, die Steffann hier 1943 errichtete, plante er als späteren Kirchenbau. Die Skizzen im Nachlass sind eindeutig, wenn sie das Gebäude als ›Scheunenkirche‹ ausweisen. Aus Trümmersteinen entstand ein Bauwerk, das in seiner Schlichtheit später vielen als vorbildlich für den Kirchenbau galt.

Wie sollte man im Deutschland nach 1945 mit Kirchenruinen umgehen? Steffann sah seine Aufgabe darin, Räume zu schaffen, die der Liturgie und den Bedürfnissen der Gemeinde Rechnung trugen. Die Berücksichtigung der erhaltenen Gebäudereste und mehr noch die Wiederverwertung des Trümmermaterials standen für ihn außer Frage. Auf einer seiner Zeichnungen hielt er fest: »Die Schutthalde ist ein idealer Baukasten voll Anregung für unsere Phantasie, seine verachteten Kostbarkeiten nicht achtlos fortzuschaffen, sondern ein Neues aus ihnen entstehen zu lassen, welches die schweren Verwundungen, die uns trafen, nicht verschweigt.«[3] Beispiele findet man im Wiederaufbau von Kloster und Kirche St. Franziskus in Köln und in der vielfach als vorbildlich angesehenen Kirche St. Bonifatius in Dortmund.

Von der neuromanischen Bonifatiuskirche aus dem Jahr 1910 ragten nach der Zerstörung 1944 nur noch die Türme in den Himmel. Drei von ihnen blieben im Neubau erhalten. Zwischen diesen entstand von 1952 bis 1958 aus dem Trümmermaterial des Vorgängerbaus die neue Kirche, die durch unterschiedliche Nebengebäude und Hofanlagen ergänzt wurde. Der Besucher nähert sich über den Vorhof im Westen. Er passiert das große Westfenster, das den Blick nach innen zulässt. Über eine Vorhalle kann der Kirchenraum von Südwesten her betreten werden. Auch vom Pfarrhof, der südlich an die Kirche angrenzt, ermöglicht ein großes Fenster den Blick nach innen, auf den Altar. Beim Betreten findet man statt der ursprüng-

St. Bonifatius, Dortmund, Deutschland, 1958
St Boniface, Dortmund, Germany, 1958

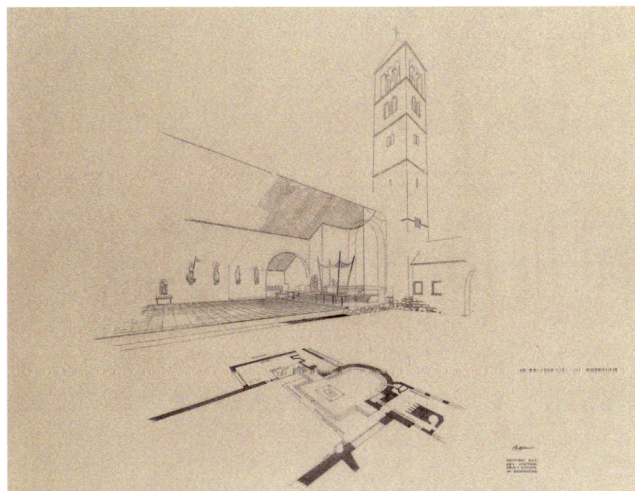

St. Bonifatius, Dortmund, Deutschland, 1958, perspektivischer Schnitt und Grundriss
St Boniface, Dortmund, Germany, 1958, perspective section and ground plan

St. Bonifatius, Dortmund, Deutschland, 1958
St Boniface, Dortmund, Germany, 1958

St. Laurentius, München, Deutschland, 1955 **St Laurence, Munich, Germany, 1955**

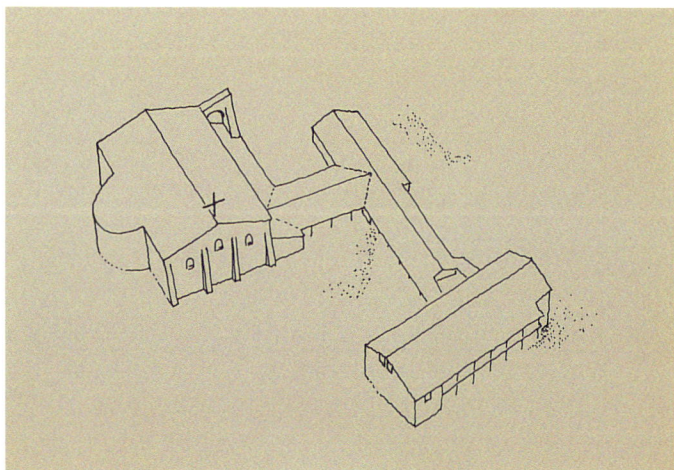

St. Laurentius, München, Deutschland, 1955, Vogelperspektive
St Laurence, Munich, Germany, 1955, a bird's-eye view

lichen dreischiffigen Basilika eine weite stützenfreie Halle vor. Im Gegensatz zur rauen Steinwand außen sieht man glatte weiße Wandflächen. Ein weit gespannter Bogen öffnet den Raum im Norden zur Werktagskapelle. Von dort gelangt man zur kleinen abgeschlossenen Sakramentskapelle, die auch direkt von außen betreten wer-

that he wanted to work as an architect. On his return to Lübeck, he trained privately and took on his first modest building projects.

He contacted Rudolf Schwarz after seeing his Frohnleichnamskirche in Aix-la-Chapelle in 1931 (see p. 24). Schwarz introduced Steffann to the Catholic youth community known as the Rothenfelser Kreis, and it was also through Schwarz that he met the theologian Romano Guardini, one of the leading proponents of the movement for liturgical reform. The community of worshippers gathering around the altar and actively participating in the concelebration of the Mass were among the aspects of liturgical renewal that Guardini helped to implement at the Second Vatican Council (1961–65). Steffann was not unaffected by these changes, as his later church buildings clearly show.

It was Schwarz who ensured that Steffann became involved in the post-World War Two reconstruction in Lorraine. Steffann saw the regional vernacular of greyish-yellow sandstone houses as a reflection of "the timeless primordial form of building in stone".[2] His work in Lorraine included rebuilding the village of Boust, eighty per cent of which had been destroyed. The vast village barn that Steffann built there in 1943 was destined to become a church. This is clearly stipulated in the plans found after his death designating the building as a "barn church". Erected from the stones of the village ruins,

179

Sakrale Orte – Kirchenbauten von Emil Steffann (1899–1968)
Sacred Places – the Religious Architecture of Emil Steffann (1899–1968)

St. Laurentius, München, Deutschland, 1955, Grundriss   **St Laurence, Munich, Germany, 1955, ground plan**

St. Laurentius, München, Deutschland, 1955
St Laurence, Munich, Germany, 1955

den kann. Der Hauptaltar der Kirche steht weit vor der Apsis, auch von der Werktagskapelle her gut einsehbar. Von ihm getrennt ist der Tabernakel, der mit dem Sakramentsaltar an die Schnittstelle der drei Kirchenbereiche gerückt wird. Anerkannt ist die Fortschrittlichkeit der Raumauffassung, die Beschlüsse des Zweiten Vatikanischen Konzils

its simplicity was later widely hailed as exemplary in the field of church design.

In response to the question of how to deal with church ruins in Germany after 1945, Steffann sought to create spaces that accommodated liturgical requirements and the pastoral needs of the community. For Steffann, it went without saying that any structural remains and materials should be used in the new building. "The heap of rubble is an ideal building set that fires the imagination, urging us not to abandon these broken treasures thoughtlessly but to transform them into something new that will not gloss over the deep wounds inflicted upon us."[3] Examples of this approach can be found in his reconstruction of the monastery and church of St Francis in Cologne, and his highly accoladed church of St Boniface in Dortmund.

After the bombing of 1944, all that remained of the neo-Romanesque church of St Boniface from 1910 was its towers. Three of these were integrated into the new building, with the new church constructed between them using the material from the ruins and extended to include various outbuildings and courtyards. Visitors to the church approach it from the west, crossing the forecourt and passing by the great west window that offers a view into the interior. The church can be entered from the south-west through a porch.

180

Sakrale Orte – Kirchenbauten von Emil Steffann (1899–1968)
Sacred Places – the Religious Architecture of Emil Steffann (1899–1968)

St. Bonifatius, Lübeck, Deutschland, 1952 **St Boniface, Lübeck, Germany, 1952**

vorwegzunehmen scheint. Bauherren waren die Oratorianer, eine Priestergemeinschaft, die der liturgischen Bewegung nahe stand und eine Rolle in der Vorbereitung des Konzils übernahm.

St. Laurentius in München (1952–1955) ist ein weiterer Kirchenbau, den Steffann im Auftrag der Oratorianer plante: ein Komplex bestehend aus Kirche und Sakristei, Wohnhaus, Gemeindesaal und Jugendräumen. Steffann schuf ein Ensemble aus miteinander verbundenen Gebäudetrakten aus Ziegelstein, das er in die natürliche Mulde des Baugeländes einbettete. Die Kirche, Teil des Ganzen, ist ein breiter gedrungener Bau mit flachem Satteldach. Es gibt keinen Turm, nur einen Glockenträger, der als Fortsetzung der nördlichen Giebelwand aufgefasst werden kann. Die Scheunenkirche tritt in Erinnerung. Die Giebelwände nach Norden und Süden werden verstärkt durch jeweils vier mächtige Strebepfeiler, und man sieht die einfachen Rundbögen der Tür- und Fensteröffnungen. Die fensterlose Westwand weitet sich zur Konche, die im Inneren den Altarraum

The parsonage courtyard to the south of the church also has a large window offering views of the interior and the altar. On entering the church, one finds a wide hall with no supporting columns instead of the original three-aisled basilica. In contrast to the rough stone masonry of the exterior, the interior walls are smooth and white. To the north, a broad-spanned arc opens up the space towards the weekday chapel. From there, one can enter the small, enclosed sacramental chapel, a space that is also directly accessible from the outside. The main altar of the church is placed at a considerable distance from the apse and can be easily seen from the weekday chapel. Separated from this is the tabernacle, which, together with the sacramental altar, is positioned at the point of intersection of the three church areas. This spatial arrangement, widely recognised as progressive, seems to anticipate the resolutions of the Second Vatican Council. The church was commissioned by the Oratorians, a community of priests closely associated with the move towards

181

Sakrale Orte – Kirchenbauten von Emil Steffann (1899–1968)
Sacred Places – the Religious Architecture of Emil Steffann (1899–1968)

hinterfängt. Man betritt die Kirche im Südosten und steht in einer schmalen Vorhalle, die sich wie ein niedriges Seitenschiff im Osten an die Kirche anlegt. Eine Arkadenreihe öffnet sie zum Hauptraum. Weit zur Mitte hin gerückt der Altar auf erhöhtem Podest, an drei Seiten umgibt ihn das Kirchengestühl. Zur Konche hin schließt die halbrunde Priesterbank den erhöhten Altarbereich ab. Ganz im Sinne der Liturgischen Bewegung gruppiert sich die Gemeinde um das Zentrum. Tabernakel und Sakramentaltar sind im Nordbereich der Vorhalle untergebracht, hier ist intime Andacht möglich. Für den nachkonziliaren Kirchenbau sollte St. Laurentius Vorbildcharakter gewinnen. Auch die schmucklose Weite des quer liegenden Kirchenraums mit den weiß geschlämmten Ziegelwänden und der einfachen Bretterdecke wurde als richtungweisend empfunden.

Eher ungewöhnlich für das Œuvre Steffanns ist die Kirche St. Bonifatius in Lübeck. Von 1951 bis 1952 entstand ein Gewölbebau im System Trautsch-Pieper. Dieses System war zuvor beim Wiederaufbau des Daches der Lübecker Marienkirche zum Einsatz gekommen. Steffann machte das Dach zur Kirche. Über Holzlehren baute man ein Gewölbe aus Schlackenbetonsteinen und eisenarmierten Betonrippen auf. Es entstand ein längs gerichteter Raum, parabelförmig überwölbt. »Der Sonderfall« titelt Susanne Grexa in ihrer Doktorarbeit.[4] Sie nennt Vorbilder und verweist dabei auch auf die Schrift *Vom Bau der Kirche*, die Rudolf Schwarz 1938 veröffentlichte. Er illustrierte seine Planfigur *Heilige Fahrt (Der Weg)* mit Skizzen eines tonnenüberwölbten Raums. Steffanns Wegekirche wird erhellt durch ein großes Fenster in der westlichen Eingangswand. Der Blick des Besuchers wird auf den Altar gegenüber gelenkt, dieser geborgen von der muschelförmigen Wand, die den Kirchenraum nach Osten hin abschließt. Die gemauerte Wandschale ist freitragend, ein schmales Fensterband folgt der Parabel der Wölbung und rahmt den Altar ein. Über den Außenbereich lesen wir auf einer von Steffanns Entwurfsskizzen: »Es wird vorgeschlagen, einen klosterhofähnlichen Vorgarten vor der Kirche zu schaffen, welcher den aus der Hast und Unruhe des öffentlichen Lebens kommenden Kirchenbesucher beim Durchschreiten zur Besinnung und Sammlung führt. Das große Fenster lädt zum Eintritt in die Kirche ein. Es öffnet sich zugleich der Außenwelt […]. In dieser Spannung der Abgeschlossenheit und des Geöffnetseins ist der Sinn der Anlage zu sehen.«[5] Wie bei St. Bonifatius in Dortmund beschreitet man einen Weg, der in die Kirche und zum Altar führt. Hier wie dort kommuniziert das Innen mit dem Außen.

Steffanns sakrale Räume sollen den Menschen aufnehmen. Die stufenweise Annäherung von außen an den Innenraum ist bedeutsam. 1932 hatte er in Lübeck eine Fronleichnamsprozession gestaltet, welche die Gläubigen von allen vier Seiten an den im Freien aufgebauten Altar heranführte. Ein undatiertes Manuskript aus seinem Nachlass hält fest, was Steffann empfand: »Jeder konnte von jedem Platz sehen und mitfeiern. [...] Der Gottesdienst richtet sich [...] allein nach innen zum Altar. Die Gemeinde selbst bildet die Grenze. Dem nach den 4 Himmelsrichtungen erteilten Segen waren allerdings keine Grenzen gesetzt.«[6] Er schreibt auch, dass »diese Prozession zum Leitbild wurde, mehr oder minder für alle Kirchen, die ich später bauen durfte, die mir aber so [...] nie mehr gelangen«.[7]

St. Bonifatius, Lübeck, Deutschland, 1952, Entwurfsskizze
St Boniface, Lübeck, Germany, 1952, preliminary drawing

liturgical renewal, a group also involved in the preparations for the Council.

St Laurence in Munich (1952–55) is another church designed by Steffann for the Oratorians: a complex consisting of church, sacristy, dwelling house, parish hall and youth centre. Steffann created an ensemble of linked brick-built tracts couched in the natural hollow of the site. The church itself is a broad, squat building with a low saddle-backed roof. There is no tower, but only a bell holder which forms a continuation of the northern gable wall. There are echoes here of the "barn church". The gable walls on the north and south are each reinforced by four massive buttresses, and one can see the simple rounded arches of the door and window apertures. The windowless west wall opens up into a concha that forms a backdrop to the sanctuary inside. Entering the church from the south-east, the visitor stands in a narrow porch attached to the east side of the church like a low side aisle. A row of arcades opens it up to the main space. Towards the centre, the altar stands on an elevated platform surrounded on three sides by pews with the semi-circular priests' bench on the concha side. In keeping with the concept of liturgical renewal, the congregation is gathered around the centre. The tabernacle and the sacramental altar are situated in the northern area of

182

Sakrale Orte – Kirchenbauten von Emil Steffann (1899–1968)
Sacred Places – the Religious Architecture of Emil Steffann (1899–1968)

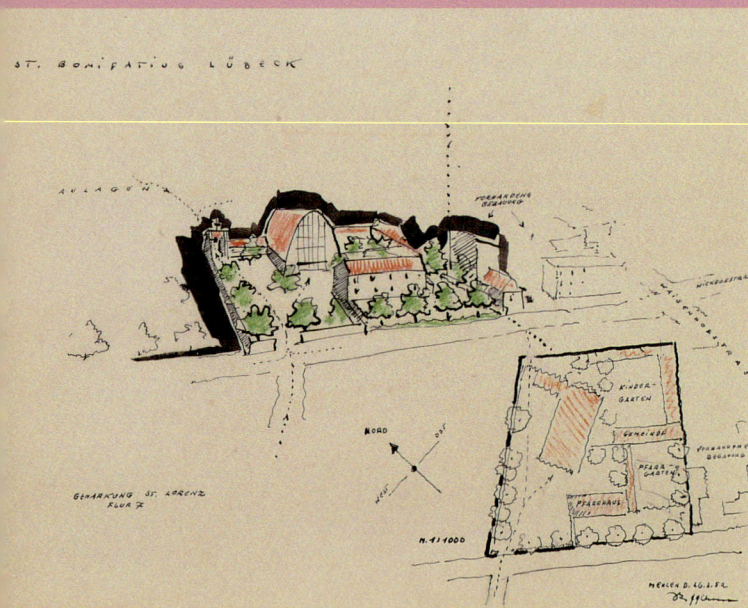

St. Bonifatius, Lübeck, Deutschland, 1952, Entwurfsskizze Gesamtanlage
St Bonifatice, Lübeck, Germany, 1952, Overall complex preliminary drawing

Man findet bei Steffann eine zeitlose Architektur, die auf handwerkliche Techniken setzt. Man denkt an die raue Wand, solide gemauert und mit altbewährter Rundbogenöffnung, doch weiß man auch, dass er keiner war, der sich technischen Neuerungen verschloss. *Von einer inneren Ordnung der Räume*[8] oder *Vollkommene Einfachheit*[9] lauten Titel von Artikeln, die sich mit der Architektur von Steffann auseinander setzen. Wolfgang Pehnt fasst zusammen: »Bei Steffann fanden sich wieder und wieder Erinnerungen an jenen Eindruck, den Lothringens verschlossene Baukultur während des Krieges auf ihn […] gemacht hatte. Steffanns Sakralbauten besaßen eine Wärme und Nähe der Gemeinde zu den wichtigsten liturgischen Orten, die sie zu einem Vorbild jüngerer Kirchenbauer nach dem Zweiten Vatikanum werden ließen – und in Deutschland zu einem stillen Gegenpol zur Formensensation von Ronchamp.«[10] (siehe S. 19)

Das Werkverzeichnis von Steffann nennt mehr als 40 Kirchen- und Klosterbauten. Es ist seinen ehemaligen Mitarbeitern Nikolaus Rosiny und Gisberth Hülsmann zu danken, dass 1986, nahezu 20 Jahre nach dem Tod des Architekten, eine geschlossene Sammlung, die mehr als 5 500 Zeichnungen und Pläne, dazu Modelle, reiches Fotomaterial und wichtige Schriftdokumente umfasst, an das Deutsche Architektur Museum übergeben werden konnte.

1 Zum Werk Emil Steffanns sind folgende Publikationen zu empfehlen, die weiterführende Literaturangaben enthalten: Gisbert Hülsmann (Hrsg.), *Emil Steffann,* Bd. 18 der Schriftenreihe Architektur und Denkmalpflege der Akademie der Architektenkammer Nordrhein-Westfalen und der Deutschen UNESCO-Kommission, Ausst. Kat. Kunsthalle Bielefeld 1981, 3. Aufl., Bonn 1984; Conrad Lienhardt (Hrsg.), *Emil Steffann (1899–1968). Werk. Theorie. Wirkung,* Bd. 2 der Reihe Kirchenbau der Diözese Linz, Ausst. Kat., 1999; Susanne Grexa, *Der Architekt Emil Steffann. 1899–1968. Der Verzicht auf Originalität als Programm,* Inaugural-Dissertation zur Erlangung der Doktorwürde des Fachbereichs Neuere Deutsche Literatur und Kunstwissenschaften der Philipps-Universität Marburg, Marburg 1996; Wolfgang Pehnt, *Die Baukunst ein Wissen des Herzens. Emil Steffann und Rudolf Schwarz: eine Freundschaft und ein Kapitel deutscher Architekturgeschichte,* Vortrag anlässlich des Symposiums Der Wille zur Gestalt. In memoriam Rolf Gutbrod 1910–1999, Universität Stuttgart, Dezember 1999, www.uni-stuttgart.de.
2 Emil Steffann, *Baufibel für Lothringen,* Typoskript, um 1943, Sammlung Deutsches Architektur Museum, Frankfurt/M., S. 3.

the porch, providing an intimate atmosphere of contemplation and devotion. The unadorned expanse of the church with its white plastered brick walls and simple ceiling planks have been greeted as a forward-looking design.

The church of St Boniface in Lübeck is something of an exception in Steffann's œuvre. It was built between 1951 and 1952 using the Trautsch-Pieper system of vault construction that had already been employed for the reconstruction of the roof of the Marienkirche in Lübeck. Steffann made the roof itself into the church. A slag concrete vault was constructed over wooden rafters and reinforced concrete ribs to create an elongated room with parabolic vaulting. Susanne Grexa's doctoral thesis describes it as a "special case" (*Sonderfall*) and presents its precursors, with reference to Rudolf Schwarz's treatise on ecclesiastic architecture, *Vom Bau der Kirche,* published in 1938.[4] He illustrated his plan of a "sacred journey" (*Heilige Fahrt* (*Der Weg*)) with sketches of a barrel-vaulted room. Steffann's pilgrimage church is illuminated by a large window in the western entrance wall. The visitor's gaze is guided towards the altar opposite, sheltered by the shell-shaped wall at the east end of the church interior. The masonry shell is self-supporting, with a narrow band of windows following the parabola of the vault and framing the altar. In one of Steffann's sketches for the design, he wrote above the outer area: "It is proposed that a cloister type garden should be created in front of the church so that visitors entering it from the hustle and bustle of public life can find calm and inner peace. The large window invites you to enter the church. At the same time it opens up to the outside world... The meaning of the complex as a whole is to be found in this tension between the closed and the open."[5] As in the church of St Boniface in Dortmund, the visitor walks a path that leads into the church and towards the altar. In both, there is a dialogue between interior and exterior.

Steffann's religious spaces are intended to welcome people. The gradual approach from outside to inside is significant. In 1932, he designed a Corpus Christi procession that led the faithful towards the open-air altar from all four sides. An undated manuscript found among his papers documents how he felt about this: "Anyone can look on and participate from any position… The religious service is directed inwardly towards the altar. The congregation itself forms the boundary. There is no boundary to the blessings given in all four directions."[6] He also writes that, "This procession became the model for more or less all the churches I was to build later, though they never again succeeded to this extent..."[7]

Steffann's timeless architecture is based on artisanal techniques – consider the rough masonry of the walls with their traditional round-arched apertures – and yet he was no stranger to technical innovation. Articles examining Steffann's architecture bear such titles as "Von einer inneren Ordnung der Räume" (From the inner order of room) or "Vollkommene Einfachheit." (Complete Simplicitiy)[8,9] Wolfgang Pehnt concludes that, "Steffann's work constantly recalls the impression that the undiscovered architecture of Lorraine made upon him during the war… Steffann's religious buildings possess a certain warmth and bring the religious community close to the most important places of the liturgy, making them models for younger

Sakrale Orte – Kirchenbauten von Emil Steffann (1899–1968)
Sacred Places – the Religious Architecture of Emil Steffann (1899–1968)

183

St. Bonifatius, Lübeck, Deutschland, 1952   **St Boniface, Lübeck, Germany, 1952**

church architects after the Second Vatican Council – and, in Germany, a quiet counterpoint to the sensational forms of Ronchamp."[10] (see p. 19)

The catalogue raisonné of Steffann's work lists more than forty churches and monasteries. It is to the credit of his colleagues Nikolaus Rosiny and Gisberth Hülsmann that, in 1986, twenty years after Steffann's death, a complete collection comprising more than 5,500 drawings and plans as well as models, photographs and key documents, could be acquired by the Deutsches Architektur Museum.

1 The following publications offer further reading on the works of Emil Steffann: Gisbert Hülsmann (ed.), *Emil Steffann*, vol. 18 in the series *Architektur und Denkmalpflege* from the Akademie der Architektenkammer Nordrhein-Westfalen and the German UNESCO Commission, exh. cat., Kunsthalle Bielefeld (1981), 3rd edition, Bonn, 1984; Conrad Lienhardt (ed.), *Emil Steffann (1899–1968). Werk. Theorie. Wirkung*, vol. 2 in the series *Kirchenbau*, Diözese Linz, exh. cat., 1999; Susanne Grexa, *Der Architekt Emil Steffann. 1899–1968. Der Verzicht auf Originalität als Programm*, inaugural dissertation for the attainment of the doctorarte in the specialised area. Neuere deutsche Literatur und Kunstwissenschaften at the Philipps-Universität Marburg, Marburg, 1996; Wolfgang Pehnt, *Die Baukunst, ein Wissen des Herzens. Emil Steffann und Rudolf Schwarz: eine Freundschaft und ein Kapitel deutscher Architekturgeschichte*, lecture at the symposium entitled *Der Wille zur Gestalt. In memoriam Rolf Gutbrod 1910–1999*, Stuttgart University, December 1999, www.uni-stuttgart.de.

2 Emil Steffann, *Baufibel für Lothringen*, ca. 1943, typoscript, Collection of the Deutsches Architektur Museum, Frankfurt/Main, p. 3.

3 The Estate of Emil Steffann, Collection of the Deutsches Architektur Museum, Frankfurt/Main, Inv. Nr. 001-041-027.

4 Susanne Grexa, ibid., p. 127 ff.

5 The Estate of Emil Steffann, Collection of the Deutsches Architektur Museum, Frankfurt/Main, Inv. Nr. 001-038-031.

6 "Not und Notwendigkeit im heutigen Kirchenbau", in Conrad Lienhardt (ed.), *Emil Steffann (1899–1968). Werk. Theorie. Wirkung*, vol. 2 in the series *Kirchenbau der Diözese Linz*, exh. cat., 1999, p. 63.

7 Ibid.

8 "Erinnerung an Emil Steffann. 30. 1. 1899–23. 7. 1968. Von einer inneren Ordnung der Räume", in *Bauwelt* 70, 19/1979, p. 776–87.

9 "Vollkommene Einfachheit", in *Die Zeit*, 5 December 1980.

10 Wolfgang Pehnt, "Groß im Kleinen", in *Heinz Dienefeld 1926–1995*, Wolfgang Voigt (ed.), Tübingen and Berlin, 1998, p.14.

3 Nachlass Emil Steffann, Sammlung Deutsches Architektur Museum, Frankfurt/M., Inv.Nr. 001-041-027.

4 Susanne Grexa, wie Anm. 1, S. 127 ff.

5 Nachlass Emil Steffann, Sammlung Deutsches Architektur Museum, Frankfurt/M., Inv.Nr. 001-038-031.

6 Zit. nach: Emil Steffann, *Not und Notwendigkeit im heutigen Kirchenbau*, in: Conrad Lienhardt (Hrsg.) *Emil Steffann (1899–1968). Werk. Theorie. Wirkung*, Bd. 2 der Reihe Kirchenbau der Diözese Linz, Ausst. Kat., 1999, S. 63.

7 Ebd.

8 *Erinnerung an Emil Steffann. 30.1.1899–23.7.1968. Von einer inneren Ordnung der Räume*, in: *Bauwelt* Nr. 70, 19/1979, S. 776–787.

9 *Vollkommene Einfachheit*, in: *Die Zeit*, 5.12.1980.

10 Wolfgang Pehnt, *Groß im Kleinen*, in: *Heinz Bienefeld 1926–1995*, hrsg. von Wolfgang Voigt, Tübingen und Berlin 1998, S.14.

DAM Jahresbericht 2002/03
Annual Report 2002–03

Das Deutsche Architektur Museum (DAM) zeigte 2002/03 folgende
große Ausstellungen:
**In 2002/03 the Deutsches Architektur Museum (DAM) hosted the following
exhibitions:**

- Aldo Rossi. Die Suche nach dem Glück.
  Frühe Zeichnungen und Entwürfe.
- **Aldo Rossi. The Quest for Happiness. Early Sketches and Designs.**
  16.08.2003–09.11.2003
- »Schönheit ruht in der Ordnung.«
  Der Architekt Paul Schmitthenner 1884–1972.
- **"Beauty is Based on Order." The Architect Paul Schmitthenner, 1884–1972.**
  16.08.2003–09.11.2003
- Lehm-Moscheen in Mali. Fotografien von Sebastian Schutyser.
- **Mud Mosques in Mali. Photographs by Sebastian Schutyser.**
  24.05.2003–03.08.2003
- Auftritte: Die Campi Venedigs.
  Sechzehn Studien zum architektonischen Raum.
- **Scenes: The Campi of Venice.**
  Sixteen Studies of the Architectural Space.
  24.05.2003–03.08.2003
- Venezia Oscura. Fotografien von Gerhard Ullmann.
- **Venezia Oscura. Photographs by Gerhard Ullmann.**
  24.05.2003–03.08.2003
- Oscar Niemeyer. Eine Legende der Moderne.
- **Oscar Niemeyer. A Legend of Modernism.**
  01.03.2003–11.05.2003
- TUD im DAM. Der Fachbereich Architektur
  der Technischen Universität Darmstadt stellt sich vor.
- **TUD in DAM. The Architecture Department of the**
  Darmstadt Technical University Introduces Itself.
  17.01.2003–16.02.2003
- Architektur zum Anfassen. FSB Greifen und Griffe.
- **Architecture within Our Grasp. FSB Handle Culture.**
  05.10.2002–05.01.2003
- Mythos Hellerau. Ein Unternehmen meldet sich zurück.
- **The Myth of Hellerau. A Company Signals Its Return.**
  05.10.2002–05.01.2003

In der Aktuellen Galerie des DAM waren folgende Ausstellungen zu sehen:
The following exhibitions were shown at the DAM's Aktuelle Galerie:

- City Scape East. Fotoausstellung.
- **City Scape East. Photo Exhibition.**
  16.07.03–24.08.03
- Die Preisträger des 'Architecture + Technology Award 2003'
  und des ›Licht Architektur Preises 2003‹.
- **The Prizewinner of the ›Architecture + Technology Award 2003‹**
  and 'The Light in Architecture Prize 2003'.
  11.06.2003–06.07.2003
- Frühlicht. Eine Spurensuche. Fotografien von Rudolf Hartmetz.
- **Dawn. Searching for Traces. Photographs by Rudolf Hartmetz.**
  16.04.2003–01.06.2003
- A New World Trade Center: Design Proposals.
- **A New World Trade Center: Design Proposals.**
  26.02.2003–06.04.2003
- In einem neuen Geiste. Die Synagogen von Alfred Jacoby.
- **In a New Spirit. Alfred Jacoby's Synagogues.**
  04.12.2002–09.02.2003

- Afghanistan Zero. Fotografien von Simon Norfolk.
- **Afghanistan Zero. Photographs by Simon Norfolk.**
  23.10.2002–24.11.2002
- Kulturspeicher Würzburg. Architekten Brückner & Brückner.
  Fotografen Peter Maney und André Mühling.
- **Kulturspeicher Würzburg. Architects Brückner & Brückner.**
  Photographers Peter Maney and André Mühling.
  13.09.2002–13.10.2002

Dauerausstellung:
Permanent exhibition:

- Von der Urhütte zum Wolkenkratzer.
- **From Primordial Hut to Skyscraper.**

Sonderausstellungen in den zwölf Höfchen des DAM:
Special exhibition in the DAM's twelve small courtyards:

- Jochen Fischer. Hofarbeiten. Weidenplastiken 2001–2002.
- **Jochen Fischer. Yardworks. Willow Sculptures, 2001–2002.**
  26.03.2003–11.05.2003
- Fero Freymark. Skulpturen.
- **Fero Freymark. Sculptures.**
  05.10.2002–15.02.2003

Kleinere Ausstellungen:
Smaller exhibitions:

- Route der Industriekultur.
- **Industrial culture route.**
  04.06.2003–20.07.2003

Zahlreiche Vorträge und Symposien widmeten sich aktuellen Fragen
der Architektur:
Numerous lectures and symposia devoted to current topics
in architecture:

- Große Architekten. Vortragsreihe.
- **Great Architects. Lecture series.**
  Toyo Ito: 25.09.2002 Hans Kollhoff: 07.11.2002 Richard Rogers:
  26.03.2003 Wolf D. Prix: 08.05.2003 Rafael Moneo: 04.09.2003
- Route der Industriekultur Rhein-Main. Eine Perspektive für die Region.
  Vortrag von D. W. Dreysse.
- **Rhein-Main Industrial Culture Route. A Perspective for the Region.**
  Lecture by D.W. Dreysse.
  02.07.2003
- Werkvortrag von Stephen Varady.
- **Lecture on Works, by Stephen Varady.**
  27.05.2003
- Digitales Zeichnen heute. Diskussionsabend.
- **Digital Drawing Today. Discussion evening.**
  11.05.2003
  Mit **With** Hani Rashid, Greg Lynn und **and** Ben van Berkel,

Moderation **chaired** by Max Hollein. In Kooperation mit der
In cooperation with Schirn Kunsthalle Frankfurt am Main.

■ Von der Baustelle: Westhafen-Tower.
Eine Diskussionsveranstaltung vor Ort.
■ **From the Building Site: Westhafen-Tower. An on-location discussion event.**
03.04.2003
Mit **With** Jürgen Hupe, Michael Schumacher und **and** Martin Wentz,
Moderation **chaired by** Ingeborg Flagge.

■ Über die Bedeutung des Lichts in den Moscheen.
Vortrag von Shahid N. Sadiq.
■ **On the Meaning of Light in Mosques. Lecture by Shahid N. Sadiq.**
26.03.2003
In einer Kooperation mit dem **In cooperation with the** Museum der Welt-
kulturen, Frankfurt am Main.

■ 2. FSB Klinkengespräch mit Christoph Ingenhoven.
■ **2nd FSB Discussion on handle culture
with Christoph Ingenhoven.**
05.01.2003

■ Architektur und Wahrnehmung. Interdisziplinäres Symposium.
■ **Architecture and Perception. Interdisciplinary symposium.**
21./22.11.2003
Mit Beiträgen von **With contributions by** Ruth Ammann, Franz Xaver Baier,
Werner Bischoff, Andres Bosshard, Torsten Braun, Gerda Breuer,
Gernot Böhme, Brigitte Franzen, Jörg H. Gleiter, Reimer Gronemeyer,
Andreas Hartmann, Bettina Köhler, Wolfgang Leuschner,
Peter Mörtenböck, Ingo Rentschler, Christian W. Thomsen, Justin Winkler,
Juhani Pallasmaa, Moderation **chaired by** Ingeborg Flagge.

■ 7. Internationaler Frankfurter Architektur Diskurs: global/local.
■ **7th International Frankfurt Debate on Architecture: global/local.**
14.11.2002, 28.11.2002, 22.01.2003
Mit **With** Paul Andreu, Layla Dawson, Winy Maas, Wolfgang Pehnt,
Christian Schittich, Werner Sobek, Moderation **chaired by** Manuel Cuadra.

■ Die Kraft des Details. Diskussionsabend.
■ **The Power of Detail. Discussion evening.**
13.11.2002
Mit **With** Christoph Mäckler, Wolfgang Lorch und **and** Jo. Franzke,
Moderation **chaired by** Fritz Straub.

■ Workshop mit dem Klinkenhistoriker Florian Langenbeck.
■ **Workshop with Florian Langenbeck, Historian of handle culture.**
13.11.2002

■ 1. FSB Klinkengespräch mit Ton Haas.
■ **1st FSB Discussion on handle culture with Ton Haas.**
17.10.2002

■ 1. Symposium Marktplätze für das Wissen.
Neue Bibliotheksbauten in Europa und den USA.
■ **1st Symposium – Marketplaces for Knowledge.
New Library Buildings in Europe and the United States.**
09.10.2002
Es wurden vorgestellt die Hauptbibliothek in Wien durch Alfred Pfoser,
Christian Jahl und Ernst Mayer; der Neubau der Sächsischen Landes-
bibliothek – Staats- und Universitätsbibliothek durch Jürgen Hering und
Manfred Ortner; der Umbau der Schweizerischen Landesbibliothek Bern
durch Jean-Frédéric Jauslin und Andreas Furrer und der Neubau der
Elmer L. Anderson Library und Umbau der Walter Library – Digital Tech-
nology Center, University of Minnesota durch Donald Kelsey und William
Beyer, Moderation: Ingeborg Flagge und Andreas J. Werner.
**Presented were: the main library in Vienna by Alfred Pfoser, Christian Jahl
and Ernst Mayer; the new building for the Saxon State and University Library by Jürgen Hering and Manfred Ortner; the conversion work on the Bern
State Library in Switzerland by Jean-Frédéric Jauslin and Andreas Furrer;
and the new building for the Elmer L. Anderson Library and the conversion**

**of the Walter Library – Digital Technology Center, University of Minnesota
by Donald Kelsey and William Beyer, chaired by Ingeborg Flagge and
Andreas J. Werner.**

Folgende Kataloge und Veröffentlichungen wurden erarbeitet:
The following catalogues and publications were produced:

■ *Aldo Rossi. Die Suche nach dem Glück. Frühe Zeichnungen und
Entwürfe*, hrsg. von Annette Becker und Ingeborg Flagge, München 2003.
Edited by Annette Becker and Ingeborg Flagge, Munich, 2003.

■ *»Schönheit ruht in der Ordnung«.
Der Architekt Paul Schmitthenner 1884–1972*,
hrsg. von Wolfgang Voigt und Hartmut Frank, Tübingen 2003.
Edited by Wolfgang Voigt and Hartmut Frank, Tübingen, 2003.

■ *Lehm-Moscheen in Mali. Fotografien von Sebastian Schutyser*,
hrsg. von Ingeborg Flagge, Hamburg 2003.
Edited by Ingeborg Flagge, Hamburg, 2003.

■ *Oscar Niemeyer. Eine Legende der Moderne / A legend of Modernism*,
hrsg. von Paul Andreas und Ingeborg Flagge, Basel 2003.
Edited by Paul Andreas and Ingeborg Flagge, Basle, 2003.

■ *Frühlicht. Eine Spurensuche. Fotografien von Rudolf Hartmetz*,
hrsg. von Ingeborg Flagge und Sunna Gailhofer, Frankfurt am Main 2003.
Edited by Ingeborg Flagge and Sunna Gailhofer, Frankfurt/Main, 2003.

■ *In einem neuen Geiste: Die Synagogen von Alfred Jacoby*,
hrsg. vom DAM, Frankfurt am Main 2002.
Edited by DAM, Frankfurt/Main, 2002.

■ *Architektur zum Anfassen: FSB Greifen und Griffe*,
hrsg. von Ursula Kleefisch-Jobst und Ingeborg Flagge,
Frankfurt am Main 2002.
**Edited by Ursula Kleefisch-Jobst and Ingeborg Flagge,
Frankfurt/Main, 2002.**

Zu den wichtigsten Neuerwerbungen für das Archiv des DAM zählen:
The most important new acquisitions of the DAM archive include:

Kohle-Zeichnungen *Bahnhof* und *Theatervision* von Hans Scharoun;
Richard Rogers/ABB Architekten, Modell *Skylight*, Deutsche Telekom
Frankfurt am Main; H. + H. Dieken, Entwürfe für Wandmalereien; Murphy/
Jahn, Grafiken und kleine Zeichnungen zum Frankfurter Messeturm; Oswald
Mathias Ungers Skizzen und Pausen zum Flughafen und zur Messe Frank-
furt; Helmut Jahn, Zeichnungen für den Frankfurter Messeturm; Heinz Rasch,
Wohnhaus Wuppertal, Bauunterlagen, Pläne und Zeichnungen; Hans
Poelzig, drei Zeichnungen zur Messe Berlin; Henn Architekten, Modell der
Gläsernen Manufaktur, Dresden; Herrmann und Valenty, Zeichnungen für ver-
schiedene Projekte; Bernhard Winking, Modell *Flutachse Hamburg* und eine
historische Fotosammlung aus Italien, um 1900.
**Coal drawings *Train Station* and *Theater vision* by Hans Scharoun;
Richard Rogers/ABB Architekten model *Skylight*, Deutsche Telekom
Frankfurt/Main; H. + H. Dieken, designs for wall painting; Murphy/Jahn,
graphics and small illustrations of the Frankfurt Messeturm; Oswald Mathias
Ungers' sketches and blueprints for the airport and Frankfurt Messeturm;
Helmuth Jahn, drawings for the Frankfurt Messeturm; Heinz Rasch, residential
house, Wuppertal, construction documents, plans and drawings; Hans Poelzig,
three drawings for the Berlin Trade Fair; Henn Architekten, a model of the
Transparent Factory, Dresden; Herrmann and Valenty, drawings for various
projects; Bernhard Winking, model of the *Hamburg flood axis* and a historical
collection of photographs from Italy, ca 1900.**

Architekturpreise:
Architecture awards:

Bisher ist das DAM an der Auslobung zweier wichtiger Architekturpreise be-
teiligt: an dem alle zwei Jahre auszulobenden ›Licht Architektur Preis‹ und an
dem 2002 erstmals von der Messe Frankfurt gestifteten ›Architecture + Technology Award. Europäischer Architekturpreis für Architektur und Technik‹.
Hinzu kommt nun ab 2003 der von der Stadt Frankfurt ins Leben gerufene
›Internationale Europäische Hochhaus Preis‹, der von der Deka Bank
Deutsche Girozentrale finanziert wird. Mit dem Preis sollen Hochhäuser aus-
gezeichnet werden, die mehr als 100 Meter hoch sind und bei Redaktions-
schluss der Ausschreibung am 30.11. nicht älter als 24 Monate sind.
To date, the DAM participates in organising two major architecture prizes:
'The Light in Architecture Prize' awarded every two years and the 'Architecture
+ Technology Award. European Architecture Prize for Architecture and Techno-
logy' which was bestowed by the Frankfurt Trade Fair for the first time in 2002.
In addition, from 2003, the 'International European Skyscraper Prize' created by
the city of Frankfurt and financed by the Deka Bank Deutsche Girozentrale will
be award. The prize is given for skyscrapers which are more than 100 metres
high and which are no more than 24 months old when the deadline for entries
closes on 30 November.

Mäzene und Sponsoren:
Patrons and sponsors:

Alle unsere Aktivitäten im vergangenen Jahr wären ohne die großzügige
Unterstützung zahlreicher Sponsoren nicht möglich gewesen. Seit Anfang
2003 ist die Ernst & Young AG Wirtschaftsprüfungsgesellschaft für drei Jahre
der wichtigste Sponsor des DAM. Zu den weiteren Sponsoren, die das
Museum durch Sach- und Geldzuwendungen unterstützt haben, zählen:
None of our activities in the past year would have been possible without the
generous support of our many sponsors. As of the beginning of 2003,
Ernst & Young AG Wirtschaftsprüfungsgesellschaft has become the most
important DAM sponsor, and has committed its support for a period of three
years. Other sponsors who have assisted the museum with professional and
financial assistance include:

Adler Real Estate Aktiengesellschaft; Akademie der Architekten- und Stadt-
planerkammer Hessen; Bilfinger Berger Projektentwicklung GmbH; Burkhard
Leitner Constructiv; Caparol Farben Lacke Bautenschutz GmbH & Co. Ver-
triebs KG; Degussa AG; Deutsche Werkstätten Hellerau GmbH; Fotografie
Forum International; Frankfurter Allgemeine Zeitung; Jo. Franzke Architekten,
Frankfurt am Main; Fraport AG; FSB Franz Schneider Brakel GmbH & Co. KG;
Gesellschaft der Freunde des Deutschen Architektur Museums e.V.; Grohe
Water Technology; Helaba Landesbank Hessen-Thüringen; Hessische
Kulturstiftung; Knauf; Dieter Köhler, Köhler Architekten, Frankfurt am Main;
Messe Frankfurt GmbH; MLP Finanzdienstleistungen AG; Prof. Gerhard
Müller-Menckens, Bremen; Röhm Plexiglas; Stadt Würzburg; Wiege Ent-
wicklungs GmbH; Wilhelmi Werke AG; Wilkahn; Zumtobel Staff Deutschland
Vertriebs-GmbH.

All diesen Förderern, aber auch manchem Mäzen, der ungenannt bleiben
möchte, gilt unser herzlichster Dank.
We owe our heartfelt thanks to all our sponsors as well as to those patrons
who wish to remain anonymous.

Gesellschaft der Freunde des DAM
Society of Friends of the DAM

Die Gesellschaft der Freunde des Deutschen Architektur Museums e.V.
wurde 1985 als eingetragener Verein ins Leben gerufen. Ihr Hauptanliegen
ist, das DAM in der Verwirklichung seiner öffentlichen Aufgaben ideell und
materiell zu unterstützen und zu fördern.
The Society of Friends of the Deutsches Architektur Museum became a re-
gistered association in 1985. Its principal concern is to support and promote
the DAM in realising its public tasks on ideal and material levels.

Zu den Aufgaben und Zielen des Vereins gehören:
- Vermittlung, Ankauf oder Überlassung von Plänen, Zeichnungen und
  Modellen internationaler Architekturprojekte und von Architekturnach-
  lässen
- Personelle und materielle Unterstützung bei Veranstaltungen und Aus-
  stellungen
- Unterstützung bei Anschaffungen
- Konstruktive Beratung und Anregung des DAM
- Hilfe bei mittel- und langfristiger Existenzsicherung des DAM
Tasks and aims include:
- **Procurement, purchase or assignment of plans, drawings and models**
  of international architecture projects and architectural events
- **Personnel and material support for events and exhibitions**
- **Support in procurement**
- **Constructive advice and stimulus for the DAM**
- **Aid in ensuring the medium- and long-term existence of the DAM**

Mitglieder in diesem Verein sind Personen, Institutionen und Firmen, deren
Anliegen es ist, einen Beitrag zur Förderung der Qualität der gebauten Um-
welt zu leisten. Der Mitgliedsbeitrag beträgt jährlich € 95 für das Einzelmit-
glied, € 35 für Studenten, € 920 für juristische Personen und Personenverei-
nigungen.
Members of the association include persons, institutions and companies who
are concerned with participating in the promotion of quality in the constructed
world. The membership fee is € 95 per annum for individual members, € 35 for
students, and € 920 for legal entities and associations.

Vorstand **Board of Management**: Rolf Toyka (Vorsitzender **Chairman**)
Dr. Evelyn Brockhoff (stellv. Vorsitzende **Deputy Chairman**), Prof. Helge
Bofinger (Schatzmeister **Treasurer)**, Marietta Andreas, Dr. Heinrich Binder,
Prof. Johann Eisele, Prof. Werner Meißner, Thomas Norweg, Joachim Wagner
und **and** Dr. Martin Wentz.

Geschäftsstelle **Office**
c/o Deutsches Architektur Museum
Hedderichstraße 104–110
D-60596 Frankfurt/Main
Telefon +49 (0)69 21 23 67 06
Telefax +49 (0)69 97 20 33 66
freundeskreis.dam@stadt-frankfurt.de

Die Autoren
The Authors

Markus Allmann
*1959. Studium der Architektur an der TU München. 1986 Mitarbeit im Büro Bétrix und Consolascio, Zürich. 1987 Gründung des Architekturbüros Allmann Sattler in München, seit 1993 Allmann Sattler Wappner Architekten. Zahlreiche Architekturpreise.
Born 1959; studied architecture at the Munich Technical University; 1986, worked in the offices of Bétrix und Consolascio, Zurich; 1987, founded Allmann Sattler architectural offices in Munich, renamed Allmann Sattler Wappner Architekten in 1993; numerous architectural prizes.

Julia B. Bolles-Wilson
Studium der Architektur an der Universität Karlsruhe; Postgraduiertenstudium bei Elia Zenghelis und Rem Koolhaas an der AA School, London. 1980 Gründung des Architekturbüros Bolles+Wilson in London, seit 1989 mit dem Büro in Münster. Zahlreiche Architekturpreise. 1981–1986 Dozentin am Chelsea College of Art & Design, London. Seit 1996 Professur für Entwerfen und CAD an der FH Münster. Seit 2001 im Gestaltungsbeirat der Stadt Salzburg.
Studied architecture at Karlsruhe University; postgraduate studies with Elia Zenghelis and Rem Koolhaas at the AA School, London; 1980, founded Bolles+Wilson architectural offices in London; since 1989, office in Münster; numerous architectural awards; 1981–86, lecturer at Chelsea College of Art & Design, London; since 1996, Professor for Design and CAD at the University of Applied Sciences, Münster; since 2001, member of the City of Salzburg Advisory Council for Architectural Planning.

Jochen Boskamp
*1936. Studium der Architektur an der RWTH Aachen. 1963–1965 Mitarbeit im Büro Hentrich, Petschnigg & Partner, Düsseldorf; 1965–1969 im Büro von Paul Schneider-Esleben, Düsseldorf. 1970 Gründung des Architekturbüros Kuhn-Boskamp-Partner in Düsseldorf, seit 1997 Architektur und Stadtplanung Boskamp, Ehlers, Wegmann. 1993–1995 Präsident des Bundes Deutscher Architekten. 1991–1996 Redaktionsmitglied der Zeitschrift *Der Architekt.*
Born 1936; studied architecture at the Aachen Polytechnic; 1963–65, worked in the offices of Hentrich, Petschnigg & Partner, Düsseldorf; 1965–69, worked in the offices of Paul Schneider-Esleben, Düsseldorf; 1970, founded Kuhn-Boskamp-Partner architectural offices in Düsseldorf; since 1997, Architektur und Stadtplanung Boskamp, Ehlers, Wegmann; 1993–95, President of the Federation of German Architects; 1991–96, member of the editorial staff at the magazine, *Der Architekt.*

Dietmar Brandenburger
Studium der Architektur an der TU Braunschweig. Seit 1970 Mitarbeit in Architekturbüros in Braunschweig, Wien, München und Hannover. 1974–1977 Referent im Bundessekretariat des Bundes Deutscher Architekten BDA. Seit 1983 im Deutschen Werkbund Nord. 1985–1990 Landesgeschäftsführer des BDA Nordrhein-Westfalen. Seit 1992 freiberuflicher Mitarbeiter des Norddeutschen Rundfunks NDR 3. Architekt BDA, außerordentliches Mitglied, und Architekturkritiker, Hannover.
Studied architecture at the Braunschweig Technical University; since 1970, worked in architectural offices in Braunschweig, Vienna, Munich and Hanover; 1974–77, consultant to the Federal Office of the Federation of German Architects; since 1983, member of Deutscher Werkbund Nord; 1985–90, provincial manager of the Federation of German Architects, State of North Rhine-Westphalia; since 1992, freelancer for North German Television (NDR 3); associate member of the Federation of German Architects and architectural critic, Hanover.

Hans-Jürgen Breuning
*1963. Studium der Architektur in Karlsruhe, Stuttgart und Florenz; 1999 Promotion. 1992–1999 Wissenschaftlicher Mitarbeiter an der Universität Stuttgart, 1999–2001 Assistent am Institut für Baukunst der Technischen Universität Graz, 2002/03 Lehrtätigkeit an der Universität Karlsruhe. Seit 2000 im Büro Prof. Lederer+Ragnarsdóttir+Oei, Stuttgart. Seit 2001 Kurator in der Architekturgalerie am Weißenhof, Stuttgart. Autor zahlreicher Publikationen zu Architektur und Städtebau.
Born 1963; studied architecture in Karlsruhe, Stuttgart and Florence, graduating in 1999; 1992–99, academic assistant at Stuttgart University; 1999–2001, assistant at the Institute for Architecture at the Technical University, Graz; 2002–03, lecturer at Karlsruhe University; since 2000, in the office of Prof. Lederer+Ragnarsdóttir+Oei, Stuttgart; since 2001, curator of the Architekturgalerie am Weissenhof, Stuttgart; author of numerous publications on architecture and city planning.

Manuel Cuadra
*1952. Studium der Architektur in Lima und Darmstadt; 1988 Promotion. 1988 Gastprofessur an der Architekturfakultät der Universidad de Belgrano, Buenos Aires. 1987–1995 Lehrauftrag am kunsthistorischen Institut der Universität Heidelberg. 1995–1997 Gastprofessur für Geschichte und Theorie der Architektur an der Städelschule, Frankfurt am Main. Seit 2003 Gastprofessur für Architekturgeschichte und Entwerfen an der Universität Kassel. Mitglied des International Committee of Architectural Critics. Architekt BDA, außerordentliches Mitglied, Autor und Ausstellungskurator, Frankfurt am Main.
Born 1952; studied architecture in Lima and Darmstadt, graduating in 1988; 1988, visiting professorship in the Faculty of Architecture, University of Belgrano, Buenos Aires; 1987–95, lecturer at the Institute of Art History at Heidelberg University; 1995–97, Visiting Professor of Architectural History and Theory at the Städel Academy, Frankfurt/Main; since 2003, Guest Professor for Architectural History and Design at Kassel University; member of the International Committee of Architectural Critics; associate member of the Federation of German Architects; author and exhibition curator, Frankfurt/Main.

Ingeborg Flagge
Studium der Philosophie, Geschichte, Sanskrit, Archäologie, Ägyptologie, Alten Geschichte, Kunst- und Baugeschichte an der Universität Köln und am University College London; 1971 Promotion. 1978–1983 Bundesgeschäftsführerin des Bundes Deutscher Architekten. 1974–1998 Chefredakteurin der Zeitschrift *Der Architekt.* 1995–2000 Professur für Baugeschichte an der HTWK Leipzig. Seit 2000 Direktorin des Deutschen Architektur Museums in Frankfurt am Main. Freie Journalistin und Architekturpublizistin.
Studied philosophy, history, Sanskrit, archaeology, Egyptology, ancient history, art history, and history of architecture at Cologne University and at University College, London, graduating in 1971; 1978–83, Managing Director of the Federation of German Architects; 1974–98, chief editor of the magazine, *Der Architekt*; 1995–2000, Professor of Architectural History at the University for Technology, Economics and Culture in Leipzig; since 2000, Director of the Deutsches Architektur Museum in Frankfurt/Main; freelance journalist and architectural publicist.

Jörg Friedrich
*1951. Studium der Architektur an der Universität Stuttgart. 1986 Gründung des eigenen Architekturbüros in Hamburg. Seit 1983 Lehraufträge in Hamburg, Wuppertal, Aachen, Genua und Rom. 1988–1999 Professur für Entwerfen und Baukonstruktion an der FH Hamburg; seit 1999 Professur für Entwerfen, Gebäudelehre und Architekturtheorie an der Universität Hannover. Seit 1995 Vorsitz der Sektion Baukunst der Freien Akademie der Künste Hamburg. Zahlreiche Kunst- und Architekturpreise. Publikationen zur Architektur.
Born 1951; studied architecture at Stuttgart University; 1986, set up his own architectural office in Hamburg; as of 1983, teaching assignments in Hamburg, Wuppertal, Aachen, Genoa and Rome; 1988–99, Professor for Design and

Architectural Engineering at the University of Applied Sciences, Hamburg; since 1999, Professor for Design and Building Instruction and Architectural Theory at Hanover University; since 1995, chairman of the architectural section of the Free Academy of Arts in Hamburg; numerous art and architectural awards; publications on architecture.

Dörte Gatermann

*1956. Studium der Architektur an der TU Braunschweig und der RWTH Aachen. 1981–1985 Projektleiterin bei Gottfried Böhm. 1984 Gründung des Architekturbüros GATERMANN+SCHOSSIG in Köln. Zahlreiche Architektur-preise. Seit 2001 Kuratoriumsmitglied der Initiative StadtBauKultur NRW. Seit 2001 im Redaktionsbeirat der Zeitschrift *Baumeister*. Seit 2001 Vor-standsvorsitzende des Internetportals koelnarchitektur.de. Seit 2002 Profes-sur für Entwerfen und Gebäudelehre an der TU Darmstadt.

Born 1956; studied architecture at the Braunschweig Technical University and the Aachen Polytechnic; 1981–85, project manager at Gottfried Böhm; 1984, founding of architectural practice GATERMANN+SCHOSSIG in Cologne; numerous architectural prizes; since 2001, on the editorial advisory council of the magazine, *Baumeister*; since 2001, chairman of the internet portal koelnarchitektur.de; since 2002, Professor of Design and Building Methodology at Darmstadt Technical University.

Annina Götz

*1976. Studium der Architektur an der Universität Stuttgart und der Hoch-schule der Künste, Berlin. Seit 2000 freiberufliche Mitarbeiterin des Deut-schen Architektur Museums in Frankfurt am Main. Freie Architekturkritikerin, Brüssel.

Born 1976; studied architecture at Stuttgart University and at the Academy of Arts, Berlin; since 2000, freelance work at the Deutsches Architektur Museum in Frankfurt/Main; freelance architecture critic, Brussels.

Johannes Kister

*1956. Studium der Architektur an der RWTH Aachen. 1982/83 Mitarbeit im Büro Suter und Suter, Basel; 1983–1988 im Büro Joachim Schürmann, Köln. 1988 Mitgründer der Architektengruppe Kölner Bucht. 1991 Förderpreis des Landes Nordrhein-Westfalen. 1992 Gründung des Architekturbüros Kister Scheithauer & Partner in Köln, seit 1997 Kister Scheithauer Gross, seit 1998 weiteres Büro in Dessau. Seit 1994 Professur für Entwerfen und Baukonstruk-tion an der Hochschule Anhalt (FH) am Bauhaus Dessau. Seit 2001 im Beirat des Deutschen Architektur Museums in Frankfurt am Main.

Born 1956; studied architecture at the Aachen Polytechnic; 1982–83, worked in the offices of Suter und Suter in Basle; 1983–88, worked in the offices of Joachim Schürmann in Cologne; 1988, co-founder of the architectural group Kölner Bucht; 1991, Promotional Prize of the State of North Rhine-Westphalia; 1992, founded Kister Scheithauer & Partner architectural offices in Cologne, renamed Kister Scheithauer Gross in 1997; since 1998, subsidiary office in Dessau; since 1994, Professor of Design and Architectural Engineering at the Anhalt University of Applied Sciences attached to the Bauhaus, Dessau; since 2001, member of the Advisory Council of the Deutsches Architektur Museum, Frankfurt/Main.

Wilhelm Kücker

*1933. Studium der Architektur in München, Wien und Zürich; 1963 Promo-tion. 1965 Gründung des eigenen Architekturbüros in München. Seit 1975 Professur für Entwerfen an der TU München. Seit 1975 im Bund Deutscher Architekten, 1983–1987 dessen Präsident. 1987–1990 Vizepräsident der Union Internationale des Architectes (UIA). Seit 1987 Ehrenmitglied des Consejo Superior de los Colegios de Arquitectos de España. Seit 1999 Honorary Fellow des American Institute of Architects. Seit 2000 im Beirat des Deutschen Architektur Museums in Frankfurt am Main.

Born 1933; studied architecture in Munich, Vienna and Zurich, graduating in 1963; 1965, founded his own architecture office in Munich; as of 1975, Profes-sor of Design at the Munich Technical University; as of 1975, member of the Federation of German Architects, and from 1983–87, President; 1987–90, Vice-President of the International Union of Architects; since 1987, honorary member of the Consejo Seperior de los Colegios de Arquitectos de España;

since 1999, honorary fellow of the American Institute of Architects; since 2000, on the Advisory Council of the Deutsches Architektur Museum, Frankfurt/Main.

Arno Lederer

*1947. Studium der Architektur in Stuttgart und Wien. 1977 Mitarbeit im Büro Ernst Gisel, Zürich; 1978 im Büro Berger Hauser Oed, Tübingen. 1979 Gründung des eigenen Architekturbüros, seit 1985 in Bürogemeinschaft mit Jórunn Ragnarsdóttir, seit 1992 mit Marc Oei. Büro heute in Stuttgart. 1985–1990 Professur für Konstruieren und Entwerfen an der FH für Technik, Stuttgart. 1990 Übernahme des Lehrstuhls für Baukonstruktion und Entwerfen an der Universität Karlsruhe. Seit 1997 Leiter des Lehrstuhls für Gebäude-lehre an der dortigen Architekturfakultät.

Born 1947; studied architecture in Stuttgart and Vienna; 1977, worked in the Ernst Gisel architectural offices in Zurich; 1978, worked in the Berger Hauser Oed office in Tübingen; 1979, set up his own architectural office; as of 1985, co-partner with Jórunn Ragnarsdóttir, and as of 1992, with Marc Oei; today, the office is in Stuttgart; 1985–90, Professor of Architectural Engineering and De-sign at the University of Applied Sciences, Stuttgart; 1990, appointed Professor of Architectural Engineering and Design I at Karlsruhe University; as of 1997, head of the Building Methodology Department at the Karlsruhe University's Faculty of Architecture.

Hilde Léon

*1953. Studium der Architektur an der TU Berlin und der Universität Venedig. 1983 Gründung des Architekturbüros léonwohlhage in Berlin, seit 1997 Léon Wohlhage Wernik Architekten. Zahlreiche Architekturpreise. 1996–1999 im Gestaltungsbeirat der Stadt Berlin, seit 2000 der Stadt Salzburg. 1997–1999 Vertretungsprofessur für Entwurf an der Hochschule für bildende Künste Hamburg. Seit 2000 Professur für Entwerfen und Gebäudelehre an der Universität Hannover. 2002 Kommissarin des Deutschen Pavillons auf der Biennale in Venedig.

Born 1953; studied architecture at the Berlin Technical University and at Venice University; 1983, founded léonwohlhage architectural offices in Berlin, re-named Léon Wohlhage Wernik Architekten in 1997; numerous architectural awards; 1996–99, member of the Architectural Advisory Council of the City of Berlin and as of 2000, of the City of Salzburg; 1997–99, Temporary Professor for Project Creation at the Academy of Fine Arts, Hamburg; as of 2000, Professor of Project Creation and Building Methodology at Hanover University; 2002, Commissioner of the German Pavilion at the Venice Biennale.

Karin Leydecker

*1956. Studium der Germanistik, Psychologie, Kunstgeschichte und Evange-lischen Theologie in Mainz, Heidelberg und Karlsruhe; 1988 Promotion. Forschung und Lehraufträge zur Architekturwahrnehmung an der Universität und der Pädagogischen Hochschule in Karlsruhe. Publikationen zur Kunst und Architektur insbesondere des 19. und 20. Jahrhunderts. Freie Kritikerin, Neustadt an der Weinstraße.

Born 1956; studied German, psychology, art history and evangelical theory in Mainz, Heidelberg and Karlsruhe, graduating in 1988; research and teaching assignments on the perception of architecture at Karlsruhe University and at the Pedagogical University in Karlsruhe; publications on art and architecture, especially on the 19th and 20th centuries; freelance critic, Neustadt an der Weinstrasse.

Niklas Maak

*1972. Studium der Kunstgeschichte in Hamburg und Paris; 1998 Promotion. 1999–2001 Redakteur für Architektur im Feuilleton der *Süddeutschen Zeitung*. Seit 2001 Redakteur für den Bereich Kunst im Feuilleton der *Frank-furter Allgemeinen Zeitung*.

Born 1972; studied art history in Hamburg and Paris, graduating in 1998; 1999–2001, architectural editor for the feature pages of the *Süddeutsche Zeitung*; since 2001, art editor for the feature pages of the *Frankfurter Allgemeine Zeitung*.

Günter Pfeifer

*1943. Studium der Architektur an der Werkkunstschule Kassel. Seit 1972 selbstständiger Architekt. 1986–1992 Zusammenarbeit mit Frank O. Gehry, Zaha M. Hadid, Tadao Ando, Alvaro Siza, mit der Firma Vitra in Weil am Rhein. Zahlreiche Architekturpreise. 1992–2001 Professur für Entwerfen und Hochbaukonstruktion an der TU Darmstadt, seit 2001 für Entwerfen und Wohnungsbau. 2001 Gründung des Architekturbüros pfeifer roser kuhn Architekten, Freiburg. Autor zahlreicher Fachbücher.

Born 1943; studied architecture at the Werkkunstschule in Kassel; as of 1972, freelance architect; 1986–92, worked with Frank O. Gehry, Zaha M. Hadid, Tadao Ando, Alvaro Siza and for the Vitra corporation in Weil am Rhein; numerous architectural awards; 1992–2001, Professor of Project Creation and Civil Engineering at the Darmstadt Technical University; as of 2001, Professor of Project Creation and Residential Construction; 2001, set up the pfeifer roser kuhn Architekten architectural offices in Freiburg; author of numerous specialist books.

Wolfgang Jean Stock

*1948. Studium der Geschichte, Politischen Wissenschaft und Soziologie in Frankfurt am Main und Erlangen. 1978–1985 Direktor des Kunstvereins München. 1986–1993 Architekturkritiker der *Süddeutschen Zeitung*. 1994–1998 stellvertretender Chefredakteur der Zeitschrift *Baumeister*. Seit 2000 außerordentliches Mitglied im Bund Deutscher Architekten. Freier Journalist und Buchautor, München. Letzte Buchveröffentlichung 2002: *Europäischer Kirchenbau 1950–2000*.

Born 1948; studied history, political science and sociology in Frankfurt/Main and Erlangen; 1978–85, director of the Kunstverein, Munich; 1986–93, architectural critic for the *Süddeutsche Zeitung*; 1994–98, deputy editor-in-chief of the magazine, *Baumeister*; as of 2000, associate member of the Federation of German Architects; freelance journalist and author, Munich; most recently published book: 2002, *European Church Architecture 1950–2000*.

Angela Wandelt

*1959. Nach einer Maurerlehre Studium der Architektur an der Hochschule für Architektur und Bauwesen Weimar. 1983–1990 Mitarbeit in verschiedenen Architekturbüros. 1989/90 Sprecherin der Initiative Leipziger Architekten. 1990 Gründung des eigenen Architekturbüros in Leipzig. 1991–1993 Vorsitzende des Landesverbands Sachsen des Bundes Deutscher Architekten. Seit 1992 im Deutschen Werkbund Sachsen. Seit 2000 im Beirat des Deutschen Architektur Museums in Frankfurt am Main. Seit 2001 im Gestaltungsbeirat der Stadt Halle.

Born 1959; after an apprenticeship as a mason, studied architecture at the University for Architecture and Building in Weimar; 1983–90, worked in various architectural offices; 1989–90, spokesperson for the Initiative Leipziger Architekten; 1990, founded her own architectural office in Leipzig; 1991–93, Chairperson of the Saxon State section of the Federation of German Architects; since 1992, member of the Deutscher Werkbund, Saxony; as of 2000, on the Advisory Council of the Deutsches Architektur Museum, Frankfurt/Main; as of 2001, on the Architectural Advisory Council of the City of Halle.

Peter L. Wilson

Studium der Architektur an der University of Melbourne und der AA School, London. 1974–1976 Assistent von Elia Zenghelis und Rem Koolhaas an der AA School, London; 1976–1988 Unit Master. 1980 Gründung des Architekturbüros Bolles+Wilson in London, seit 1989 mit dem Büro in Münster. Zahlreiche Architekturpreise. 1994–1996 Gastprofessur für Entwerfen an der Kunsthochschule Weißensee, Berlin. 1998–2000 External Examiner an der University of Cambridge, UK.

Studied architecture at the University of Melbourne and at the AA School, London; 1974–76, assistant to Elia Zenghelis and Rem Koolhaas at the AA School, London; 1976–88, unit master; 1980, founded Bolles+Wilson architectural offices in London, since 1989 with offices in Münster; numerous architectural awards; 1994–96 Guest Professor for Project Creation at the Weissensee Art Academy, Berlin; 1998–2000, external examiner at the University of Cambridge, UK.

Konrad Wohlhage

*1953. Studium der Architektur an der TU München und der TU Delft. 1983 Gründung des Architekturbüros léonwohlhage in Berlin, seit 1997 Léon Wohlhage Wernik Architekten. Zahlreiche Architekturpreise, u. a. Deutscher Kritikerpreis für Architektur. 1987–1990 Wissenschaftlicher Mitarbeiter an der TU Berlin, Gastvorträge und Lehraufträge. Seit 2000 im Gestaltungsbeirat der Stadt München.

Born 1953; studied architecture at the Munich Technical University and the Delft Technical University; 1983, founded léonwohlhage architectural offices in Berlin, renamed Léon Wohlhage Wernik Architekten in 1997; numerous architectural awards including the German Critics' Award for Architecture; 1987–90, assistant at the Berlin Technical University, guest lectures and teaching duties; since 2000, member of the Architectural Advisory Council of the City of Munich.

Inge Wolf

*1955. Studium der Kunstgeschichte in Frankfurt am Main. Seit 1994 Mitarbeiterin des Deutschen Architektur Museums in Frankfurt am Main, seit 1996 Betreuung der Plan- und Modellsammlung.

Born 1955; studied art history in Frankfurt/Main; since 1994, member of staff at the Deutsches Architektur Museum in Frankfurt/Main; since 1996, in charge of the Plans and Models Collection.

Ingo Andreas Wolf

*1956. Studium der Stadt- und Regionalplanung in Köln und Aachen. Studium der Architektur an der Hochschule der Künste, Berlin. Freischaffende Mitarbeit an der Internationalen Bauausstellung Berlin 1987. 1985 Gründung des eigenen Büros für Planung und Baukunst. Wissenschaftliche Mitarbeit an der TU Berlin und der TU München. Seit 1992 Professur für Entwerfen und Städtebau an der HTWK Leipzig. Seit 1995 Mitglied der Deutschen Akademie für Städtebau und Landesplanung. Seit 2001 im Gestaltungsbeirat der Stadt Halle.

Born 1956; studied city and regional planning in Cologne and Aachen; studied architecture at the Berlin Academy of Arts; freelanced at the International Building Exhibition in Berlin in 1987; 1985, founded his own planning and architecture office; assistant at the Berlin Technical University and the Munich Technical University; as of 1992, Professor for Project Creation and City Planning at the University for Technology, Economics and Culture in Leipzig; as of 1995, member of the German Academy for Town and Country Planning; as of 2001, member of the Architectural Advisory Council of the City of Halle.

Erwin H. Zander

*1929. Studium der Architektur an der RWTH Aachen. 1956 Gründung des eigenen Architekturbüros in Köln. 1972–1976 im Redaktionsbeirat der Zeitschrift *Werk und Zeit*. 1973–1980 im Beirat für Raumordnung des Bundesministeriums für Raumordnung, Bauwesen und Städtebau. 1974–2002 Vorsitz des Kölnischen Kunstvereins. 1976/77 Vorsitz des Deutschen Werkbundes Nordrhein-Westfalen. 1977–1990 Vorsitz des Kunstbeirats der Stadt Köln. 1978–1994 Professur für Technischen Ausbau und Entwerfen an der FH Düsseldorf.

Born 1929; studied architecture at the Aachen Polytechnic; 1956, established his own architectural office in Cologne; 1972–76, on the editorial advisory council of the magazine, *Werk und Zeit*; 1973–80, on the Advisory Council for Zoning attached to the Federal Ministry for Area Planning, Building Industry and Urban Construction; 1974–2002, Chairman of the Cologne Kunstverein; 1976–77, Chairman of Deutscher Werkbund, North Rhine-Westphalia; 1977–90, Chairman of the Advisory Council for Art of the City of Cologne; 1978–94, Professor for Technical Engineering and Project Creation at the Düsseldorf University of Applied Sciences.

Abbildungsnachweis
Illustration Credits

■ Umschlag **Cover**
Gemeindekirche Christus König, Radebeul
Parish Church of Christ the King, Radebeul
Architekten **Architects**: Staib Architekten mit **with** Günter Behnisch
Fotografie **Photography**: Christian Kandzia, Stuttgart

■ Frontispiz **Frontispiece**
Domviertel, Magdeburg
Cathedral District, Magdeburg
Architekten **Architects**: Bolles + Wilson
Fotografie **Photography**: Christian Richters, Münster

■ **Essays**
■ **Essays**

■ Essay Wolfgang Jean Stock
9, 10 Dietmar Tollerian, Linz, Österreich **Austria**
Conrad Lienhardt (Hrsg.), *Sakralbau im Umbruch*, Reihe Kirchenbau, Bd. 4.,
Regensburg 2003 (in Vorbereitung **not yet published**).
12, 13 Bruno Klomfar, Wien **Vienna**, Österreich **Austria**
14, 15 Per Berntsen, Rjukan, Norwegen **Norway**
16, 17 Klaus Kinold, München **Munich**

■ Essay Karin Leydecker
18 © VG Bild-Kunst, Bonn 2003
19 Achim Bednorz, Köln © FLC/ VG Bild-Kunst, Bonn 2003
20 Robert Häusser, Mannheim
21, 24 Achim Bednorz, Köln **Cologne**
22 Wolfram Janzer/ artur, Köln **Cologne**
23 Ernst Herb, Frankfurt/ Main
25 Keith Collie, London, Großbritannien **United Kingdom**

■ Essay Niklas Maak
29 Michel Denancé/ Archipress
30 Photograph by Mitsuo Matsuoka courtesy of
Tadao Ando Architect & Associates
31 Photograph by Erika Barahona Ede © FMGB Guggenheim Bilbao Museoa.
2003. All rights reserved. Total or partial reproduction is prohibited.
32 Jens Weber, München **Munich**
33 Werner Huthmacher/artur, Köln **Cologne**
34 Nigel Young, London, Großbritannien **United Kingdom**
35 Studio Atkinson, New York, NY, USA
37 Red Saunders, London, Großbritannien **United Kingdom**

■ **Kirchen in Deutschland**
■ **Churches in Germany**

Die Rechte für Zeichnungen liegen bei den jeweiligen Architekten.
The copyright holders as regards drawings are the respective architects.

■ Zwischenseiten 38/39 **Opening Pages 38–39**
Gemeindezentrum, Köln
Community Centre, Cologne
Architekt **Architect**: Nikolaus Bienefeld
Fotografie **Photography**: Lukas Roth, Köln **Cologne**

■ Gemeindezentrum, Köln
Community Centre, Cologne
40–49 Lukas Roth, Köln **Cologne**

■ Pfarrkirche St. Theodor, Köln
Parish Church of St Theodore, Cologne
51, 56 Mitte **centre** Architekturbüro Paul Böhm, Köln **Cologne**
53, 54/55, 56 oben **top**, 56 unten **bottom**, 56/57 Jochen Helle/artur,
Köln **Cologne**

■ Doppelkirche für zwei Konfessionen, Freiburg
Dual Denominational Church, Freiburg
58–65 Christian Richters, Münster

■ Pfarrzentrum St. Franziskus, Regensburg
Parish Community Centre of St Francis, Regensburg
67, 70/71, 72/73, 74 unten **bottom**, 75 Gerhard Hagen, Bamberg
69 Jens Willebrand, Köln **Cologne**
74 oben **top** Königs Architekten, Köln **Cologne**

■ Gemeindekirche Christus König, Radebeul
Parish Church of Christ the King, Radebeul
77, 80/81, 82/83, 83 unten **bottom** Christian Kandzia, Stuttgart
79, 80 oben **top** Gerald Staib, Stuttgart

■ Autobahnkirche, Medenbach
Highway Chapel, Medenbach
85, 87 oben **top** 88/89 Thomas Ott, Mühltal
87 unten **bottom** Renate Gruber, Darmstadt
88 oben **top** Gerhard Hagen/artur, Köln **Cologne**

■ **Architektur in Deutschland**
■ Architecture in Germany

Die Rechte für Zeichnungen liegen bei den jeweiligen Architekten.
The copyright holders as regards drawings are the respective architects.

■ Zwischenseiten 90/91 **Opening Pages 90–91**
Sächsische Landesbibliothek – Staats- und
Universitätsbibliothek, Dresden
Saxon State and University Library, Dresden
Architekten **Architects**: Ortner & Ortner
Fotografie **Photography**: Stefan Müller, Berlin

■ Verbandsgebäude der Südwestmetall, Reutlingen
Südwestmetall Federation Building, Reutlingen
93, 95, 98, 99 Jens Passoth, Berlin
96/97 Florian Holzherr, München **Munich**

■ Domviertel, Magdeburg
Cathedral District, Magdeburg
100–107 Christian Richters, Münster

■ Haus S, Ludwigsburg
House S, Ludwigsburg
108–113 David Franck, Ostfildern

■ Erzbischöfliches Archiv, Freiburg
Archiepiscopal Archives, Freiburg
114–119 Roland Halbe/artur, Köln **Cologne**

■ Museum und Park Kalkriese, Bramsche
Kalkriese Museum and Park, Bramsche
120–127 Heinrich Helfenstein, Zürich **Zurich**

■ Bürogebäude Neumühlen, Hamburg
Office Building, Neumühlen, Hamburg
128–135 Werner Huthmacher/artur, Köln **Cologne**

■ Werner-Otto-Saal im Konzerthaus Berlin
Werner-Otto-Saal, Konzerthaus Berlin
136–141 Roland Halbe/artur, Köln **Cologne**

■ Sächsische Landesbibliothek – Staats- und
Universitätsbibliothek, Dresden
Saxon State and University Library, Dresden
142–151 Stefan Müller, Berlin

■ Bäckereikette Dat Backhus, Hamburg
'Dat Backhus' Bakery Chain Outlet, Hamburg
152–159 Klaus Frahm/artur, Köln **Cologne**

■ Neues Stadtquartier Westhafen, Frankfurt am Main
New City Quarter, Westhafen, Frankfurt/Main
160–167 Waltraud Krase, Frankfurt/Main

■ Kindertagesstätte, Berlin
Day-Care Centre, Berlin
168–173 Werner Huthmacher/artur, Köln **Cologne**

■ **Aus dem Archiv des DAM**
■ From the Archives of the DAM

■ Zwischenseiten 174/175 **Opening Pages 174–175**
St. Bonifatius, Lübeck, 1952
St Boniface, Lübeck, 1952
Architekt **Architect**: Emil Steffann
Sammlung des DAM **DAM Collection**

■ Essay Inge Wolf
176–183 Sammlung des DAM **DAM Collection**

Die Herausgeber und der Verlag danken den Inhabern von Bildrechten, die freundlicherweise ihre Erlaubnis zur Veröffentlichung gegeben haben. Etwaige weitere Inhaber von Bildrechten bitten wir, sich mit den Herausgebern in Verbindung zu setzen.
The editors and the publisher would like to thank those copyright owners who have kindly given their permission for material from previously published works to appear in this volume. The editors would be pleased to hear from any copyright holder who could not be traced.

Impressum
Imprint

Herausgegeben von **Edited by**
Ingeborg Flagge und **and** Annina Götz
im Auftrag **on behalf of** des Dezernats für Kultur und Freizeit,
Amt für Wissenschaft und Kunst
der Stadt Frankfurt am Main

Redaktion **Editing** Annina Götz

© Prestel Verlag, München · Berlin · London · New York, 2003
© Deutsches Architektur Museum, Frankfurt am Main, 2003
© Für die abgebildeten Werke bei den Künstlern,
ihren Erben oder Rechtsnachfolgern
For the artworks with the artists, their heirs or assigns

Urhebernennungen stammen von den beteiligten Architekten selbst.
Für die Richtigkeit dieser Angaben übernehmen das
Deutsche Architektur Museum
und der Prestel Verlag keine Gewähr.
Names of copyright holders of the material used have been
supplied by the architects themselves. Neither the Deutsches Architektur
Museum nor Prestel Verlag shall be held responsible for any
omissions or inaccurancies.

Die Deutsche Bibliothek verzeichnet diese Publikation in
Die Deutsche Nationalbibliografie; detaillierte bibliografische Daten
sind im Internet über http://dnb.ddb.de abrufbar.
Die Deutsche Bibliothek lists this publication in
Die Deutsche Nationalbibliografie; http://dnb.ddb.de

Library of Congress Catalog information is available

Prestel Verlag
Königinstraße 9
D-80539 München
Telefon +49 (0) 89 38 17 09-0
Telefax +49 (0) 89 38 17 09-35
info@prestel.de
www.prestel.de

Prestel Publishing Ltd.
4 Bloomsbury Place
London, WC1A 2QA
Telefon +44 (0) 20 73 23 50 04
Telefax +44 (0) 20 76 36 80 04

Prestel Publishing
175 Fifth Avenue, Suite 402
New York, N.Y. 10010
Telefon +1 (2) 12 9 95 27 20
Telefax +1 (2) 12 9 95 27 33

www.prestel.com

Deutsches Architektur Museum
Schaumainkai 43
D-60596 Frankfurt am Main
Telefon +49 (0) 69 2 12-3 63 13
Telefax +49 (0) 69 2 12-3 63 86
info.DAM@stadt-frankfurt.de
www.DAM-online.de

Übersetzungen **Translations** Ishbel Flett, Jeremy Gaines
(deutsch-englisch **German-English**)

Koordination **Coordination** Kirsten Rachowiak
Lektorat **Copyediting** Kirsten Rachowiak (deutsch **German**),
Claudine Weber-Hof (englisch **English**)
Gestaltung und Herstellung **Design and production** Cilly Klotz
Reproduktion **Lithography** Longo, Bozen
Druck und Bindung **Printing and binding** Appl, Wemding

Gedruckt auf chlorfrei gebleichtem Papier
Printed on acid-free paper

Printed in Germany

ISSN 1611-1370
ISBN 3-7913-2916-2